SIXTH EDITION

Leading Young Children to Music

B. Joan E. Haines
Professor Emerita, Southern Connecticut State University

Linda L. Gerber
Professor Emerita, Western Connecticut State University

Merrill
an Imprint of Prentice Hall
Upper Saddle River, New Jersey   Columbus, Ohio

Library of Congress Cataloging-in-Publication Data
Haines, B. Joan E. (Beatrice Joan Elizabeth)
     Leading young children to music / B. Joan E. Haines, Linda L.
Gerber. — 6th ed.
        p.   cm.
     Discography: p.
     Includes bibliographical references and index.
     ISBN 0-13-976275-2
     1. School music—Instruction and study.   I. Gerber, Linda L.
II. Title.
MT1.H13 2000
372.87′044—dc21   99-11595
                                                        CIP

Cover photo: Image Bank
Editor: Ann Castel Davis
Production Editor: Sheryl Langner
Production Coordination: Linda Zuk, WordCrafters Editorial Services, Inc.
Photo Coordinator: Sandy Lenahan
Design Coordinator: Diane C. Lorenzo
Cover Designer: Rod Harris
Production Manager: Laura Messerly
Director of Marketing: Kevin Flanagan
Marketing Manager: Meghan McCauley
Marketing Coordinator: Krista Groshong

This book was set in Century Schoolbook by Carlisle Communications and was printed and bound by Banta Company, Menasha, WI. The cover was printed by Banta Company, Menasha, WI.

© 2000 by Prentice-Hall, Inc.
Pearson Education
Upper Saddle River, New Jersey 07458

Printed in the United States of America

10 9 8 7 6 5 4 3 2 1

ISBN: 0-13-976275-2

Prentice-Hall International (UK) Limited, *London*
Prentice-Hall of Australia Pty. Limited, *Sydney*
Prentice-Hall of Canada, Inc., *Toronto*
Prentice-Hall Hispanoamericana, S. A., *Mexico*
Prentice-Hall of India Private Limited, *New Delhi*
Prentice-Hall of Japan, Inc., *Tokyo*
Prentice-Hall (Singapore) Pte. Ltd., *Singapore*
Editora Prentice-Hall do Brasil, Ltda., *Rio de Janeiro*

Preface

It has been more than twenty years since the cooperation began that gave rise to our book and guided it to this sixth edition and the opening of a new century. We have learned much along the way through experience, study, and the contributions of others. All have reinforced in us the beliefs we professed at the very beginning:

> We believe that music is every child's birthright. Wherever children are born, they have the right to the music of their heritage and culture. We believe that music benefits all children by enriching their lives, fostering positive feelings about themselves and others, promoting acceptance and understanding of differences, and offering a learning climate free from pressure and competition. Music has such flexibility that it can serve at a moment's notice, under any circumstances. It has such power that it can set limits or expand them. It has such feeling that it can create, express, or change a mood. It is so versatile that it can support and enhance the whole school curriculum. It transcends all barriers of time and tongue. Our beliefs were strengthened by the 1994 passage by Congress of Goals 2000: Educate America Act, which wrote arts education into federal law.

The sixth edition of *Leading Young Children to Music* is built on these convictions and deals with music and music-related experiences for preschoolers through eight-year-olds. The materials it contains are designed for use by both music specialists and classroom teachers, in day-care centers, nursery schools, and the primary grades. They are adaptable to each teacher's ability and the readiness of the children. In addition, the contents are in line with the National Standards in Music Education (Music Educators National Conference, 1994).

The design of *Leading Young Children to Music* is a simple, architectural one: First lay the foundation and then build the house! "The Rationale" establishes the foundation. Part One, "Music in Education," contains three chapters. Chapter 1, "Children and Music," describes young learners at several stages of their early development, along with the five kinds of musical experiences in which they readily become involved. In Chapter 2, "Teachers and Music," both music specialists and classroom teachers are the topic since they share similar qualities and abilities, as well as responsibility for preparing the music environment and planning the musical experience. Chapter 3 deals with "Diversity and Music." Under the heading "Cultural Diversity," we examine and illustrate the multiethnic role of music as an early source of understanding and tolerance in children. "Individual Diversity" heads a section meeting the special needs of children who come to us as part of the processes of mainstreaming and inclusion.

With these foundations in place, Part Two addresses the main structure: the musical experience itself. Chapters 4 through 9 cover speech, chant, and finger plays; action songs and singing games; songs and the singing voice; moving to music; playing musical instruments; and listening to the music of others. A sequence of activities is presented under each chapter heading, arranged from the simpler to the more complex. We have omitted the prescriptive use of grade levels in the hope that each teacher will choose from the materials and activities offered at a level appropriate to the children's abilities and interests. A section on related student activities is included at the end of each chapter. In addition, teachers should feel free to implement the chapters in any order that seems most meaningful to them, or to dip back and forth from one chapter to another, as we do ourselves.

Part Three, "The Curriculum and Music," establishes a link between music and other areas of learning. Chapter 10, "Music and Integrated Learning," contains materials based on the premise that music is a natural means of unifying and enriching every area of the early childhood curriculum. Six activity clusters demonstrate this.

In this sixth edition you will find some new materials and a careful revision of both content and organization. We hope these will make the book even more user friendly.

ACKNOWLEDGMENTS

Thanks to our reviewers, whose comments aided us in preparing this sixth edition: Clifford D. Alper, Towson University; Kimberly M. Golden, Lycoming College (Williamsport, PA); Patricia Hofbauer, Northwest State Community College; Margaret M. Kelly, Illinois State University; and Marie Stern Plemons, University of Houston–Victoria. Thanks also to Ann Davis, our editor at Merrill/Prentice Hall; and to Linda Zuk, our production coordinator.

We pay special tribute to all those with whom we share our joy in music making—music education students and specialists, classroom teachers, mothers and fathers, boys and girls. Their influence on us is as enduring as our gratitude to them.

B. Joan E. Haines
Linda L. Gerber

Discover Companion Websites: A Virtual Learning Environment

Technology is a constantly growing and changing aspect of our field that is creating a need for content and resources. To address this emerging need, we have developed an online learning environment for students and professors alike—Companion Websites—to support our textbooks.

In creating a Companion Website, our goal is to build on and enhance what the textbook already offers. For this reason, the content for each user-friendly website is organized by topic and provides the professor and student with a variety of meaningful resources. Common features of a Companion Website as described below.

FOR THE PROFESSOR

Every Companion Website integrates **Syllabus Manager**™, an online syllabus creation and management utility.

- **Syllabus Manager**™ provides you, the instructor, with an easy, step-by-step process to create and revise syllabi, with direct links into Companion Website and other on-line content without having to learn HTML.
- Students may logon to your syllabus during any study session. All they need to know is the web address for the Companion Website, and the password you've assigned to your syllabus.
- After you have created a syllabus using **Syllabus Manager,** students may enter the syllabus for their course section from any point in the Companion Website.
- Class dates are highlighted in white and assignment due dates appear in blue. Clicking on a date, the student is shown the list of activities for the assignment. The activities for each assignment are linked directly to actual content, saving time for students.
- Adding assignments consists of clicking on the desired due date, then filling in the details of the assignment—name of the assignment, instructions, and whether or not it is a one-time or repeating assignment.
- In addition, links to other activities can be created easily. If the activity is online, a URL can be entered in the space provided, and it will be linked automatically in the final syllabus.
- Your completed syllabus is hosted on our servers, allowing convenient updates from any computer on the Internet. Changes you make to your syllabus are immediately available to your students at their next login.

FOR THE STUDENT

- **Topic Overviews**—outline key concepts in topic areas
- **Electronic Blue Book**—send homework or essays directly to your instructor's email with this paperless form
- **Message Board**—serves as a virtual bulletin board to post–or respond to–questions or comments to a national audience
- **Web Destinations**—links to www sites that relate to each topic area
- **Professional Organizations**—links to organizations that relate to topic areas
- **Additional Resources**—access to topic-specific content that enhances material found in the text

To take advantage of these resources, please visit the *Leading Young Children to Music* Companion Website at www.prenhall.com/haines.

Contents in Brief

Contents

The Rationale

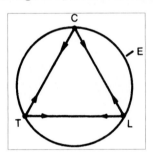 This photograph shows children and their teacher in an active music classroom setting. It is a perfect illustration of the rationale for *Leading Young Children to Music.* This book is built on our belief that learning in the early years is based on the interaction of the child with the people and objects in the environment. The quality and relevance of learning in school are affected profoundly by the nature and content of the young child's interactions with his teachers. The Horowitz Model for Teaching and Learning, shown in Figure 1, illustrates this concept graphically.

Figure 1 ◆ The Horowitz Model for the Teaching and Learning Process.

In the figure, *L* represents the child as an active, participating learner; *T* stands for the teacher. The two are joined in communication with each other. The arrows show that this communication, which is frequently nonverbal, is a two-way process. The eyes, facial expression, and the posture and movement of the body all contribute to the interchange of feelings and attitudes. This affective interchange is ongoing in the early childhood classroom and, when positive, contributes significantly to successful learning. In addition, teacher-learner communication is often verbal and at the cognitive level. It is "about something," whether it be feeling, fact, or fantasy. *C* represents the content about which *T* and *L* communicate. This content (sometimes in the form of a curriculum) has meanings that are available to both *T* and *L* as they interact about it; hence the two-way arrows on the two arms leading to *C.* All of this takes place in a setting or environment indicated by the circle *E,* which touches and contains the elements and the processes uniting them.

This model emphasizes the dynamic, reciprocal nature of teaching and learning and can readily be applied to the teaching of music. Most children are born with the capacity to move and to make sound—two ingredients fundamental to enjoyment and learning in music—and so they are ready and able to take part in their own musical education almost from birth. Through the ongoing development, refinement, and enrichment of these abilities, the child becomes a communicating, expressive human being, aware of and interacting with her total environment. As educators from the time of Plato to the present have spelled out, musical education can and should contribute to this growth. For this reason, the child has a right to musical experiences in her education. Movement and words, combined with rhythms, rhymes, melody, and other musical elements, enable the child to grow and develop through pleasurable activity. The intimate relation between music and the sound and movement natural to the young child provides a basis for musical understanding and the fulfillment of individual potential.

In 1994, the National Committee for Standards in the Arts announced America's first nationwide voluntary standards for K–12 education in the Arts. These standards apply to dance, music, theater, and visual arts. They describe the cumulative skills and knowledge to be given the highest priority in teaching. *The School Music Program: A New Vision,** published by the Music Educators National Conference, presents the music component of these standards. The standards recommended for prekindergarten and K–4 are consonant with our beliefs and will be an important aid to readers of *Leading Young Children to Music.* A summary of these appears in Appendix D.

The School Music Program: A New Vision. 1994 Music Educators National Conference. Reston, VA.

Part One

Music in Education

The first three chapters of this book lay the foundation for the materials and techniques that follow in Part Two, with particular attention to the diverse settings in which they are used. Chapter 1 delineates the role of music in early childhood, relating stages of child development to appropriate musical experiences and learning. Chapter 2 describes the part played by the teacher in this process. Attitude, approach, and ability are surveyed, and attention is paid to the classroom setting and the planning of musical experiences. Today's classrooms are characterized by a broad spectrum of cultural origins and an unprecedented range of individual abilities. Chapter 3 focuses on these two aspects of diversity found increasingly in our schools.

An understanding of all these components is basic to the development of sensitive and skillful teaching. It also provides the foundation for the building of a sound music curriculum.

Chapter 1

Children and Music

In music, as in other areas of the curriculum, developmentally appropriate activities and materials are essential if learning is to be meaningful and enjoyable. Teachers who understand the characteristics of young children's growth are able to provide musical experiences appropriate to each stage of their development. Learnings from these interactions include musical skills and knowledge and a positive lifelong attitude toward music.

Learners: A Developmental Overview

The development of a child follows consistent patterns common to all in the human species. Normal body growth and the acquisition of physical skills follow predictable patterns. Children stand before they walk, walk before they skip, babble before they talk, eat with their fingers before they use a tool, wherever they happen to be born and grow up. Similarly, constant patterns occur in their mental or cognitive growth, emotional development, and relationships with the world and the people and things in it. In fact, so predictable are these sequences that we can count on and plan for them as we live with children at home and in school.

Along with these similarities we observe individual characteristics, attributes, and behaviors that make each child unique. Our society values these differences and our schools foster their development. We do not expect any one child to match exactly every characteristic described for a particular stage in a developmental profile. Rather, we use norms to assess the general appropriateness of a behavior or ability and as a basis for planning good environments and programs for children as they grow from one stage to the next. For example, most three-year-olds talk a great deal—to other people, to themselves, and to the things in their world. We therefore plan nursery schools with much opportunity for individual activity and spontaneous interaction with peers and adults. We invite children into small groups for comparatively short periods of quiet listening, and we rarely ask for no talking, often only at naptime.

Developmental profiles provide useful guidelines. They give direction in planning for children's optimum growth. They indicate the sequences of behavior and skills we may expect many children (though not all) to exhibit during a particular chronological period.

As we plan musical experiences for very young children, it is important to know the patterns of early growth. We need to identify what **abilities relevant to music** we may expect to find as children move through the early years.

Abilities Relevant to Music

1. Hearing, auditory acuity, and auditory discrimination are basic to learning skills.
2. Vision, body awareness, gross and fine motor skills, directionality, and laterality determine the ability to move expressively in response to directions and in the use of musical instruments.
3. Growing acquisition of receptive and expressive language, articulation, diction, and expressive use of the voice in speech influence the child's ability to sing.
4. The cognitive abilities of memorization, sequencing, imitation, classification, and making relationships and choices affect each child's ability to create new (for him) lyrics, melodies, harmonies, and rhythms, and to express perceptions of dynamics, mood, form, and timbre.
5. Over all of these related academic skills lies the ability to pay attention—not only to perceive on the instant using the senses (sight, sound, and kinesthetic awareness) but to internalize that perception and to process and retain it for use in the immediate situation or in future ones.

The developmental profiles that follow will help teachers in choosing music materials and ways of teaching them to young children. Bear in mind that children may function developmentally at a younger or older level than their chronological age. Suggestions for the music education of children with special needs are found in Chapter 3, "Diversity and Music."

The Infant and Toddler

To set the stage for the early group behaviors observable at about three years, we begin with some comments on musical responsiveness and involvement from infancy to early toddlerhood. As they read them, educators will see that their techniques as caregivers for this age group will differ from those in the group teaching situations presented in this book. They will, however, find material appropriate for their use with premobile and early mobile children.

For the first months of life, the baby is receptive to music, reacting with her eyes, turning her head toward its source, and often becoming very calm and falling asleep, even though the music is quite lively. Physical and vocal responses soon follow, as the baby begins to respond more overtly to the stimulus of music, although her movements and sounds may seem unrelated to what is heard. More active listening seems to replace the passive hearing stage, and pleasure or distaste are readily seen. Imitation of sounds and movements made by others also appears, showing the ability to focus attention, and the child may subsequently repeat these sounds and movements spontaneously to gain the attention and approval of an adult or older child.

With the ability to sit up alone, crawl, creep, and ultimately walk comes the first use of expressive language. The young toddler can add the last words to familiar rhymes, say or sing an opening fragment, find a specific recording, and then use movement and environmental sounds to participate when it is played. These skills are fostered through personal, one-to-one interaction with a sympathetic adult (or older child) in an informal, homelike setting. Patting, stroking, crooning, humming, rocking, bouncing, finger plays, and body rhythms obviously give pleasure and lead to participation in both words and movement. Children at this stage also sing and croon when alone in bed or at play and enjoy making loud and often rhythmic sounds with whatever objects are at hand.

The eighteen-month-old has many ways to reach places and things (crawling, creeping, walking, rolling) and uses his hands with growing versatility. He enjoys rhythmic movements initiated by himself or an adult and bounces to music or a rhythmic sound or to his own inner rhythms. He likes to be held, rocked, or swayed, and sung to when he is tired, sad, or hurt and shows especially happy responses to favorite songs and peekaboo-type chants. In a secure setting, the one-and-a-half- to two-year-old will often launch himself trustingly into adult arms for a quasi-hazardous swing or a rhythmic ride on a lap that opens up to drop him almost to the floor at the end! The unexpected change in rhythm from the safe and gentle to the more active, dramatic drop, stop, or lift gives great delight and holds the child's attention for more turns than the grown-up often wants to give. Chanted words or a rhyme appear to enhance both the suspense and the pleasure.

Listening to music on radio, television, or records has short-lived charm for the toddler unless it is to something already known and loved. The turning record or the TV image does not usually hold the child's attention when a cookie, a cat, a car, or a potentially more rewarding object is perceived. Hitting, banging, and pounding with palm or fist all intrigue the eighteen month old, are often rhythmic in themselves, and are violent and loud. Pianos and big drums are sizable targets, and the resulting sound is hard for adults to tolerate. Soft sounds do not seem to satisfy the child as much, and at this stage he seems concerned with the energy he expends and the volume he produces.

The Two-Year-Old

The two-year-old has made significant gains in gross and fine motor skills. She uses her arms expressively, for balance, and to respond to music, which she enjoys. She will imitate rhythms and tempi when playing with adults. The desire to be independent and to attempt things alone, such as eating and dressing, contrasts with the pleasure she shows in the repetition of familiar stories, rhymes, chants, and songs by grown-ups, the latter giving pleasure in the music as much as in the meaning. By this time, the beginning of singing may often be overheard in the chanting of a descending minor third to "bye-bye," "mom-my," "ni-ni," or other sounds that herald the approach of sleep or follow awaking in a quiet house. She will also try out different vocal pitches and qualities in solitude.

Games with large balls and bean bags can be shared with one adult. Dolls and soft toys are rocked and crooned to. Favorite records begin to be identified visually, and tunes on radio and TV are recognized and responded to with obvious pleasure. (The overwhelming popularity of Barney and his songs on television is a vivid example of this.) Percussion instruments are hit at; a mallet or striker may be used by choice, with some rhythmic impulse but little accuracy. The child who marches around the kitchen banging two pot lids together is doing more than making an irritating noise. She is using her increasing ability to remember as she recalls the actions of the cymbal player in last week's parade and using her reasoning and perceptual powers as she chooses her replica of the musician's instrument. If, however, she has several pot lids to choose from, she is likely to take two that are similar in size rather than try them out for sound. All through these early years, visual rather than auditory discrimination is her first criterion.

The Three-Year-Old

The maturing three-year-old shows several strands of his development coming together and has an aura of wholeness and competence about much of his doing. He is still very active, and both gross and fine motor control have increased. Skills in climbing, swinging, riding, and pushing are acquired through practice. Awareness of the body in space shows in an increased ability to stop and start and move adroitly in the environment. The whole body comes under finer control. Fingers are used more nimbly and can pick out individual keys on the piano or strum across a stringed instrument. Often a regular beat can be established and maintained by shaking or tapping in relation to music played or sung by others. Improvised dancing changes from the toddler's jogging up and down to include arm movements and a variety of steps. Often this creativity is quite a private affair and may stop if it draws attention, unlike that of the more extroverted four-year-old.

Language competency grows apace, both in vocabulary and syntax. Songs with repetitive words are added to the growing repertoire. Threes like to sing together, and, although a group may sing in several keys, individual children may well be singing in tune. Talking, chanting, and singing accompany many activities. The labeling of objects and actions seems to give three-year-olds new control over themselves and their worlds. The three-year-old with her doll and carriage may sing a rambling but quite tuneful aria, with phrases beginning "Now I'm going to" or "Then we'll have a" that provides a running commentary combined with plans for action.

Threes love to please adults and to try to enter into their world in ingratiating ways. They like grown-ups to play with them and to give them tasks, puzzles to solve, or sounds and simple rhythmic patterns to imitate. Clapping in different tempi and at different levels can be quite accurate when modeled by an adult. Success in interacting with adults is greeted with laughter, delight, and requests for more. Failure or ridicule may result in sulking, tantrums, or refusing to play.

In nursery school, threes respond more quickly to the new adults and the new toys and equipment than they do to their peers, to whom they relate best when an adult is present or readily accessible. To be the doer of the many activities that nursery school teachers provide brings its own intrinsic reward, and it is only toward the end of the three-year-old's year that she begins to focus on the product of her actions and wants to share it at home. Thus singing, playing, and moving are particularly suitable for small groups of threes, who live very much in the present.

The Four-Year-Old

The world of four is much bigger than that in which the three-year-old functions. Stunts and tricks now enter the motoric repertoire. The four is confident and capable on the jungle gym, slide, and rope nets and at riding and steering. For instance, arm and leg muscles can be used rhythmically to travel quite fast and safely on a tricycle. A budding sense of competition adds to her desire to master new physical skills. Singing games in circles or with partners are now within the four-year-old's interest and ability.

Fine motor development involves drawing objects purposefully, painting with beginning control of the medium, and skill with scissors, puzzles of numerous pieces, and percussion instruments. The ability to sort and match objects also indicates perceptual gains and can readily be extended to include matching and classifying sounds in terms of source, volume, pitch, and duration. This is a big step that all too often receives little attention in our visually oriented society until as a five-year-old the child is confronted with structured auditory discrimination tasks in a fairly formal reading readiness program.

Not only can the four-year-old order, classify, and reproduce sounds, tones, and rhythmic patterns vocally and with instruments, but he can use these creatively to help him express his ideas in a story or the words and feelings of a song. He can also improvise simple melodies on pentatonic instruments and sustain one- or two-tone accompaniments to familiar songs.

The singing voice is more secure at four, and an increasing portion of every group of fours can sing in tune as the year progresses. Autoharps and guitars give a firm tonality to which many fours are sensitive. Singing time draws almost all fours, who love to invent new topical or humorous lyrics to songs that are familiar favorites, especially if they are about members of the group. Appropriate finger plays, rhythmic chants, and action songs are quickly memorized and gladly repeated from day to day. Willingness to sing or chant alone may indicate quite a competitive spirit. However, self-confidence and self-consciousness are never far apart, and the attention-seeking four may blush profusely and disappear into the sidelines when he realizes that he has twenty pairs of four-year-old eyes on him in addition to the adult's which he originally sought.

The Five-Year-Old

In describing the five-year-old, Arnold Gesell tells us, "Although he is by no means a finished product, he already gives token of the man he is to be."[1] It is as if we could look at him and see all the skills, abilities, and individual talents and traits coming together and uniting to carry a unique person forward into life. The kindergarten year is often a year of refining and consolidating rather than exploring new territory, almost as though the child is organizing his resources and identity as he begins his life in the primary school. The five can meet most of his own physical needs, enjoys his social group, and may also have an inner circle of special friends. He can lead his peers when opportunity is afforded him, and he can also follow and be a member of a group. This state of social grace is a far cry from that of the one-year-old just beginning to differentiate between his own and other selves.

Associated with this development is poised and often graceful use of the five-year-old body, which can lead to skating, skiing, riding a pony or a two-wheeler, hammering, sawing, and similar activities. Intellectually and motorically the five-year-old can now learn simple dance steps and adapt them to musical rhythms. She can move in response to visual symbols. She can play instruments with accuracy, both in memorized patterns and in response to nonverbal directions. She can work with peers or alone to create simple orchestrations and accompaniments that she can then play from a chart. She can create and notate her own melodies. In a very real sense, then, the five-year-old can both write and read music.

The Six-Year-Old

The six-year-old moves into first grade in top gear and normally maintains this high energy level throughout his encounters during a full day at school, with reading, writing, and number skills, and quite often with several teachers concerned with one aspect or another of the learning spelled out for him in the school curriculum. This world of first grade contains more that is different than any new environment he has experienced so far. The six-year-old has the physical, mental, and emotional resources to meet all these challenges and enough left over, both in school and at home, to be exasperating and endearing.

Most sixes have some formal encounter with music during the year, either with their own teacher or a music teacher who comes to their room or whose music room they visit on a regular basis. They like to sing, especially their own choice of song, and will release emotional and physical energy by shouting, especially early in the year. However, a skillful teacher who knows the capabilities of the group can interest them quite easily and teach them to sing tunefully, with good tone and sensitivity to the meaning and mood of a variety of songs. The aural discrimination being emphasized in early reading helps concentration, tonality, and diction in singing, which in turn improves reading and listening skills. Sixes have a strong sense of rhythm, can understand the concept of beat and rhythmic pattern, and play tuned and untuned instruments with growing ability. On instruments such as xylophones, metallophones, glockenspiels, and resonator bells they can create and play simple *ostinati* (rhythmic or melodic patterns) to accompany singing and creative movement. They like to share their products with other classes and in school assemblies, and they enjoy working hard and doing well.

The Seven-Year-Old

David Elkind describes the seven-year-old entering her eighth year of life as reflective and serious, organizing and integrating previous life experiences, and he refers to second grade as a period of digestive work.[2] The development of the seven's reasoning powers predominates over the physical and sensorimotor powers previously observed. Thinking and feeling, especially about the self, tend to turn inward.

Creative output in movement and dance may not be great during this year, but by the same token it is a good time for learning the steps and sequences of partner dances and simple folk dances. Seven-year-olds welcome practices and rehearsals, and the movement of boys and girls away from each other, both in and out of school, still lies ahead. It will be some time before the teacher can again interest a whole class in this kind of activity.

With the acquisition of basic skills, especially reading, new worlds of interest open up and the ability to read music may be readily taught, especially when melody instruments are used. Singing is increasingly accurate and of good, light tone. Seven-year-olds will work assiduously to perfect their performance and can learn to sing simple canons or hold a melody while the teacher sings or plays another part. When this is done with a listening ear, rather than by blocking out the other sound, a complex state of perception and coordination has been reached, indicating the productiveness of this year of consolidation.

The Eight-Year-Old

The trend is outward again as the eight-year-old moves forward from his carefully secured position of strength. Interest and skill in music may be fostered in both boys and girls by group activities such as primary choirs, extracurricular recorder groups, or other instrumental groups. In their regular school music program, eight-year-olds are reluctant soloists but show great satisfaction when they have been coaxed to perform alone. Similarly, boys will not choose girls for partners in dances or games, or vice versa, but if assigned to each other appear to enjoy the activity. Increased motoric skills allow them to play intricate rhythmic patterns on a wide range of tuned and untuned instruments. Singing while playing a second part is readily accomplished. When physical development is accompanied by continuing vocal training, eight-year-olds are well able to sing canons, rounds, and simple two-part songs. While eights can learn the skills of reading and notating music, they frequently prefer to hark back to the familiar rote music of earlier years rather than persevere in unlocking the new—a reminder that their scholastic independence is only recently acquired and maintained with considerable effort.

Musical Experiences

Based on an understanding of child growth and development, the teacher initiates musical experiences that develop appropriate skills, concepts, and attitudes. Teachers should remember, however, that "in musical development, as in all growth processes, each child is unique, and each child's musical growth pattern must be understood and respected."[3]

Specifically, a musical experience may be composed of any or all of the following. Although they are listed separately, each is dependent upon the others and all are essential components of the music program. **Active listening** is the continuing generator.

- Listening
- Moving
- Singing
- Playing
- Creating

The child listens to the music in his environment and responds to it experientially. In so doing, he becomes increasingly creative and expressive in his ability to move, sing, and play instruments. It is essential to bear in mind the interrelatedness of the different musical experiences of children as we examine each one in turn.

Listening

Most children are born with the ability to hear. The ability to listen, however, involves not only hearing but focusing the mind on the sounds perceived. *This ability to pay attention is not innate but is a learned skill, and the young child needs training and help to acquire it.* Such *active listening* is essential for him to make sense of the environment and to communicate within it.

The development of the active listening skill is fundamental to moving, singing, playing, and musical creativity and later to reading, writing, and performing music. By these means, the young child grows in his ability to enjoy, appreciate, understand, and contribute to the aural art of music which is a part of the human environment.

On taking a closer look at active listening, we find that it has three component skills:

> . . . auditory awareness, auditory discrimination, and auditory sequencing and memory. The first, **auditory awareness,** is concerned with the simple recognition of the presence of sound. The second, **auditory discrimination,** requires the ability to distinguish between sounds and to group them into categories such as fast-slow, loud-soft, high-low, etc. The third section, **auditory sequencing,** deals with the ability to reproduce a sequence of sounds in the correct order and therefore requires the exercise of auditory memory as well.[4]

Auditory Awareness.   When a three-week-old baby turns his head in the direction of the sound of dripping water as his mother squeezes a washcloth into his bathtub, he is recognizing and responding to the presence of sound in a simple yet dramatic fashion: auditory awareness is already evident.

Auditory Discrimination.   The ability to distinguish between sounds is observed in the toddler who runs to the front door when he hears a two-tone bell rather than to the telephone, which has an intermittent ring.

Auditory Sequencing.   The preschooler is using auditory sequencing and memory when he sits with his teacher and plays a game of echo clapping—the teacher clapping a pattern and the child imitating it as accurately as possible.

As the young child matures and encounters increasingly sophisticated and complex auditory stimuli in daily life, skill in these aspects of active listening is refined and developed. The infant bangs rhythmically with her spoon as the radio plays, not differentiating between the loud and rousing or the soft and soothing, but relating rather to the rhythmic impulses she hears. The four-year-old, however, will try several sounds—a bell, a drum, or a pair of sticks—carefully choosing and playing one that sounds good with the music he hears and changing it when he hears a marked change in tempo and dynamics. The toddler tries to imitate with his voice many sounds in his environment as he becomes aware of them and their significance. Fours and fives develop listening skills that enable them to sing in tune and to match pitches. Primary children rely on even more refined and discriminating listening abilities. They create melodies, rhythmic and harmonic accompaniments, and orchestrations, choosing what they want to include or discard and noting what the ear tells them is most pleasing or appropriate.

Although the listening component of music education in schools focuses customarily on recorded compositions, we believe that, for very young children, a more active involvement with the music of others should come first. We find that early development of aural skills and music appreciation is enhanced through live performances and through recording of the children's own music-making. We have supported Alice Yardley's viewpoint, "Although children enjoy short spells of direct listening, much of what they hear is intimately bound up in other aspects of their daily experience."[5] Currently, however, the impact of media-generated materials (tapes, videos, and electronic games) seems to be bringing about a change in the direction of young children's daily experiences, turning them toward the more receptive aspects of listening and viewing. Some of these materials, identified as developmentally appropriate and presented by a skillful teacher, can add a wide variety of listening activities to the music program.

Part Two includes a chapter devoted to the use of recorded materials. The other activity chapters also contain a wide variety of suggested listening experiences.

Moving

The ability to move is evident in the first moments of the newborn's life. In fact, the ability to move autonomously distinguishes animate from inanimate life forms. Every movement of the young child is an assertion of his vital existence and an expression of his selfhood.

The young child's movement falls into two main categories: unconscious and conscious. Unconscious movement characterizes the early years, decreasing (though not disappearing) with intellectual and physical maturity.

Unconscious movement may be in response to the inner environment of the child: spontaneous and/or reflexive reaction to a perceived stimulus. The drumming heels and pounding fists of a four-year-old during a temper tantrum are expressive of the frustration and anger within, rather than a conscious effort to get at the cookie jar that is out of reach. The external environment also provides stimuli for unconscious movement. Eyes blink when the wind blows on them, limbs shiver when the air is cold, the whole body jumps in response to a loud noise.

Conscious movement may be both planned and spontaneous. The kindergartner may decide quite deliberately to cross the room for a doll carriage, take a few walking steps, and then skip the rest of the way for pleasure in the movement itself.

Much of the young child's movement is rhythmic. In infancy, rhythm is largely unconscious, coming from within. As the child grows, she begins to make rhythmic body movements in response to strongly accented vocal sounds or music. When new ways of moving are explored, such as skipping, hopping, or using a drum stick, they may at first be random and arhythmic. As control over the new movement is acquired, inner rhythm takes over and is later complemented by the ability to skip, hop, or play the drum in rhythm with music. This is the beginning of creative movement to music, of later learning of dance steps and patterns, and of playing musical instruments in middle and later childhood.

Movement plays an important role in the acquisition of musical concepts by the young child. He uses his whole body to explore and express changes in tempo, dynamics, or pitch or to express the line of a phrase or the mood of a song. These kinesthetic actions seem to go directly and deeply from the muscles and the senses to the brain to implant lasting learnings that lie beyond verbalization. Such internalized experiences become the unique property of the child and are readily observed in his ensuing responses when he comes into direct contact with appropriate music.

We observe that throughout the early years movement is a great source of pleasure to the child. Her eagerness to be physically free to move at will, her happy face, her laughter and chanted accompaniments to her own motions, her spontaneous physical response to music, even when it interrupts an ongoing activity—all show her joy in movement for its own sake. "The transfer of these experiences to musical concepts can be a natural and enjoyable process leading to the growth of a human being who understands and loves music."[6]

Singing

All young children love to sing. They begin to make singing sounds in their first six months of life. Cooing, babbling, and experimentation with pitches and vocal inflections lead to imitation of environmental sounds. This continual use of sound is extended to form an accompaniment to some of the activity of two- and three-year-olds. Tonally it lies somewhere between speech and song and may be classified as *chanting*. Sometimes it is long and meandering and contains a few recognizable words to a wandering pitch:

"Give Teddy cookie—num, num, num—eating a cookie—num, num."

At other times it may be a short, rhythmic, repeated phrase with syllables, rhythm, and pitch intervals that can be notated:

If this chanting is echoed and extended by an adult, it can become the entrance to the world of song. Feelings can lend intensity to the chanting, newly acquired words can be added and practiced in the repeated phrases, new pitches can be added, and different meters can grow out of these spontaneous beginnings.

The young child develops this spontaneous chant into creative song as his vocabulary and listening skills increase. At the same time, he increases his vocal skills into imitative singing as he listens to the singing of others. Frequently sung lullabies, nursery rhymes, folk tunes, children's songs, and the popular music of the day elicit both rhythmic physical movement and vocal participation. Initially, the young child joins in with the last word or tone of a phrase. As he gains control of his voice, he sings more and more of the melody with increasing accuracy of interval and rhythm, especially in a range of his own choice.

We cannot overemphasize the importance of singing to and with the young child. Listening to good singing is the most significant factor in vocal development and ability. Many and varied singing experiences catch and focus attention, heighten pleasure, and stimulate participation. Throughout the early childhood years, rote singing is the primary means of adding enjoyment, variety, and accuracy to the young child's repertoire. Happy and successful singing is, in turn, the key to the child's total musical growth.

Playing

Young children should have the opportunity to hear and produce as many different kinds of sounds as possible: big sounds, little sounds, and the sound of silence. In considering playing and producing sound, we do not restrict ourselves to the use of musical instruments but include those objects in the everyday environment that provide unique and interesting tone quality. Particularly important for the very young child is the exploration of environmental sounds as she begins to discover the world of sound around her. Water dripping, paper tearing, pounding of nails, striking spoons together—all afford elemental experiences that sharpen her awareness and enrich her daily life.

In no way, however, do these environmental activities detract from the importance of making sound with musical instruments. Although we hope the teacher will provide and encourage opportunities to make environmental music, the young child needs to experience valid musical sound to grow musically.

Classroom instruments provide opportunities for children to make their own music. Through playing them they discover tonal qualities and expressive elements of music. As their understanding of music grows and their physical coordination develops, their playing can reinforce and secure learning of pitch, duration, and dynamics, and they can add appropriate accompaniments to singing and movement activities. Instruments that are tonally accurate and produce good musical timbres are essential. The child must be exposed to good musical sound, for anything less will inhibit or damage her awakening sensitivity. We believe that out-of-tune pianos with poor tone quality or missing keys or untuned autoharps are harmful to the development of the aural and vocal abilities of little children.

Although the child's experimentation with sound is essential in the first stage, the teacher must be prepared to guide or sometimes to structure playing activities at any given moment. Without direction in how to play the instrument and guidance in when to play, the young child might be content with hitting or rattling for an indefinite period. This more sophisticated development in the making of music requires an observant teacher who also understands both the musical and physical problems that exist in instrument playing. Apart from pleasure in the activity for its own sake, little musical value results from giving the child an instrument that he is not yet able to control to some degree.

With instruments appropriate to their level of competence, children as young as four may begin to learn the new musical skills associated with ensemble playing. Here they will meet the challenge of playing in rhythmic unison with one group, of playing differently from another group, and of following the directions of a conductor. Making music as part of a group is as essential to musicianship as are the individual skills already stressed.

Creating

Much has been said and written about creativity and the nature of the creative process. Here we look at each of the musical experiences we have identified and point out ways in which the young child can contribute from his own uniqueness. We believe that every child has the capacity to take the ingredients of music and to make from them a recipe, however simple, that is peculiarly his own, that delights and satisfies him, and that can often be shared with others. As this creativity develops, the child needs a basic vocabulary of musical experiences and skills, just as he needs a vocabulary of words and events to express his ideas and feelings in language. As these are acquired, from experiences such as those that follow in Part Two of this book, so the creative acts of music making will appear. It is the teacher's task not only to foster the skills but to provide a supportive and accepting climate that values both effort and achievement and stimulates further exploration and discovery.

Creating through Active Listening.   Active listening, as we have discussed earlier, is the means whereby the child adds to her understanding of and feeling about her environment from the sounds she hears in it. She also learns about herself by listening to the sounds she herself makes, with her own voice and body, and by acting, either spontaneously or deliberately, on objects around her. The six-year-old leans over a bridge, drops a pebble, and listens to hear it hit the water. It is a simple act but one that creates in her, the creator of the sound, feelings of mastery and of self-worth. Attentive listening in musical activities gives rise to unique and innovative responses in moving, singing, and playing. Hence, the act of taking in is as much a part of the creative process as is the ultimate giving out.

Creating through Moving.   The young child's movement is characterized by its creativity, expressing his feelings and aiding his communication with others. Walking turns to skipping as his feeling of well-being bubbles over or to running with outstretched arms as he sees his parent at the end of the school walk. In a musical context, children move just as creatively. At the sound of a rousing march, quiet activities will stop and children will spontaneously clap or tap to the beat, get up and march around, or go to the music corner and seize a drum to play. At the conscious level, a child will create arm, head, and body movements to express the meaning of a song about autumn leaves. At this conscious level children need many guided experiences in moving in different ways and with different parts of the body to varied rhythms, tempi, dynamic ranges, and moods. Through such activities, a repertoire of many responsive movements will be developed, along with freedom to make choices and inner control to enact them.

While these educational experiences are essential to creative movement and dance, opportunities for spontaneous movement to both words and music must be continued. This keeps the channels open for creative expression of feelings while helping each child to extend his movement skills and repertoire. The balance between spontaneous and planned movement in response to verbal and musical stimuli is important. All too often, in the name of creativity, children are urged to move as the music makes them feel, to "do what it tells them," when they have in fact a very small repertoire of conscious movements on which to draw.

Creating through Singing.   Singing affords the child another medium for the expression of her creativity. Here again we observe the dual thread of spontaneity and planning discussed previously. Spontaneous song appears early in two forms: chanting repeated phrases and chanting long, meandering arias accompanying activities, often improvised in a *minor* or *pentatonic scale* (see Glossary). The teacher who catches a repeated chant can give it back to the child exactly as she sang it or add new words, encouraging her to repeat, extend, or change her first song. A creative musical dialogue can be initiated in this way. The narrative singing referred to above does not invite adult participation in the same way, but can be observed and recorded for use as an indicator of the child's growing freedom to express herself with words and melody.

Making up new words to known songs is a creative activity that comes readily to preschoolers and primary grade children, whose unlimited freedom with the spoken word gives them an advantage over older children. Countless songs and chants invite substitution of lyrics from the child's personal experience or group creations about shared activities. (See Songs for Informal Settings, pp. 74–80.) Creation of new melodies can be initiated by improvising phrases between teacher and child, beginning with the invitation to add an ending tone and extending to the composing of complete phrases, sung to a neutral syllable. Children as young as four years old can create their own songs and dictate them, words and melody, to the teacher. They can also notate their own tunes with the use of color-coded piano keys, xylophone bars, or resonator bells and crayons and paper. We stress here the importance of all creative singing, spontaneous and learned, as a factor in affective and cognitive growth. Valuing the songs of the young child, in or out of tune, enhances a child's positive self-concept and feelings of self-worth and leads to his increased joy, effort, and achievement in singing.

Creating through Playing.   The playing of percussion and melody instruments is an integral part of early childhood musical education and develops naturally from early interest in environmental sounds. Although the young child, even as a toddler, loves to play instruments for the sensorial satisfaction she derives, she is probably about four years old before she has sufficient control and perception to use them in a consciously creative way. When she does reach this level of physical and intellectual maturity, she can use many of the traditional classroom instruments to create rhythmic and dynamic accompaniments for her singing and moving. Tuned or melody instruments in pentatonic scales allow her to improvise melodies without discord and to play in consonance with others long before she acquires the skills of music reading. Thus the creative powers of the young child are released very early and can be refined as the sensitivity of her ear, her muscular coordination, and her intellectual powers develop.

In conclusion, we can see that the flow of creativity from the young child into all phases of his musical life depends to a large degree on the positive attitude of the teacher—toward him as a unique and worthwhile individual and toward music as a vital and important part of life for both child and adult. This attitude fosters creative teaching and releases creative learning.

Musical Learnings

All experiences lead to learning, from the simplest rhythmic experiences of being rocked to sleep to the more sophisticated challenge of playing one rhythmic pattern while singing another. When musical experiences are related to the developmental continuum, the learning is acquired without difficulty. As concepts are internalized and integrated by the child, he grows in his ability to interpret and create. The satisfaction and pleasure he derived from his earliest spontaneous musical expressions are now extended to his conscious use of what he has learned. The most important areas of musical learning are as follows:

- Rhythm
- Melody and Harmony
- Timbre
- Dynamics
- Form
- Mood

Rhythm

In its musical context, *rhythm* is the all-encompassing word we use to describe the time-based or temporal components of music: beat, meter, duration of sounds, rhythmic patterns, and tempo. In this sense, rhythm is the organizing element that makes music out of tonal sounds.

In a broader context, we recognize other related meanings in the fundamental rhythms of human life: the heartbeat, breathing, walking, running, speech patterns, sleeping, and waking, to name a few. In the environment we observe the change of seasons, night and day, the phases of the moon, and the rise and fall of the tide. Rhythm is basic to our universe and to our daily lives and provides a ready link between us and the expressive arts. The young child begins to develop an understanding and mastery of music through conscious rhythmic experiences.

Melody and Harmony

Melody may be described as a sequence of changing or repeated tones. The human voice produces melody, as does a vast array of tuned instruments reaching us from primitive times and from many cultural and ethnic settings around the world. From one age to another and from one culture to another, differences develop in what pleases and is considered melodious. Twentieth-century technology, however, has broadened tremendously our understanding and acceptance of the melodies of other times and cultures.

Most children are born with the ability to sing tunes spontaneously. In its simplest form this seems to be an innate skill in many cultures, and certain common qualities may be observed. From this springboard, vocal and instrumental melody making can readily be developed in the young child. In conjunction with rhythm, a multitude of musical concepts and skills can be learned experimentally in the early childhood years. These lead the child to independence in reading and performing music from the printed page.

Harmony is a sequence of one or more changing or repeated tones added to a predominant melody line, to enrich and elaborate it. Generally, the young child is not ready to grasp the concept of harmony. She responds, however, to harmonic sounds in moving, singing, and playing with some degree of auditory discrimination and creativity. She enjoys hearing harmonically rich music and with guidance can use tuned instruments such as the autoharp, resonator bells, guitar, and piano to augment melody making, movement, and other activities.

Timbre

Timbre refers to the unique qualities of sound made by a voice or instrument enabling the listener to identify the source. The young child begins to acquire this concept as she responds appropriately to the familiar tonal qualities of her mother's voice in contrast to that of a stranger. The preschooler recognizes the vocal timbre of his peers, in a blindfold guessing game. Good teaching fosters the understanding of this concept and the skills which it engenders—for example, the ability of a student to identify the instrument families of the orchestra, sight unseen. The aesthetic power of the listener/performer/creator relies heavily on the development of this concept.

Dynamics

In moving, singing, and playing, the young child encounters loudness and softness in music, gradual and sudden changes in volume, and the accenting of certain tones. These three elements are the *dynamics* of music. At the experiential level, the child can deal with them well since they are expressive and affective. The deeper understandings that these three dynamic elements give to music—its movement forward in time, its intensity, and its vitality—are more abstract notions and must wait for the child's later cognitive maturity.

Form

Form is the framework that organizes and gives meaning to the elements of music. Simple concepts of form can be experienced and understood by the young child as he encounters music. Musical phrase, the basic unit of form, is easily identified by the child as he moves, sings, and plays instruments. Through these experiences he develops an awareness of repeated or contrasting phrases and the special qualities inherent in each. He differentiates between like and unlike phrases in both his musical performance and discussion. As he internalizes the concept of phrase, the young child is increasingly able to use the phrase creatively in composing and improvising. Larger musical forms—the canon, round, verse-chorus, ABA song form, and rondo—can also be understood through guided listening and movement and used in singing, playing, and composing.

Mood

Within the context of this book, *mood* is understood to be the combination of musical elements—rhythm, melody, harmony, timbre, dynamics, and form—that causes an emotional or affective response in the listener or performer. This interaction with music is a personal and subjective one. The quality of this interaction depends on three factors: (1) the clarity of the musical message; that is, the successful organization of musical elements into an integrated whole; (2) its suitability to the intellectual, emotional, and physical development of the listener; and (3) the sensitivity of the listener's ear and her readiness to perceive the feelings the music conveys and to respond to them, within herself or with some outward and relevant form of expression.

The young child often reacts spontaneously to the feelings music expresses. He may talk, move, sing, or play in response to them. The teacher should also stimulate and extend his perception through guided listening, and point out to him, in simple language, how music is able to affect him, through tempo, rhythm, melodic intervals, major and minor modes, and dynamic range.

This brief discussion of mood completes our journey through the ideas put forward at the outset on leading young children to music in "The Rationale." We are reminded of Rachel Carson's important statement about the relationship between feeling and knowing: "Once the emotions have been aroused . . . then we wish for knowledge about the object of our emotional response. Once found, it has lasting meaning."[7]

We hope the musical activities that follow in Parts Two and Three will enliven the bare bones of our rationale. Throughout them we have tried to stress the importance of the young child's pleasure and joy in active music making and to show how these feelings can lead to musical knowledge and understanding. We have experienced that progression as the natural and the lasting way of learning. Concepts and skills acquired happily from spontaneous and experiential beginnings become part of the child's inner resources to be tapped again and again as she grows in depth of feeling and intellectual ability.

NOTES

1. Gesell, Arnold, & Frances Ilg. (1946.) *The child from five to ten.* New York: Harper and Row, p. 62.

2. Elkind, David. (1978.) *A sympathetic view of the child from birth to sixteen* (2nd ed.). Boston: Allyn and Bacon.

3. McDonald, Dorothy, & Gene M. Simons. (1989.) *Musical growth and development: Birth through six.* New York: Schirmer, p. 52.

4. Birkenshaw, Lois. (1982.) *Music for fun, music for learning* (3rd ed.). St. Louis, Mo.: MMB Music, p. 33.

5. Yardley, Alice. *Senses and sensitivity.* New York: Citation, p. 111.

6. Andress, Barbara, et al. (1973.) *Music in early childhood.* Washington, D.C.: Music Educators National Conference, p. 4.

7. Carson, Rachel. (1960.) *A sense of wonder.* New York: Harper and Row, p. 45.

RELATED ACTIVITIES FOR STUDENTS

1. Read in your learning theory or developmental psychology texts about the function of the child's environment in his early learning. Write a short summary of your findings, citing your authorities.

2. Choose any three of the age levels described in this chapter. Write an anecdote for each one based on your own childhood or that of a child whom you know well. Each event described should clearly illustrate at least one developmental trait mentioned in the text.

3. Visit an early childhood setting and identify three "typical" children who appear to be functioning at different developmental levels. Observe them for at least forty-five minutes, keeping careful notes for each. After your visit, and with your text to guide you, write up short profiles of these youngsters, giving each a pseudonym. Suggest the age level at which each child is functioning in at least two areas of growth and development.

4. Write a description of a child you know who has a special need. Describe the child briefly and explain the ways in which he or she differs from peers. (a) What might be a suitable musical activity for you to share together? (b) How could you approach the child to best ensure his or her participation and success? (c) What might this child achieve because of your time together?

5. Make a list of the early listening skills discussed in this chapter. Test them by visiting a group of preschool children. Observe informal and directed listening activities and record them under the headings prepared.

6. Visit a preschooler in his or her home. Sing a familiar song together and involve the child in creating new words to the music. Tape-record your visit or write a full description of what happened.

7. Visit a music activity period in a preschool. Observe and record the activities that take place during your visit. List them under the experiential headings identified in this chapter.

Chapter 2

Teachers and Music

Teachers

In the school setting, two groups of adults bring musical experiences to young children. Early childhood educators, or generalists, are teachers whose professional preparation often involves all curriculum areas, including music and the other arts. They usually provide the musical component in day-care centers and other preschool settings. In primary and elementary schools they may also be responsible for their own classroom music.

In addition, some schools have music teachers or music specialists, whose preparation includes child development and general methodology but who have concentrated in the area of music education. When a specialist is responsible for the music program in the primary curriculum, the classroom teacher should reinforce and extend it whenever possible.

The orientation and abilities of teachers in these two groups differ considerably, but they should share the qualities of enthusiasm about music and interest in young children. Readers should approach this chapter from their own professional viewpoint as classroom teachers or music specialists.

Attitude and Approach

The teacher's positive attitude and approach to musical experiences are crucial factors in the young child's success in music. Interest in and enthusiasm about music are the most important teacher attributes. Children are great imitators; if the teacher is involved in music and uses it in a variety of interesting and challenging ways, the young child will become interested too. Active participation in music, by both teacher and child, ignites the fire that stimulates further exploration and discovery of the world of music. This participation must begin in the early childhood years, as the teacher responds to developmental clues and begins to guide the child toward musical goals. Techniques of observing, recording, and using the clues found in the child's behavior are important throughout the early years. The teacher's role in providing activities and materials for musical learning grows with the child's developing intellect, body skills, and enthusiasm for increasingly purposeful activities.

In the Preschool.   Particularly in the preschool years, opportunities for children to begin musical activities on their own are enhanced by an informal physical environment and a curriculum that is usually flexible and often based on the child's own expressed interests. Child-initiated musical activities occur more frequently here partly because of the young child's greater spontaneity and lack of inhibition in expression and communication. Another factor that can and should encourage spontaneous music making in the preschool is the attitude of the teacher toward it and the provisions made for it to take place. If the teacher shows acceptance and appreciation for the young child's spontaneous songs, expressive movements, and purposeful experimentations with the sounds of the environment, these activities will increase. The teacher may go further, providing adequate space for free movement, indoors and out; setting out intriguing sound-making materials, including percussion and melody instruments, for experimental use; being willing and un-self-conscious enough to enter into singing, dancing, and playing when given opportunity to do so. In these ways the teachable moment is caught, the child's confidence and skill confirmed, and musical concepts identified and reinforced.

In the Primary Grades.   A degree of spontaneous music making continues to occur in the primary grades. The teacher's responsibilities are the same, with increasing emphasis on identifying and reinforcing concepts at the conscious level. This teaching, though incidental, is not unplanned. Here the teacher may well include the use of playground and street games and chants in the classroom. These favorites of the children can be worked out on melody instruments and then used to teach rhythmic and melodic notation and reading with a high degree of interest. A group of third graders can compile a small anthology of their favorites, notated, written, and illustrated by the children themselves.

Ability

Emphasizing the teacher's attitude and approach does not mean that the teacher's musical capabilities and knowledge are unimportant. These capabilities are just as essential for planning and organizing appropriate musical experiences. Classroom teachers should extend their musical skill by:

1. asking for help from music specialists and colleagues
2. taking lessons in singing or playing
3. using carefully chosen teaching aids
4. capitalizing on the musical abilities of children in the group
5. committing themselves to their own musical growth.

Music specialists should expand their understanding of their younger pupils by talking with classroom teachers, observing both teachers and children in nonmusic activities, and reading professional literature.

There are no shortcuts to acquiring and extending the rich and diverse range of songs and activities that teachers must have to meet the needs of growing, learning children. Books such as this and others listed in Appendix D are useful resources.

For all who teach music, attending workshops is a good route to the goal of building a musical repertoire and improving teaching skill. State organizations, in-service programs, teachers' centers, and college extension programs offer such workshops. Tapes and recordings are also sources of new material and approaches that can enrich music teaching.

The Setting for Musical Activities

The physical setting in which musical learning takes place is important, as is the quality of equipment and materials.

Preschool

Since preschool children need ample room for large muscle movement, access to a large area of clear space is important. In a small classroom, this may mean moving back the furniture or taking the children outside or to a large hall. If the facility is oversized, such as a school gymnasium, it may be necessary to define the space to be used by balance beams, furniture, or even chalk marks on the floor. In a classroom or kindergarten of appropriate size, we recommend that the basic floor plan include a permanent meeting and moving space.

Primary

A large space is also needed in the primary grades, in either a classroom or a music room. Primary grade children have more fine motor control but they are larger, and so they need plenty of space. The use of outdoor space, an auditorium, gym, cafeteria, or other available area can help, but the teacher is urged to have the arrangement of classroom furniture as flexible as possible.

Music Materials

Musical equipment includes percussion and tuned instruments, CDs and CD player, tapes and tape player/recorder, head sets, and a piano. These should all be of the best quality possible so that the child hears good musical sound, allowing her ear and listening skills to become more sensitive and discriminating. Instruments and pianos should be kept in good tune and repair. Storage and maintenance of musical equipment is part of the teacher's ongoing responsibility for high-quality musical experiences.

The teacher is also responsible for building a collection of appropriate teaching materials, including teaching aids and source books. Since source books are so abundant, it is often difficult to choose good collections. Music workshops are not only sources of good material in themselves, but often give guidance on what publications to select. Helpful reference lists also are found in basic music series, activity texts, and curriculum guides. These books often include classified lists of good children's recordings.

The Planned Musical Experience

The approach to the teacher-initiated experience is a complex one. In the first place, the teacher needs clearly articulated musical goals, with consideration for individual differences. In line with these goals, materials and activities are chosen and teaching strategies planned. The teacher may wish to follow a specific approach to music education, such as that developed by *Carl Orff* or *Zoltan Kodaly* (see Glossary), each of which is widely used in the United States today. An eclectic approach may be taken, in which teachers choose parts of these and other methods and materials, combining them to suit their abilities. The more adventurous or musically able teacher frequently creates original methods, collecting and developing materials to meet prescribed goals. Developmentally appropriate goals for prekindergarten through fourth grade may be found in the National Standards in Music developed by the Music Educators National Conference (see Appendix D).

One of the most crucial tasks for the teacher is planning a music lesson. (In preschool, kindergarten, and programs with an integrated curriculum, the term *activity* is preferred. The reader should substitute *activity* for *lesson* when appropriate.) In a music lesson the teacher has a block of time (perhaps ten or fifteen minutes for the youngest children, up to thirty minutes for the older ones) that has been specifically set aside for the purpose of teaching music. Whatever the scheduling, the lessons must be planned to achieve optimum musical growth.

There is no single correct way to teach a lesson. This also holds true for preparing one. It is important, however, that the teacher have a basic philosophy and some convictions about music education to plan for children's musical growth and development. This is not easy for the beginning teacher. While we recognize the tremendous importance of methods and approaches and their distinct contributions to the advancement of music education, we support an eclectic music curriculum. It is the individual teacher's responsibility to be aware of current trends and choose those materials and skills that are best suited to the needs of the children and to his own particular teaching style.

Whatever methods are chosen, the clarity of the teacher's goals gives validity and focus to the teaching of music throughout the child's school program. This eliminates noise making, that is, banging on percussion instruments, indiscriminate use of recordings, and running around in the name of movement. An understanding of the young child, a basic philosophy of music for children, musical goals, a variety of music materials, and strategies for presenting those materials give the teacher a foundation for teaching young children music. Only through trial and error and the teacher's willingness to learn, however, will music programs grow and thrive.

Good music programs for children should include experiences that are carefully integrated with other classroom activities, in addition to planned music lessons. This is particularly true for the very young child. Songs and creative movements may be related to a topic being explored by the children, such as the first snowfall or a visit to the fire station. Instruments may be used to accompany them or to work out interesting representations of the sounds heard. Children may be given recordings of appropriate music for independent listening. They may also work together with the teacher to create a poem, a chant, or a song to record their experiences. When music is woven into the daily program, it increases its value and relevance to the child as an integral part of life.

Planning a Lesson

Before planning can begin, teachers need to know the musical concepts appropriate to the developmental levels of young children. Based on the premise that experience, participation, and involvement are the foundations of a good music program, and that skills, concepts, and appreciation are the outgrowth, the teacher sets up music objectives for the group, selecting what is to be learned and the mode of activity through which each objective will be accomplished.

To review, musical learnings appropriate to the early years relate to

- ◆ Rhythm
- ◆ Melody and Harmony
- ◆ Timbre
- ◆ Dynamics
- ◆ Form
- ◆ Mood

Since these elements are present in all music and are essential to its understanding, involvement with them should be as varied as possible, including playing, singing, and moving. Starting with the simplest concepts, and keeping in mind the children's abilities and developmental stages, you are ready to plan sequential musical experiences for your group. (See the teachers' guides to current music series for age-appropriate musical learnings in Appendix D.) Of course, active listening is an integral part of every lesson. Always include some singing and several other music activities to add diversity and keep interest high.

A Lesson Plan

Musical Objective(s):

Materials:

Procedures:
1. Familiar material and warm-up activities:

2. Reinforcement of previous skills:

3. New learning:

4. Culminating activity:

Evaluation:

Objectives

The first step in lesson planning is to decide on the concept to be experienced, learned, or applied. The concept should be one that is based on the child's previous learning, lies within her competence, and challenges her intellect. When this concept is identified, the best teaching vehicle for it must be chosen (i.e., singing, moving, playing), and its introduction and application planned. This requires choosing suitable materials, activities, and equipment. The teacher's plan usually begins with familiar music, followed by reinforcement of a previous learning. Then comes the introduction of new material. The lesson should not last beyond the children's highest point of interest and involvement, and it is relaxing and enjoyable to end with a known activity of their own choice.

Procedures

Having decided on the musical objectives for a specific lesson, develop your procedures in four phases:

1. Start with familiar material that is stimulating and creates an atmosphere of enjoyment, interest, and enthusiasm.
2. Extend, reinforce, or complete learning that took place at a previous time.
3. Initiate, introduce, or develop new learning through singing, playing, or moving.
4. End with one or two familiar but relaxing and calming music activities, often including one chosen by the children. Close the period on a note of success and pleasure.

Reminder: It is important to "revisit" songs previously learned from time to time. This helps to build a living musical repertoire in the children's memory.

Phases 2 and 3 of the lesson plan depend on the objectives chosen for a particular lesson. These parts may be interchanged or blended depending on your objective. Often it is in this part of the lesson that the children's discovery and creativity can be encouraged and used by the teacher to reinforce the learning.

Evaluation

To help you assess the success of your lesson and to guide you in preparing the next step, conclude your plan with simple evaluation procedures. They may be informal, including these questions: Was the musical objective achieved? Can the children perform or understand what was taught (e.g., sing the song, play the ostinato, move to the rhythmic pattern, hear and show the accent in 4/4 time)? If you are unsure of your success, try out the new skill or knowledge as a review or reinforcement activity in the next lesson. Teach it again if necessary, using new or simpler material to maintain interest. If the objective has been achieved, your children should have added to their repertoire and acquired a skill or understanding that they can use in a new context, transferring what has been learned.

The sample lesson plan on page 23 shown uses material found in Part Two. Other examples are found in Appendix A.

Alternative Procedures:

Sometimes the suggested form for a lesson may not be appropriate.

1. On occasion, the teacher may want to start with a new learning and extend it throughout the entire lesson, integrating all activities around the new skill, concept, or idea.
2. At other times, a familiar beginning activity may be extended, leading to new learning and developing into a culminating activity.
3. Variety within the lesson plan format is good and helps to keep the ongoing music program interesting and alive. Keep in mind that no one format is sacred.

When planning is built on sound objectives, music activities are varied and geared to the interests and developmental level of the children, and the teacher is willing to be flexible and responsive to children's contributions, the elements of a successful lesson are present.

A Lesson Plan

The following is a fifteen- to twenty-minute lesson plan for five- and six-year-olds in a kindergarten class working outdoors on a warm spring morning.

Musical Objective.   The children will participate in an active singing game to extend vocal repertoire and reinforce beat and rhythmic pattern.

Materials
1. "A Little Black Dog" (p. 99)
2. "Here We Come, Zudio" (p. 98)
3. "I Have Lost My Little Partner" (p. 104)
4. "Three Crows" (p. 86)

Procedures
1. *Familiar material and warm-up activities:*
   Circle game: "A Little Black Dog"
   Partner game: "Here We Come, Zudio,"
2. *Reinforcement of previous skills:*
   Return from partners to standing in circle formation. Review clapping and stamping skills, using the following pattern:

   Stamp, stamp,   clap, clap, clap

When this is secure, the group sits in a circle.

3. *New learning:* "I Have Lost My Little Partner"
   Teach this game by walking inside the circle and demonstrating the actions. You and your partner both stay in the game as it is repeated for 4, then 8, then 16 children. If your group has fewer or more than the "magic numbers" of 1, 2, 4, 8, 16, or 32, pause before the last repeat to pair up the children, opting to stay in or out yourself to ensure that all have a partner for the finale: "I have found my little partner."
4. *Culminating activity:*
   At the end of the game bring all the children around you by using a signal that you chant and clap:

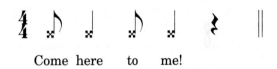

   Come here   to   me!

They will join in the clapping as they gather and may then be seated for a familiar song such as "Three Crows"

Evaluation.   Can most children sing the new song and play the game simultaneously? Do the children participate accurately in the rhythmic pattern involving stamping and clapping? Can some play the game walking naturally to the beat?

Incidental Teaching

There are many occasions for music making in the primary classroom. A change of activity, the need for physical movement or relaxation, a new lesson topic, and many other occasions are enhanced by the addition of music. With young children at any level, the teacher should be able to thread the day with music, introducing musical experiences at different times and in response to specific needs or opportunities. She should be able to produce an appropriate song, game, or activity on the spur of the moment.

The Apple Farm: An Example of Incidental Teaching

A group of children visits an apple farm where they gather their own windfalls and watch the workers. Back at school, the trip leads to activities in science, mathematics, language, art, and music. The teacher observes a boy walking in a circle, stooping and stretching up as he goes. He is chanting, "Apples on the ground, apples in the tree," reenacting his work and that of the apple pickers in rhythmic movement and chant. The little boy is outgoing and sociable, so the teacher offers him a basket from the housekeeping corner for the apples he is gathering. As his activity continues, the teacher adds a soft accompaniment of high and low tones on the piano or the resonator bells. Other children come over, interested in joining in. The teacher says: "Peter, here are two more apple pickers to help you. Let's tell them how we're doing the work! Some of the apples are high up on the trees and some have fallen on the ground." The three repeat the activity without music. Now the teacher adds: "I can play this high music (illustrates) for you to pick apples from high on the tree, and this low music (illustrates) for you to pick up the windfalls from down on the ground. There's a basket for your apples if you want to use it. I'll play this kind of music (illustrates middle tones) while you walk around among the trees." The activity may be sustained for several minutes, while the children's attention is focused on high and low tones in association with high and low movement, identifying and reinforcing the children's perception of changes in musical pitch and the use of appropriate language.

Begin now to acquire a repertoire of music that you really enjoy yourself and with which you are so familiar that you can select and adapt from it at a moment's notice. Be sure that you learn and use new material every week. By the end of the year your repertoire, skill, and confidence in incidental teaching will have expanded greatly.

RELATED ACTIVITIES FOR STUDENTS

1. Based on your study of the teacher's role in teaching music, write a short essay describing an adult who taught you some musical activities during your first six years. Note particular characteristics in attitude, personality, and ability, and describe the specific musical game, skill, or song you learned.

2. Using as models the sample lesson plans in Appendix A, write a complete lesson plan for teaching the concept of moving to the rhythmic pattern of a melody. Use the singing game "Wind, Wind, Wind the Thread" (page 000). If possible, arrange for an opportunity to teach this lesson. Find out and include opening and closing material familiar to the children. Include with your plan an observation and evaluation by a professor, teacher, or fellow student.

3. Tape-record yourself teaching a planned musical activity to children. Use this as the basis for discussion and self-evaluation in class.

4. Describe three occasions appropriate for the incidental teaching of a song. List a song from the text to suit each occasion.

Chapter 3

Diversity and Music

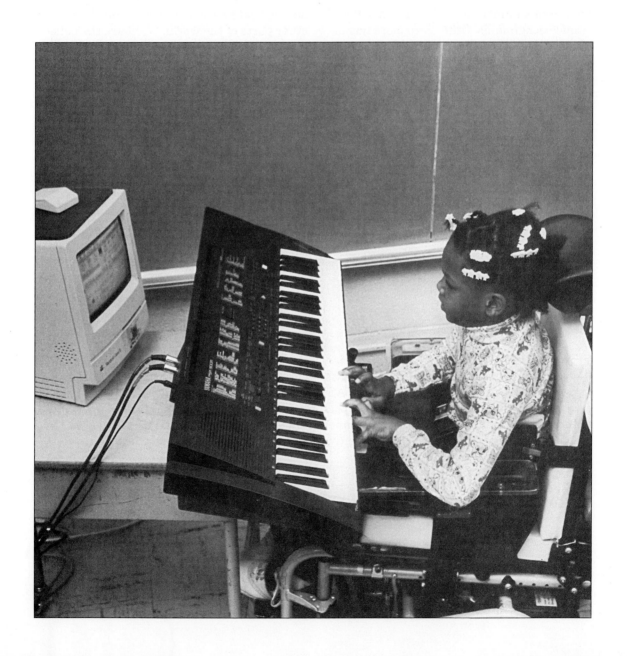

As our society approaches the twenty-first century, diversity, with all that term implies, is a major challenge to our educational system. The malleable nature of young children makes them particularly open to the development of attitudes and dispositions of tolerance and understanding. Opportunities for these qualities to grow and flourish are found in music; music is a part of every world culture and a universal means of communication between individuals. Our concept of diversity, as it relates to young children and music, develops along two strands of thought/meaning—cultural and individual, both of which are to be seen in every classroom setting.

Cultural Diversity

The range of cultural origins of the children in today's classrooms is as varied as a map of the world itself. Many classes contain children from a number of different racial and ethnic backgrounds. Others are more homogeneous in culture. Children in *all* these settings need to develop a sensitivity to and understanding of the diverse nature of today's society. Only in this way can they grow into contributing members in their own communities and the world.

Multicultural music education offers opportunities to reach these goals through songs, singing games and dances, instrumental music, stories, poetry, and guided listening. Ethnic music resources are plentiful and increasingly available, especially for older children. We have chosen developmentally appropriate music activities from four diverse world cultures, widely found in the United States today, to be a launching pad for your exploration of music from many other parts of the world. We share the belief of prominent ethnomusicologist David P. McAllester: **"It's better to learn anything about other cultures, any little bit of information—a 'smattering'—than nothing at all. Culture is contagious, and we learn smatterings or much more, depending on the opportunities presented to us."** * In that spirit, the multiethnic materials in this book serve as an introduction to the cultures they represent.

*Campbell, Patricia. "David P. McAllester on Navajo music." *Music Educators Journal* (July 1994), p. 18.

Cultural Diversity

African American Musics

A strong sense of beat and rhythmic patterns, syncopations, call-and-response singing/chanting, and work songs are characteristics of African American music appropriate to the music education of young children. Children respond readily to the highly rhythmic and repetitive nature of the music and experience its connection with much of the music heard outside school. This active enjoyment forms a positive sensory basis on which true cultural understandings can develop.

OH, CHILDREN, SHOUT FOR JOY!

Key: C
Starting tone: G

African American

Oh, chil-dren, shout for joy! Oh, chil-dren, shout for joy!

Ear-ly in the morn-ing, shout for joy! Ear-ly in the morn-ing, shout for joy!

Oh, chil-dren, shout for joy! Oh, chil-dren, shout for joy!

Mark each * with a shout: YEA! Repeat the song, using other action words: clap, jump, dance. Use a strong, short motion or sound at each *.

OBWISANA

Key: D
Starting tone: F#

African

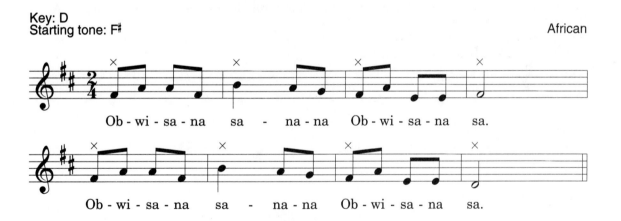

Ob - wi - sa - na   sa - na - na   Ob - wi - sa - na   sa.

Ob - wi - sa - na   sa - na - na   Ob - wi - sa - na   sa.

In this singing game from Ghana a child says: "Oh Grandma, I've hurt my finger on this stone!" The vowels are all short so the words are easy to learn.

The children sit on the floor in a circle to learn the song. Each child taps his right hand on the floor in front, on the first beat of each measure. On the second beat, each right hand moves to the right and taps the floor in front of the neighboring child.

When this is secure and rhythmic, put in front of each child a stone he can easily grasp. Now repeat the song, moving the real stones from child to Grandma on each measure.

Be sure to keep a steady beat. Children enjoy trying the game at a faster tempo.

Hispanic Musics

Singing, dancing, and the strumming of guitars are characteristic of Hispanic cultural life, whether in Spain, the many countries of Central and South America, or the United States. It is not surprising, therefore, that several versions exist of many popular folk songs and dances, with variations in melody and lyrics. Young children respond readily to the characteristics of this music. The repetitive verse-chorus form, the strong and lively syncopated rhythms, and the lilting melodies all come naturally to young children. In addition, they easily learn the Spanish words. Teaching the songs in Spanish is not difficult, and it is important to do this since it increases the children's exposure to their world of many cultures.

SAN SERENI

Key: C
Starting tone: G

Spanish

San Se - re - ní de la bue - na, bue - na vi - da,

San Se - re - ní de la bue - na bue - na vi - da, A -

sí, a - sí, a - sí, a - sí, a - sí, a - sí.

San Serení means a place where life is good.

EL COQUÍ
(The Frog)

Key: C
Starting tone: C

Puerto Rican

El co - quí sings a lul - la - by soft-ly. I can hear el co - quí all night long; Though I fall fast a - sleep when it's bed-time, In my dream comes his sweet lit - tle song: Co - quí, Co - quí, Co - quí, quí, quí, quí! Co - quí, Co - quí, Co - quí, quí, quí, quí!

This little lullaby from Puerto Rico uses both Spanish and English to tell about a sound in the night. *El coquí,* the frog, sings his own name.

The Spanish for mouse is *el ratón*. Sing a verse about him and his quiet song. Maracas make a quiet rhythmic accompaniment.

Asian Musics

The pentatonic scales and the free-flowing rhythms in Asian music contrast strongly with the music of the West, evoking less familiar moods and images. Young children are responsive to these subtleties, sensing some of the quality of Asian culture.

YANG WA WA
(Smiling Doll)

Key: F pentatonic
Starting tone: A

Taiwanese

AKI NO YŪHI NI
(Red Maple Leaves)

Key: F
Starting tone: A

Japanese

This song is about a Chinese child singing to a smiling doll.

Composed for school children after the Meiji revolution, this song tells of a red maple tree glowing on the hillside.

Native American Musics

The music of the American Indian is primarily vocal and closely integrated into daily and ceremonial life. Much of it focuses on the natural world and often includes dance and hand gestures accompanied by rattles and drums. Here, as with African American musics, young children respond to the strong recurrent rhythms and the repeated movement patterns. We emphasize the importance of sharing truly authentic Native American music with our children and avoiding the disrespectful use of contrived materials, so widespread today.

Key: C pentatonic
Starting tone: G

Hopi
Collected by David McAllester

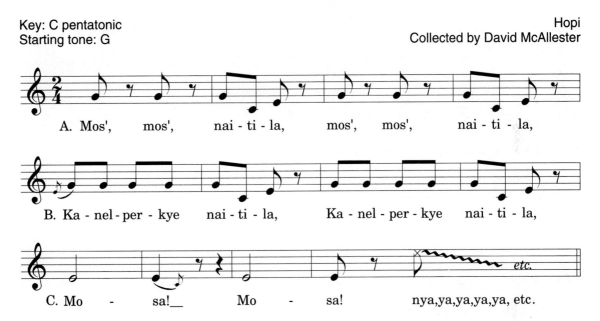

A. Mos', mos', nai - ti - la, mos', mos', nai - ti - la,

B. Ka - nel - per - kye nai - ti - la, Ka - nel - per - kye nai - ti - la,

C. Mo - sa!__ Mo - sa! nya,ya,ya,ya,ya, etc.

This Hopi children's singing game comes from Arizona. It describes a cat who steals sheepskins and goatskins from the village. Teach it as an echo song, "pawing" with both hands on the beat for A and B. At C "paw" once for each word.

HI YO HI YO IP SI NI YAH
(Happy Song)

Key: C pentatonic
Starting tone: G

Navajo

A. Hi   yo,   hi   yo   ip   si   ni   yah,

B. Hi   yo,   hi   yo   ip   si   ni _____ yah,

C. Hi _____ yo,   hi   yo   ip   si   ni   yah,

D. Hi _____ yo,   hi   yo   ip   si   ni   yah,

E. Hi   yo,   hi   yo!
   (pat   pat   pat   pat)

The simple, repeated words of this chant have no literal translation. They are the syllables Navajo sing to the rhythm of the melody. They are called "vocables."

Children sit cross-legged in a circle on the floor. Sing the whole chant to them and add this patting sequence to phrase E:

knees, knees, knees, knees

Sing the whole song, till it is secure, with the class patting at the final phrase E. Stress that this small patting pattern comes at the end of *every* repeat.

Teach, one at a time, the patting sequence for phrases A–E for each of four repeats of the chant:

1. knees, knees, floor (in front), floor (in front), knees, knees
2. knees, knees, floor (at sides), floor (at sides), knees, knees
3. knees, knees, 1 knee left, 1 knee left, knees, knees
4. knees, knees, 1 knee right, 1 knee right, knees, knees

Note: At 3, "1 knee left" puts the left hand on neighbor's right knee, right hand on own left knee. At 4, the reverse occurs.

Children enjoy changing the above sequence and inventing new patterns, always using E as a resting place.

Individual Diversity

Most of the children we teach can be identified within the developmental profiles that cluster around their chronological ages. There is a small group, however, who do not "fit the descriptors" for one or more reasons. These atypical children are often described as children with "special needs," and in times past their education was provided in special schools and classes, by teachers qualified in special education.

In 1975 the federal government enacted Public Law 94–142, the Education for All Handicapped Children Act. This requires schools to "mainstream" or bring such children into regular classrooms to the extent that they can benefit from this "least restrictive environment."

The current policy of inclusion in the public education process of those with particular needs comes about through Civil Rights Rider #504, appended to Public Law 94–142. Along with the right to be in a regular classroom, it brings with it ramifications in terms of staffing, school facilities and materials, and modifications to both curriculum and instructional techniques.

To help in planning appropriate music experiences and fostering optimal growth in these children, teachers need to understand the effects of some of their disabilities and the role of music in helping them overcome them. **All young children need the joy, security, and comfort that musical activity brings, and this is particularly true for the individually diverse.** In addition, learnings stimulated by musical activity lead to other areas where difficulty is being experienced. Communication and language abilities, physical coordination, purposeful use of feelings, and focusing of attention, as well as the subject matter itself, are all enhanced by the musical participation of these children. The resulting growth in self-esteem is immeasurable.

Individual Diversity

Limited Vision

Children who are visually limited or blind may be hesitant to move freely in the primary classroom, holding back from the physical and social exploration of their environment so characteristic of their peers. They often wait for adults to direct and lead them and appear somewhat passive or slow to catch on in their early school days. Their auditory and tactile skills, however, are increasingly sensitive; and speech and song are rewarding and beneficial modes of expression. Singing, playing, and moving with sighted children gives the visually impaired child important social skills and the ability to become a member of the group.

Limited Hearing

Children with hearing problems often have associated speech difficulties in the early years. The acquisition of a functional vocabulary and understandable speech patterns is a slow process, even with mechanical aids, and such children may become tense, lacking a sense of flow in their physical movement. In the early childhood setting, they may follow their teachers continually to stay in touch with their source of security and not miss out. They become adept at placing themselves advantageously in group situations and may particularly enjoy and benefit from movement activities and the playing of instruments, feeling the vibrations through fingers and limbs. Their singing is often hearty though limited in tonal range. The hearing-impaired child's confidence is built through the use of many modalities, especially movement and visual clues.

Limited Mobility

Orthopedic problems in the early years may have been present at birth or caused by illness. Limited mobility or motor control characterizes such handicaps, and the degrees of difficulty encountered vary widely. Listening and singing are not particular problems for these children, and their responses to music may also include simple rhythmic movements of head, trunk, and limbs. A growing ability to play musical instruments appropriate to their manipulative skills brings social and emotional growth as well as musical enrichment to children who are motorically limited.

Limited Understanding

We find slow learners and children who are somewhat developmentally delayed in our classrooms today, some of them full-time and some part-time. These youngsters are limited in their cognitive abilities, resulting in developmental delays such as poor motoric and speech development, short attention span, difficulty in following directions, and lack of initiative and interest, especially in group settings. Slow learners enjoy and often eagerly participate in moving, playing, and singing activities, incidentally acquiring useful skills and knowledge and developing positive attitudes toward others. Poor coordination and lack of ability to sing in tune are secondary to the joy experienced through participation, and teachers will need to accommodate these varying abilities tactfully.

Learning Problems

Initially, children who are learning disabled may appear in the early childhood classroom as children with emotional or behavior problems. If a child does not adequately process the input from her own sensorimotor experience, she may be considered stubborn, hostile, or a reluctant learner. Professional assessment, however, may reveal that such patterns of behavior result from a problem in the central nervous system. She may have specific perceptual problems in paying attention and remembering (attention-deficit disorder), sequencing and directionality (dyslexia), listening, or looking. Many of these problems originate before birth. Such disabilities make children's efforts to learn songs or to play active games and simple instruments uneven and sporadic, although the will and desire to do so may be present. Responses and achievement vary from child to child but often improve in simple, low-key settings.

Emotional Problems

Emotional problems in children may be the cause of disruptive social behaviors in the early years. Children who have suffered traumatic experiences sometimes respond to their world with destructiveness, hostility, or aggression. They also may reject it by becoming sulky or withdrawn. Behavior may be consistent in any one of these modes or it may be unpredictable and erratic as the child is swayed by the feelings of the moment. Even a clumsy attempt by such a youngster to participate in any musical activity may be his very best effort to relate to his peers and teachers. When his interest is nurtured carefully, he may be able to interact with music at his affective level and enjoy the soothing influence of the activity.

You may have mainstreamed children in your class and other individuals for whom you have specific musical or behavioral goals. The following examples offer ways of integrating mainstreamed children into the musical experience through adaptations to individual needs. The alert and sympathetic teacher can readily apply these techniques to other materials in this book as she comes to understand the needs of these children. More examples and discussion of disabilities is provided in Lois Birkenshaw-Fleming's book, *Come on, Everybody, Let's Sing.*[1]

The first example is a suitable singing game for such a kindergarten class, in the second month of school. The class contains five children with individual needs:

Albert: restless, moves constantly, in a group has difficulty focusing attention.

Betsy: hearing impaired, wears a hearing aid, participates well but speaks only in a whisper.

Carol: verbal, assertive, quick to learn but finds many ways to dominate others, who resent her.

Derek: mildly developmentally delayed, highly motivated, happy nature, some speech problems, needs extra time on skills.

Eddie: cerebral palsy, wears leg braces but walks with assistance.

BALLOONS FOR SALE!

Key: F
Starting tone: C

Words and Music: J. Haines

Bal - loons for sale! Bal - loons for sale! Here comes the col - or man!

Bal - loons for sale! Bal - loons for sale! I'll buy one if I can.

The children sit in a circle with the balloon man in the center. He holds a bunch of colored balloons and walks around as the children sing. At the end of the song he sells a balloon to the child where he stops, as follows:

Q. Would you like to buy a balloon today? A. Yes, please.

Q. What color would you like? A. Red, please.

Q. Here you are. Do you have ten cents? A. Yes, I do.

Q. Thank you!

And on he goes. When all the balloons are sold, the balloon man may stand in the middle of the circle and call the colors home.

In addition to the regular plan, individual objectives may be as follows:

Albert: He will sustain in the circle, beside the teacher, for five minutes, and participate if chosen.

Betsy: She will respond to the balloon man audibly.

Carol: She will take the balloon man's part, and let others have turns without interfering.

Derek: He will point to and correctly name a color he "knew" yesterday.

Eddie: He will choose three favorite colors and sell the balloons himself, with assistance in walking.

Presented in a similar format to the above is an echo song. It helps develop in-tune singing in a first grade, in the spring of the year. The class includes:

Francesca: speaks only Spanish at home, cries if unsuccessful.

Gerry: legally blind, good oral language.

Helena: in a wheelchair, no speech, can use hands.

Ivan: hostile, fists up to everyone.

AS I LOOKED OUT MY WINDOW

Key: C pentatonic
Starting tone: G

Words and Music: M. Burnett

This charming echo song gives groups and individuals call-and-response practice. Change "cock robin" to the names of other birds, animals, and people in the children's lives. Accept a variety of suggestions and adjust the rhythm as needed.

Suggested individual goals are:

Francesca: She will echo in Spanish first, then English.

Gerry: He should have no difficulty.

Helena: She will wave "Hello" and "I'm just fine."

Ivan: He will sit between an adult and a reliable child and participate.

A singing game offers children a welcome change of pace and the opportunity for movement, even in a room with desks formally arranged.

Third graders enjoy "Tony Chestnut." Such a class may include:

Judy: dyslexic, nonreader, mainstreamed for music/art.

Keith: obese, poorly coordinated, low self-esteem.

Lavene: nonparticipant, appears depressed, "spaced out."

Moishe: mild Down's syndrome, limited speech, eager participant.

TONY CHESTNUT

Key: C
Starting tone: G

Camp Song

Teach the song by rote, then write text on the board:

To - ny   Chest - nut   knows I   love   you

Discuss motions and add below text:

toe   knee   chest   head   nose   eye   hug   point

Repeat the song, adding the motions as the words indicate. When the song and motions are very secure, repeat the whole motion sequence four more times, and leave off the *sung* words, one at a time, in the following order:

- nut

Chest - nut

- ny Chest - nut

To - ny Chest - nut

Continue four more times, deleting these additional words (this is more difficult):

you

love you

I love you

knows I love you

Suggested individual goals are:

    Judy: She may help with the board work and the sequencing.

    Keith: With encouragement he will try hard to do motions.

    Lavene: She will use a pointer to show the word order.

    Moishe: He will focus on and imitate the teacher's model.

◆ —————————————————————————— ◆

We conclude this necessarily brief overview of diversity in its two major manifestations. First come differences in culture, traditions, values, language, and even appearance. Many of these differences tend to divide us, but music from the world's children brings unity out of its very diversity, if teachers are prepared and eager to initiate and sustain the cross-cultural experience. Next, but of equal importance and challenge, are differences in individual potential—physical, mental, and emotional—which tend to divide a child from his peers and to label him, to his detriment. These differences, too, can be minimized if teachers are willing and prepared to bring children closer to each other in spite of their disparities, uniting them through the shared musical experience.

NOTES

1. Birkenshaw-Fleming, Lois. (1989.) *Come on, everybody, let's sing.* Toronto: Gordon V. Thompson. Chapter 13 (pp. 239–276).

RELATED ACTIVITIES FOR STUDENTS

1. Write a description of your own early childhood as it was impacted by children with different cultural backgrounds and/or individual disabilities. Comment, if you can, on ways in which your teachers helped or hindered you in developing positive attitudes and behaviors toward these children.

2. Visit the children's department of your local library. Find and document at least ten books relating to cultural diversity, appropriate for young children. Indicate briefly the focus on the content. For one title add a paragraph commenting on the quality of the text and the illustrations.

3. Choose and learn one of the musical examples from the Cultural and Individual Diversity parts of this chapter. Teach it to a small group of children, noting their responses. Share these with your classmates and discuss the role of music in the antibias curriculum.

4. Refer to the five children described in the plan for "Balloons for Sale," page 35. Write individually appropriate goals for each child using any other musical selection in Chapter 3.

5. Identify a child with a specific learning challenge. Choose, prepare, and teach her a music activity that can improve her ability. Write up or record this project and evaluate its success.

Part Two

Musical Experiences

Chapters 4 through 10 contain music experiences for children from preschool to about age eight. In each chapter the content is arranged from the simple to the complex. We have avoided assigning age levels to the material to encourage teachers to choose from it without regard for the artificial barriers of age and grade. A particular group of children may be able to sing quite difficult songs but may need the simplest movement activities. Another group may have the opposite abilities. Teachers are urged to choose freely from the range of material offered, evaluating their choices by the enthusiasm and understanding shown by the children.

Having chosen material, the teacher needs to learn it thoroughly. Only when the words and melody, the beat and rhythmic patterns, and the sequences of movement or instrumentation are truly familiar can they be shared with children, enabling them to internalize and make the learnings their own.

We have not isolated active listening and creative experiences in separate sections but have integrated them with the singing, moving, and playing material of the following chapters. Active listening is clearly part of every music activity, whether incidental or intentional. Creative musical acts do not occur in a vacuum but in a specific setting and in conjunction with some particular aspect of music in which a child engages.

While listening opportunities occur in each chapter, Chapter 9 is devoted to the use of recordings and live performances as listening sources. For such experiences to be meaningful to young children, teachers need to develop the skills discussed and illustrated in that chapter.

A REMINDER ABOUT CHILDREN WITH SPECIAL NEEDS

Many special needs children will enjoy and benefit from the materials in the following chapters. Give them frequent opportunities to take part in musical activities during the school day, in both group and individual settings. In your mind, or on paper, establish appropriate goals for each of your special learners. Sometimes small modifications in your teaching will be all that is needed; at other times you will need to observe a child's response in the group and tailor specific activities for specific needs.

Here are some suggestions:

1. A quiet song with a gentle rhythmic activity can enhance self-control in a group, soothe an overactive individual, or reassure a tearful or withdrawn child.
2. A supportive adult's hands and arms help children overcome hearing, visual, and

motor limitations to achieve the right rhythmic movement, learn action songs, and play instruments.

3. Hands and fingers on drums, piano keys, bells, and the lips and throats of singers give deaf and blind children the feel of the sounds they cannot hear or see.

4. Children who hear or contribute their names or information about their families, pets, and personal lives in the words of songs develop interest, concentration, and a positive self-image.

5. Frequent repetition of old favorites, even in the primary grades, enables learning-disabled or intellectually slower children to internalize their learning by working within their own styles and speeds.

The overall principle in teaching special learners is to make the learning steps small and frequent, so that each child has optimal opportunity to like and learn music and to make music her own. Thus, success and joy are built into the daily musical life of every child and even the least able finds herself to be a worthy member of the group.

Chapter 4

Rhymes, Finger Plays, Chants, and Song-Stories

Rhymes

Children respond to their environment from the very beginning with vocal and physical reactions that are both rhythmic and repetitive. To encourage and stimulate this awareness, to capture and hold the child's attention, we play with her often, using the rhythmic word patterns and motions of nursery rhymes and traditional verses.

Rhythm and repetition are also an integral part of music, so that when we sing and play with young children we are, in fact, laying the foundation of their musical awareness and responsiveness. Unlimited potential exists in these rhymes for fostering language and speech development by teaching awareness of pitch (high, low), dynamics (loud, soft), tempo (fast, slow), and meter (e.g., rocking, marching). Children should also have the opportunity to perceive and organize rhythm for themselves, to make rhythmic and vocal skills firmly their own through activities they originate and help shape.

As children come together in groups in preschool and primary settings, use nursery rhymes and songs such as those that follow. Teach them to the children through participation and then add the rhythmic beat by such movements as clapping, patching, tapping, or marching. (*Patsching* is a German term found in the Orff method meaning "slapping the thighs with the open hands.")

When the words are known, simple percussion instruments may sometimes be used to keep the beat, add tone color, illustrate the words, or give interest and variety. Suitable instruments for keeping a clear beat are rhythm sticks, drums, tambourines, wood blocks, and cymbals. For special effects add jingle clogs, triangles, bells, and maracas.

Participation is the goal when instruments are first used. Some children are tentative while others overreact in the beginning; in either case the rhythm may falter. Encourage gentle playing by a few children at a time, avoiding drill on keeping the beat. As children have frequent opportunities to play, the feel of the beat will soon be captured and rhythmic playing will develop to accompany rhythmic singing.

As children grow older, they develop new skills such as imitating, remembering, and carrying out a sequence of physical movements. They acquire a repertoire of actions on which they can draw in creating their own movements for rhymes and songs. They also learn how to do two things at once, such as singing or speaking while marking the beat, speaking while moving to an internal rhythm, or doing hand motions while singing a simple melody.

Today hundreds of nursery rhymes and games are available in books and on cassette, including many that adults remember from their own childhood and many from diverse cultures. Try some of the following rhymes, adding a rhythmic swing, bounce, or patsch to keep the beat.

Twinkle, twinkle, little star,
How I wonder what you are.
Up above the world so high,
Like a diamond in the sky.
Twinkle, twinkle, little star,
How I wonder what you are.

◆ ─────────────── ◆

Baa, baa, black sheep, have you any wool?
Yes sir, yes sir, three bags full.
One for my master and one for my dame,
and one for the little boy who lives
   down the lane.

◆ ─────────────── ◆

Hickory dickory dock.
The mouse ran up the clock.
The clock struck one, the mouse ran down.
Hickory dickory dock.

Hickory dickory dare.
The pig flew up in the air.
The man in brown soon brought it down.
Hickory dickory dare.

◆ ─────────────── ◆

See-saw, Margery Daw.
Johnnie shall have a new master.
He shall have but a penny a day
Because he can't work any faster.

◆ ─────────────── ◆

Jack be nimble, Jack be quick,
Jack jump over the candle stick.

♦ —————————————————— ♦

Humpty Dumpty sat on a wall.
Humpty Dumpty had a great fall.
All the king's horses and all the king's men
Couldn't put Humpty together again.

♦ —————————————————— ♦

Hot cross buns!
Hot cross buns!
One a penny, two a penny,
Hot cross buns!
If you have no daughters
Give them to your sons,
One a penny, two a penny,
Hot cross buns!

♦ —————————————————— ♦

Lucy Locket lost her pocket,
Kitty Fisher found it.
Not a penny was there in it,
But a ribbon round it.

♦ —————————————————— ♦

Little Boy Blue, come blow your horn.
The sheep's in the meadow, the cow's
    in the corn.
But where is the boy who looks after
    the sheep?
He's under the haystack, fast asleep!

♦ —————————————————— ♦

Pussy cat, pussy cat, where have you been?
I've been to London to visit the Queen.
Pussy cat, pussy cat, what did you there?
I frightened a little mouse under the chair.

♦ —————————————————— ♦

Older children will enjoy "The Nursery Rhyme Rap" found on page 51.

Finger Plays

Finger plays appeal strongly to the very young child because they give him the attention of the important adults in his life. Physical nearness and imitation, eye contact, and shared expressions of feeling all stimulate activity and build ego-strength. Musically, such games are strongly rhythmic, often involving the chanting of simple melodic intervals and rhythmic patterns. In addition, the movement of fingers, hands, and other parts of the body develops kinetic awareness and muscular coordination. Nursery school and kindergarten children show interest in the content and mime found in many rhymes of topical and seasonal interest.

Here are some rhymes with specific hand movements. Speak the words with vocal inflection and a strong rhythm.

Rhyme:	*Hand movement:*
Give a little whirl,	Roll the hands one around the other.
Give a little twirl,	Reverse direction.
Give a little clap,	Clap once, on the word.
Lay them in your lap.	Clasp the hands and fold them on the lap.

♦ —————————————————— ♦

Five little peas in a pea pod pressed,	Clench fingers of one hand.
One grew, two grew, and so did all the rest.	Raise fingers slowly.
They grew and grew and did not stop,	Stretch fingers wide.
Until one day the pod went POP!	Clap loudly on "pop."

♦ —————————————————— ♦

This is a nest for a robin.	Cup hands together.
This is a hive for a bee.	Put clenched fists together.
This is a hole for a bunny.	Make a circle with thumb and finger.
And this is a house for me.	Make a roof overhead with fingers touching.

♦ —————————————————— ♦

Thumbkin Left and Thumbkin Right	Hold up both thumbs.
Met each other late at night.	Move thumbs toward each other.
Thumbkin Left said: "How are you?"	Wag left thumb.
Thumbkin Right said: "Fine! And you?"	Wag right thumb.
See them nod each sleepy head.	Move thumbs apart, nodding.
Now each Thumbkin's gone to bed!	Tuck thumbs away behind back.

◆ ——————————— ◆

Here's a bunny with ears so funny,	Hold up two crooked fingers on one hand.
And here's a hole in the ground.	Make a round shape with the thumb and finger of the other hand.
At the first sound he hears, he pricks up his ears,	Raise and wiggle the ear fingers.
And pops right into the ground!	Pop the rabbit ears into the hole made by the other hand.

◆ ——————————— ◆

I see a ball,	Thumb and forefinger touching.
And I see a ball,	Two thumbs together, two forefingers.
And a great big ball I see.	Both arms raised over the head.
Shall we count them?	
One! Two! Three!	Repeat the motions in unbroken sequence.

◆ ——————————— ◆

Five little squirrels	Hold up all the fingers of right hand.
Lived in a tree.	Show the shape of a big tree with both arms.
This one said:	Touch the right thumb.
"What do I see?"	Peer around, hand shading eyes.
This one said:	Touch index finger, right hand.
"I hear a gun!"	Cup hand to the ear.
This one said:	Touch middle finger, right hand.
"Oo! let's run!"	Draw back with arms bent and fists by shoulders.
This one said:	Touch ring finger, right hand.
"Let's hide in the shade."	Peek through a lattice of crossed fingers, held over the eyes.
This one said:	Touch little finger, right hand.
"I'm not afraid!"	Give three rhythmic beats on the chest, with the right hand.
When BANG went the gun,	Give one loud clap.
And they ran, every one!	Let the fingers of both hands run away behind the back.

This can be repeated using the fingers of the left hand as the squirrels. It can also be used for solo and group speech.

◆ ——————————— ◆

Five little jack-o'-lanterns sitting on a gate.	Holds up all fingers of one hand.
This one said: "My it's getting late!"	Look at watch.
This one said: "Who goes there?"	Scan the sky.
This one said: "There are witches in the air!"	"Fly" with arms.
This one said: "Let's run, let's run!"	Draw back both arms.
This one said: "It's Halloween fun!"	Gesture *It's nothing* with hands.
When WHOOSH went the wind, and OUT went the light,	Both hands sweep from the mouth and out to the sides.
Away went the jack-o'-lanterns, Halloween night!	All the fingers run and hide behind the back.

This rhyme uses the same pattern as "Five Little Squirrels" for indicating each jack-o'-lantern.

Chants

Chanting develops an awareness of the beat underlying music and introduces young children to the experience of accent and meter.

There are two kinds of chants: spoken chants and chants with limited vocal pitch. In the first, the *speaking voice* is used and the words are given strong rhythmic stress. In the second, which can be written on the staff, the *singing voice* is used with a small range of pitches and the strong rhythmic emphasis still occurs.

Spoken Chants

> Clap your hands as slowly,
> As slowly as can be,
> Clap them very quickly,
> Just like me.

This verse lends itself to rhythmic chanting in two contrasting tempi, with countless additional verses involving many verbs and body parts: (1) "Snap your fingers . . . ," (2) "Shake . . . ," (3) "Rub . . . ," (4) "Stamp your feet . . . ," (5) "Tap your head . . . ," (6) "Blink your eyes . . . ," and many more.

◆ ——————————————————————— ◆

> My mother said I never should
> Play with the alligators in the wood.
> If I did, she would say:
> "Naughty girl to disobey!"

Partners face each other to clap their own hands and then their partner's in rhythm with the chant.

◆ ——————————————————————— ◆

> Freight train! Freight train! Number Nine!
> Going down Chicago line.
> If the train goes off the track,
> Do you want your money back?
> 1. Yes (high pitch)
> > or
> 2. No! (low pitch)
> > or
> 3. Maybe so! (medium pitch)

Chant this verse rhythmically, rubbing the palms of the hands back and forth to imitate the train. Use the three endings in turn and add a hand motion for each, paralleling the pitch of the voice used.

◆ ——————————————————————— ◆

The following chants have notated rhythms added to them to make them easier to teach and to ensure rhythmic accuracy, especially where off-beat rhythms occur. It should be noted that such syncopation is not difficult for children to learn when it is closely related to word patterns. In fact, the frequent use of rhythmic speech is basic to a good early childhood music program.

THE APPLE TREE

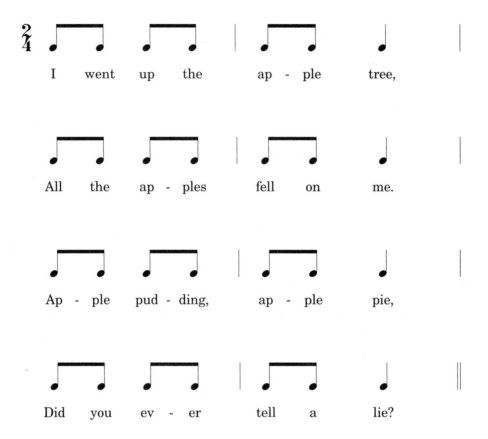

Patsch the beat with light hand slaps on the thighs and use the names of other fruits to vary this chant. Instruments may be added for tone color.

FOUR LITTLE MONKEYS

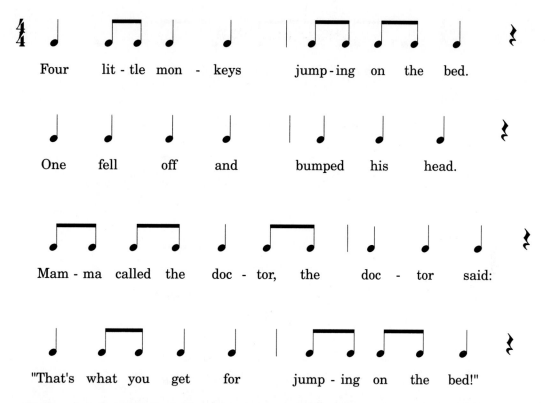

Four lit - tle mon - keys jump - ing on the bed.

One fell off and bumped his head.

Mam - ma called the doc - tor, the doc - tor said:

"That's what you get for jump - ing on the bed!"

Explore hand and body motions to accompany this rhyme or act out the words. Additional verses can begin with three, two, and one.

I HAVE FEET

I   have   feet   that   tap,   tap,   tap,

Tap feet three times.

I   have   hands   that   clap,   clap,   clap,

Clap hands three times.

I   have   eyes   to   see   who's   who,

Make goggles with fingers and look around.

Pol - ly   John - son,   I   see   you!

Point to the person named.

THREE LITTLE MUFFINS

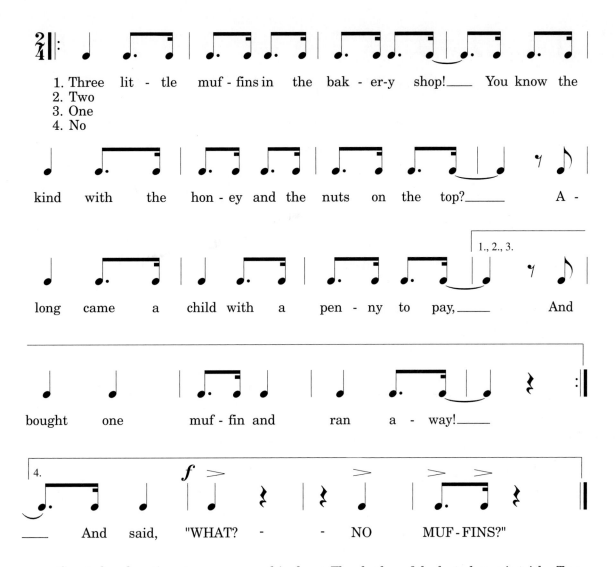

1. Three lit - tle muf - fins in the bak - er-y shop!___ You know the
2. Two
3. One
4. No

kind with the hon - ey and the nuts on the top?_____ A -

long came a child with a pen - ny to pay,___ And

bought one muf - fin and ran a - way!___

4. And said, "WHAT? - - NO MUF - FINS?"

Create hand motions to accompany this chant. The rhythm of the last phrase is tricky. Try:

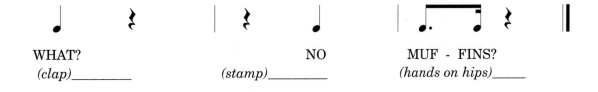

WHAT?   NO   MUF - FINS?
(clap)_____   *(stamp)_____*   *(hands on hips)_____*

NOT LAST NIGHT BUT THE NIGHT BEFORE

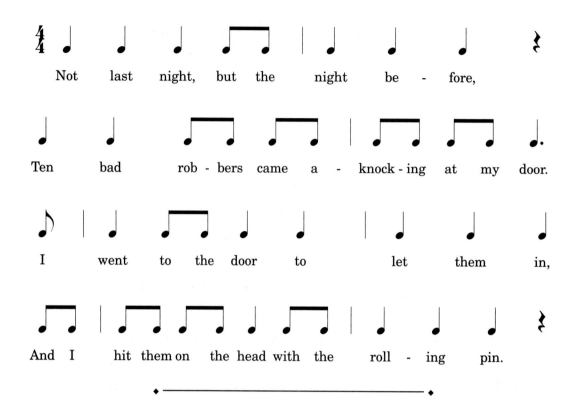

Not last night, but the night be - fore,

Ten bad rob - bers came a - knock - ing at my door.

I went to the door to let them in,

And I hit them on the head with the roll - ing pin.

EENIE, MEENIE, GYPSA LEENIE

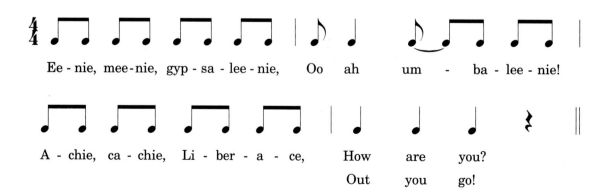

Ee - nie, mee-nie, gyp - sa - lee - nie, Oo ah um - ba - lee - nie!

A - chie, ca - chie, Li - ber - a - ce, How are you?
                                                    Out you go!

THE NURSERY RHYME RAP

Refrain   Mark Weeks

Ev' - ry - bod - y   clap,   ev' - ry - bod - y   clap.

Ev' - re - bod - y   clap   to   the   nurs - ery   rhyme   rap.

Lis - ten   to   the   words,   and   it   won't   take   long,   'til you're

mov - ing   to   the   rhy - thm   and   you're sing - ing   to   the   song.

1. Baa, baa, black sheep, have you any wool?
   Yes sir, yes sir three bags full.
   One for my master and one for my dame
   And one for the little boy who lives down the lane.

   Refrain

2. Humpty Dumpty sat on a wall,
   Humpty Dumpty had a great fall.
   All the king's horses and all the king's men
   Couldn't put Humpty together again.

   Refrain

Add more familiar rhymes. Be sure to keep to the same steady beat.

MY FAV'RITE TREAT

Joan Haines

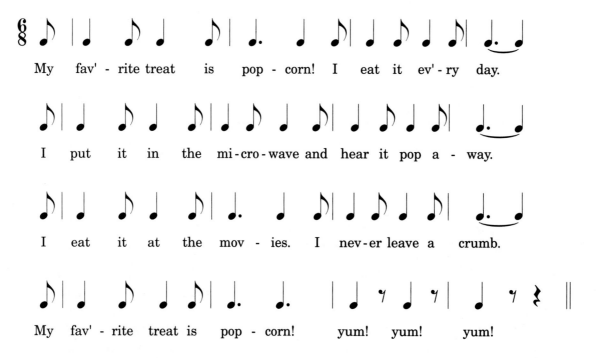

Keep the beat of this chant with a steady, light patsch throughout, with three loud claps on "Yum, Yum, Yum!" at the end. Substitute other two-syllable microwaveable foods of the children's choice, and repeat.

DOCTOR KNICKERBOCKER

American Traditional

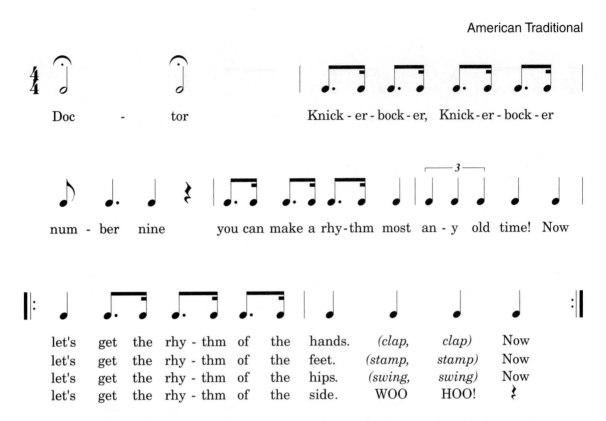

Doc - tor   Knick - er - bock - er,   Knick - er - bock - er

num - ber   nine   you can make a rhy-thm most an - y old time! Now

let's	get	the	rhy - thm	of	the	hands.	*(clap,*	*clap)*	Now
let's	get	the	rhy - thm	of	the	feet.	*(stamp,*	*stamp)*	Now
let's	get	the	rhy - thm	of	the	hips.	*(swing,*	*swing)*	Now
let's	get	the	rhy - thm	of	the	side.	WOO	HOO!	

This chant is played standing in a circle. Patsch continuously on "Doctor." Then clap own hands and those of players on either side in a two-beat rhythm and substitute additional actions as indicated.

HEY THERE!

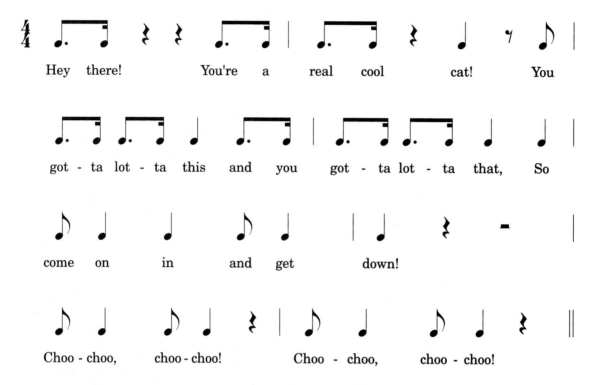

Hey there!   You're   a   real   cool   cat!   You

got - ta lot - ta this   and   you   got - ta lot - ta that,   So

come   on   in   and   get   down!

Choo - choo,   choo - choo!   Choo - choo,   choo - choo!

The chant "Hey There!" is useful for familiarizing both teachers and children with people's names. Establish an easy walking beat by saying, "A-one, a-two, a-three, a-four," snapping and swinging your arms from side to side on the numbers. Keep the snapping and swinging going, and start walking to the beat. Go around the group, chanting the words. When you come to the half-note rest (▬) after "down!" stand still and call someone's name. That person joins on behind you during "Choo-choo, choo-choo! Choo-choo, choo-choo!"

Repeat from "Hey there!" adding a new person after the next "down!" Add as many children as you wish in this fashion. Of course, the children themselves may take over the calling of names when they know the chant well enough. When the train is long enough, "choo-choo" around a few times and slow down as if coming to a station.

WHO STOLE THE COOKIE?

Introduction   American Traditional Game

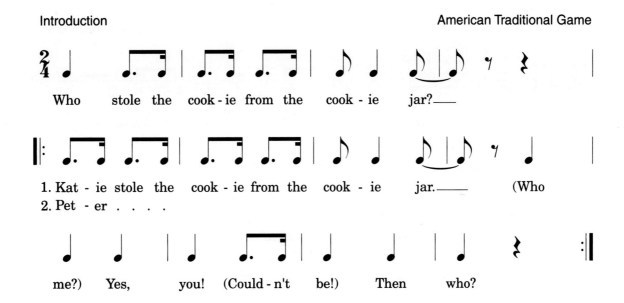

This chant is a game, done in circle formation, with specific goals. To be successful, all the children must sing, speak, and move as one; the rhythmic patterns must be unerringly accurate and the beat regular and unflagging.

Establish a basic two-beat rhythm in the circle: children clapping their own hands, then those of their neighbors on both sides. This continues, uninterrupted, throughout the game. The teacher is a member of the circle and assumes the leader's role until the children are ready to take over. All speak the first phrase. The teacher takes the second phrase, giving a child's name. The rest of the dialogue is between that child and the whole group. Each time the second phrase comes around, a new name is given. When the group is ready, the leadership changes, each time passing the chanted dialogue around the circle in unbroken rhythm to the clapped accompaniment. Ultimately, numbers or letters may be assigned instead of using names, though this is difficult. Of course, those who fail to keep the rhythm unbroken leave the game until two or three unflagging children are acclaimed as winners.

Melodic Chants

In addition to chants that use the speaking voice, there are many with limited-range melodies. These melodic chants develop and reinforce tuneful singing.*

Three Ways to Start a Melodic Chant

1. Identify the starting tone from the written music. Then sound the tone on any tuned instrument, such as piano, resonator bells, metallophone, recorder, or pitch pipe.

2. Start the chant and sing it through. If the pitch seems too high or too low for the singers, start over by using a little higher or lower tone. This trial-and-error method leads to increasing skill and accuracy. The tendency is usually to pitch a song too low. Beware of it!

3. Ask a reliable, tuneful singer in the group to start a familiar chant. A comfortable range is usually achieved. This is another skill that will grow.

---

*For ideas on selecting and teaching song materials, see Appendix A.

OH MY, NO MORE PIE!

Key: D min
Starting tone: A

American Traditional

Oh my,   (Oh my,)   Wan-na piece o' pie! (Wan-na piece o'pie!)

Pie's too sweet, wanna piece o' meat!
Meat's too red, wanna piece o' bread!
Bread's too brown, think I'll go to town!
Town's too far, better take a car!
Car's too slow, fell and stubbed my toe!
Toe gives me pain, better take a train!
Train had a wreck, nearly broke my neck!
Oh my, no more pie!

SARDINES

Key: E min
Starting tone: D

Camp Song

Sar - dines (hey) and pork and beans (hey). Sar - dines on a Mon - day.

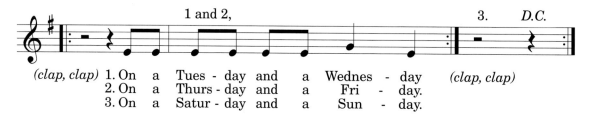

(clap, clap) 1. On a Tues - day and a Wednes - day (clap, clap)
            2. On a Thurs - day and a Fri - day.
            3. On a Satur - day and a Sun - day.

The camp chant "Sardines" is built on three tones. It involves children in devising simple two-beat body rhythms. On each "hey" make a circle in the air with open hands at shoulder level. Teach the song with the "clap, clap" as indicated and the children will readily suggest other motions such as stamp, snap, and sway.

HAMBONE, HAMBONE, WHERE YOU BEEN?

Key: F pentatonic
Starting tone: A

American Traditional

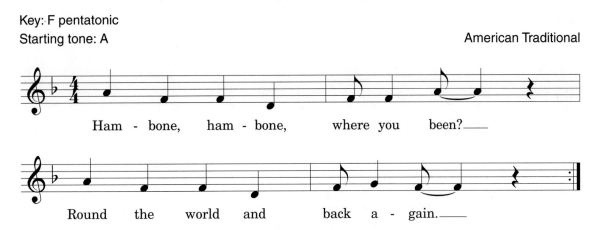

Ham - bone, ham - bone, where you been?___

Round the world and back a - gain.___

Hambone, hambone, where's your wife?
In the kitchen cooking rice.
Hambone, hambone, have you heard?
Poppa's gonna buy you a mockin' bird.
If that mocking bird don't sing,
Poppa's gonna buy you a diamond ring.
If that diamond ring don't shine,
Poppa's gonna buy you a street car line.
If that street car line gets broke,
Poppa's gonna buy you a billy goat.
If that billy goat runs away,
Poppa's gonna buy you a load of hay.
If that load of hay burns down,
Poppa's gonna buy you a wedding gown.
If that wedding gown gets tore,
(Whisper:) Poppa's gonna kick you out the door!
(Shout:) HAMBONE!

HEY, MR. KNICKERBOCKER

Key: E♭
Starting tone: G

Playground Chant

Clap   1   2   3   4   5   6   7   8

On each repeat, name a new body part at the asterisk, moving it appropriately during the counting sequence.

Song-Stories

Song-stories combine chanting and singing to tell the story with motions to keep the beat. Based on folk or nursery tales, they contain much repetition and follow the syncopated rhythms of natural speech. As long as the beat is constant, these patterns should come easily. The rhythmic notations that follow are a guide only and need not be followed exactly. Children well-versed in jumprope and hopscotch chants are very good at this activity.

♫ ACTIVITY 1: THE THREE BEARS' JIVE _____

Establish the 4/4 beat with a steady patsch-clap, snap-clap. Repeat it twice before beginning the chant. Keep it constant throughout, except on "Someone has broken my chair!" and "Bye, bye, bye, bye, bye, bye, bye." These are triplet sequences and are most effective when the rhythmic pattern itself is patsched.

THE THREE BEARS' JIVE

Traditional

Once upon a time in a nursey rhyme there were three bears—
A momma and a poppa and a wee bear.
They all went a-walking and a-talking in the woods.
Along came a girl with long curly hair.

Key: D
Starting tone: A

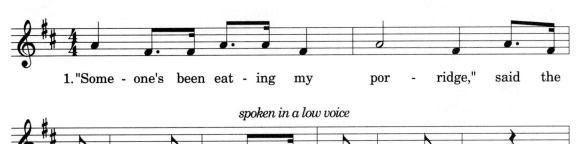

1. "Some - one's been eat - ing my por - ridge," said the

spoken in a low voice

pop - pa bear,— (said the pop - pa bear. ___)

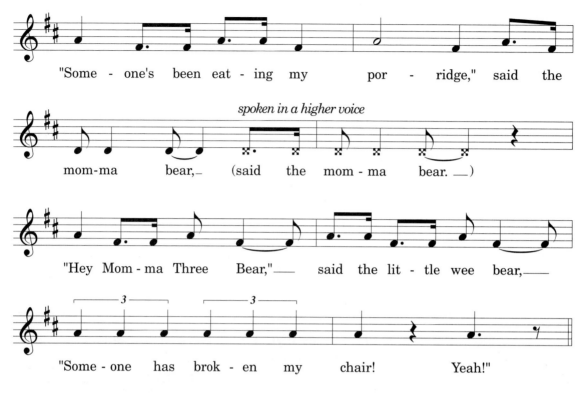

"Some - one's been eat - ing my por - ridge," said the

spoken in a higher voice

mom-ma bear,— (said the mom - ma bear. —)

"Hey Mom - ma Three Bear,"— said the lit - tle wee bear,—

"Some - one has brok - en my chair! Yeah!"

2. "Someone's been sitting in my chair," said the poppa
   bear (said the poppa bear).
   "Someone's been sitting in my chair," said the
   momma bear (said the momma bear).
   "Hey Momma Three Bear," said the little wee bear,
   "Someone has broken my chair! Yeah!"

3. "Someone's been sleeping in my bed," said the poppa
   bear (said the poppa bear).
   "Someone's been sleeping in my bed," Said the momma
   bear (said the momma bear).
   "Hey Momma Three Bear," said the little wee bear,
   "Someone has broken my chair! Yeah!"

ACTIVITY 2: THE LITTLE PIGS' JIVE

For the next song-story use the 4/4 pattern suggested earlier, or devise a pattern of your own. When beginning a new song-story, it is helpful to use a simple four-beat patsch. Use both hands or alternate hands and be sure to keep the rhythm very steady and unflagging. The memorizing of the words comes naturally with a few repetitions.

THE LITTLE PIGS' JIVE

L. Gerber and J. Haines

This is a story by Old Mother Goose,
About three little pigs who were out on the loose.

1. The first little pig built his house of straw—
   The cutest little house that you ever saw.

Refrain

The   big   bad   wolf   said:___   "Let   me   come   in!"___

"Oh   no,   by   the   hair   on   my   chin - ny   chin - chin!"___

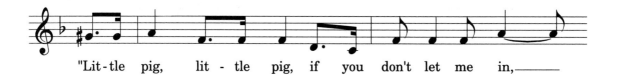

"Lit - tle   pig,   lit - tle   pig,   if   you   don't   let   me   in,___

I'll   huff   and   I'll   puff   and   I'll   blow   your   house   in!"

And he huffed (*huff, huff*) and the puffed (*puff, puff*)
And the little pig ran to the second pig's place.

2. The second little pig built his house of sticks,
   But the big bad wolf was up to his tricks.

Refrain

And he huffed (*huff, huff*) and he puffed (*puff, puff*)
And the little pig ran to the third pig's place.

3. The third little pig built his house of bricks.
   They were stronger than straw, they were
       stronger than sticks.

Refrain

And he huffed (*huff, huff*) and he puffed (*puff, puff*)
and the little pigs stayed in the third pigs place.

4. The big bad wolf said, "Let me come in,
   Or I'll slide down the chimney and I'll do you in!"

"Come in, come in! We are read - y for you,——

And you nev - er will guess what we're go - ing to do!"——

And the three lit - tle pigs made the fire red - hot——

And they boiled up the wat - er in the big—— black pot!

And he slid (*swish, swish*)! Yes, he did (*swish, swish*)!
And he fell in the water in the middle of the night,
And the little pigs laughed because
   IT SERVED HIM RIGHT!

ACTIVITY 3: LITTLE RED HEN RAP

This is a familiar tale in a new mode. Establish a steady, easy rhythmic accompaniment in double time, such as patsch-clap or patsch-clap, snap-clap, and keep it going throughout. Narrate the whole rap several times. The children will begin to join in the spoken parts and sing the choruses.

When the class is joining in freely, put up charts of the chorus, finale, and spoken texts. One child may now speak for the little red hen, and a group of any size may be the uncooperative neighbors. The rest of the class, or another group, may be the supportive friends, singing the first five choruses. Everyone, led by the little red hen herself, should sing the finale, with two good claps and a shout on "ALL GONE!"

LITTLE RED HEN RAP

J. Haines

Once upon a time there was a little red hen.
She hadn't had a meal since dear knows when.
She went for a walk and she looked all around.
She saw some grains of wheat; they were lying on the ground.

The little red hen took the wheat back home.
She showed it to the neighbors, 'cause she didn't live alone.
She said: "If you help me we can make it grow."
The neighbors all answered; "No, no, no!"

Chorus

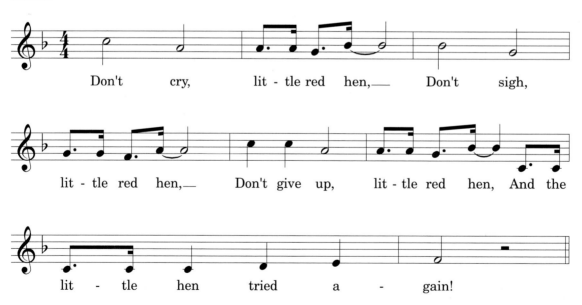

The little red hen she planted all the seeds.
She watered them well and she pulled up all the weeds.
She said: "If you'll help me we can cut this grain."
The neighbors all answered: "No again!"

Chorus

The little red hen she cut the wheat.
She tied it in a bundle so it looked real neat.
She said: "If you'll help me we will thresh it today."
The neighbors all answered: "Nay, nay, nay!"

Chorus

The little red hen she threshed all day.
She filled her sack with grain and she was on her way.
She said: "If you'll help me we will take it to the mill."
The neighbors all answered: "No-one will!"

Chorus

The little red hen got a bag full of flour.
She brought it home in half an hour.
She said: "If you'll help me we can make some dough."
The neighbors all answered: "No, no, no!"

Chorus

The little red hen made a loaf out of dough.
She put it in the oven for an hour or so.
She took it out and it looked so nice!
The neighbors all said: "WE'LL TASTE A SLICE!"

Finale

♫ ACTIVITY 4: THE BROTHERS GRUFF AND THE TROLL _____

The familiar story of the Billy Goats Gruff and the Big Bad Troll is presented as a song-story. There are speaking parts for a narrator, three goats, and a troll, indicated as follows:

- *N* = Narrator
- *T* = Troll
- *G1* = First Goat
- *G2* = Second Goat
- *G3* = Third Goat
- *3G* = All three goats together

The musical interludes are sung by a chorus. The troll joins them where shown.

THE BROTHERS GRUFF AND THE TROLL

J. Haines

Trip, trap, trip, trap, trip, trap, trip.—   Trip, trap, trip, trap, trip, trap, trip.—

N: Let me tell you all the story of the Billy Goats Gruff.
They were three different sizes. They were all quite tough.
They'd eaten all the grass in the field near home,
So the far hillside was where they'd like to roam.

On the way to the hillside was a bridge they had to cross,
With a Troll living under it who thought he was the boss.
His eyes were big as saucers and his nose was like a pole!
A very scary creature was the Big Bad Troll!

Trip, trap, trip, trap, trip, trap, trip.—   Trip, trap, trip, trap, trip, trap, trip.—

N: The smallest Billy Goat, he was a brave little kid.
He stepped up on the bridge and made it squeak
    Yes, he did!
The Big Bad Troll, he stuck his head way out.
He saw the smallest Billy Goat and he began to shout:

"Who's that mak - ing that trip - trap noise?____ I'm going to gob - ble up you lit - tle Bill - y Goat Boys!"

G1: "Oh no, Mister Troll, please don't do that.
      Just wait for my brother, he's really big and fat!"
T: "OK," *N*: said the Troll, *T*: "If you're the smallest of the bunch,
      I'll wait for your brother, before I have my lunch!"

N: The first little Billy Goat, he made it to the hill,
     Where the grass grew green and he could eat his fill.

Trip, trap, trip, trap, trip, trap, trip.— Trip, trap, trip, trap, trip, trap, trip.—

N: The second Billy Goat, he was a middle-sized kid.
     He stepped up on the bridge and made it squeak—Yes, he did!
     The Big Bad Troll, he stuck his head way out.
     He saw the second Billy Goat and he began to shout:

"Who's that mak - ing that trip - trap noise?____ I'm going to gob - ble up you lit - tle Bill - y Goat Boys!"

G2: "Oh no, Mister Troll, please don't do that.
Just wait for my brother , he's really big and fat!"
T: "OK," N: said the Troll, T: "If you think that you are thinner,
I'll wait for your brother, before I have my dinner!"

N: The second little Billy Goat, he made it to the hill,
Where the grass grew green and he could eat his fill.

Trip, trap, trip, trap, trip, trap, trip.— Trip, trap, trip, trap, trip, trap, trip.—

N: The third Billy Goat, he had horns and a beard,
And a big hoarse voice that made him sound real weird.
He stepped up on the bridge and when he made it squeak,
The Troll stuck out his head and he began to speak:

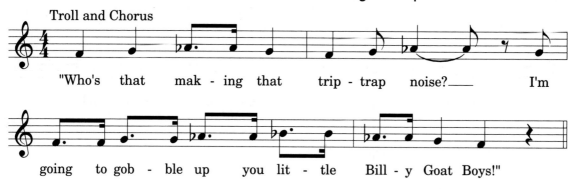

"Who's that mak - ing that trip - trap noise?____ I'm

going to gob - ble up you lit - tle Bill - y Goat Boys!"

G3: "Well, come on out!" N: roared the Billy Goat Gruff,
G3: "Put your feet up on the bridge so I can do my stuff!"
N: When the Troll came out, he went a-flying through the air,
'Cause the Billy Goat he butted him—fair and square!

Then he ran to his brothers who were grazing in the sun,
He told them what he'd said, and he told them what he'd done!

Trip, trap, trip, trap, trip, trap, trip.— Trip, trap, trip, trap, trip, trap, trip.—

3G: "We're safe!" *N:* said the Goats, from their grassy green patch,
3G: "'Cause the Big Bad Troll has met his match!"
 N: Then they stepped up on the bridge and they made it squeak,
    And they did it every day for a whole long week!

All: They did? *N:* Yes, they did! *All:* They did? *N:* Yes, they did!
All: And they did it every day for a WHOLE LONG WEEK!

"Who's   that   mak - ing   that   trip - trap   noise?___   We're

ver - y   glad   to tell   you it's   the   Bill - y   Goat Boys!"

THE GINGERBREAD MAN JIVE

Joan Haines

Chorus

The Gin - ger - bread Man! The Gin - ger - bread Man!

We'll tell you all the sto - ry of the Gin - ger - bread Man!

N: There was once a little woman made a Gingerbread Man.
She put him in the oven in a baking pan.
When she opened up the oven door — away he ran!
"You can't catch me 'cause I'm the Gingerbread Man!"

Chorus

The Gin - ger - bread Man! The Gin - ger - bread Man!

You can't catch him 'cause he's the Gin - ger - bread Man!

The woman tried to catch him. She was far too slow!
Her husband stood beside her as they watched him go.
"See ya later, alligator!" — and away he ran!
"You can't catch me 'cause I'm the Gingerbread Man!"

Chorus

The Gin - ger - bread Man! The Gin - ger - bread Man!

You can't catch him 'cause he's the Gin - ger - bread Man!

He ran about a mile until he met a horse.
She said "I would like to eat you!" and he said "Of course!"
She took a step towards him — and away he ran!
"You can't catch me 'cause I'm the Gingerbread Man!"

The Gin-ger-bread Man! The Gin-ger-bread Man!

You can't catch him 'cause he's the Gin-ger-bread Man!

He ran about a mile until he met a cow.
She said "I would like to eat you but I don't know how!"
She took a step towards him — and away he ran!
"You can't catch me 'cause I'm the Gingerbread Man!"

The Gin-ger-bread Man! The Gin-ger-bread Man!

You can't catch him 'cause he's the Gin-ger-bread Man!

He ran down to the river and he met a fox.
She said "Jump up on my back and you'll escape the rocks!"
When she reached the other riverbank, she tossed her head,
And she gobbled up the little man of gingerbread!

The Gin-ger-bread Man! The Gin-ger-bread Man!

There's noth-ing else to tell a-bout the Gin-ger-bread Man!

RELATED ACTIVITIES FOR STUDENTS

1. Cooperate with your classmates to prepare an anthology of rhymes, chants, and finger plays to supplement those in the text. Useful resources are your own childhood memories, those of family and friends, visits to local playgrounds, and anthologies of children's verse.

2. Arrange to teach a small group of children two or three items from this chapter or your class anthology. Tape this activity and share it with your classmates, encouraging their evaluative comments.

3. Practice the following rhythmic sequence in a steady walking tempo: patsch, patsch, clap, clap (repeat). Find two children's rhymes that fit this simple movement pattern well. Teach them to your classmates.

4. When chanting rhymes, a beat is often felt and moved to *after* the last word in a line. Here is an example (the underlines mark the accents or beats):

Hot cross buns ____,
Hot cross buns ____,
One a pen-ny, two a pen-ny,
Hot cross buns ____.

Using this principle, create an appropriate sequence of *four* movements that repeat, using the following chant. Teach it to a classmate.

Big A, Little A, Bouncing B.
Cat's in the cupboard and he can't catch me.

Chapter 5

Songs for Doing

Action songs and singing games are part of the musical heritage of many cultures. Some of them are hundreds of years old, and some, like certain nursery rhymes, bore political undertones in their original forms. Common elements occur in most societies; circles, partners, choosing, and chasing are found worldwide. A strong underlying pulse or beat is usually present and is often stressed by clapping, stamping, or drumming. Rhythmic patterns of varying complexity may be superimposed vocally or by hand motions, ropes, balls, and hoops.

The songs in this chapter usually require a more expanded use of the singing voice than the three-tone chants in Chapter 4. They carry the meaning of the activity and are often highly repetitive and melodically simple. They contribute to the development of the young child's singing voice and to good listening skills and should have a place in every music period as well as occurring informally during the school day.

Teach action songs and singing games for the enjoyment they give, knowing that they are a springboard to every aspect of musical growth. Interweave the material in this chapter with that of the next five to ensure a varied yet balanced program.

In the United States, much of the repertoire of early childhood songs for doing comes from folklore and the oral tradition and contains elements of several cultures. Singing games that have stood the test of time are those most readily learned and enjoyed. Small differences may be found in melody, lyrics, and motions from one part of the country to another, but songs such as "Ring around the Rosie," "Bluebird, Bluebird," and "I Have Lost My Little Partner" have a universal appeal.

When selecting action songs and singing games, begin with the traditional literature. As you acquire skill in choosing and teaching activities appropriate to the ability of your group, expand your resources to include some specially created or composed materials. These should meet the criteria for choosing songs given in Chapter 6 (page 132). In addition, movements should suit the overall mood and rhythm of the song and stay within the competency of the students. Avoid very frequent changes of motions with the youngest and build gradually toward the inclusion of specific dance steps with older groups.

Songs with movement are best taught through participation. At first the singing may take second place while very young children concentrate on the actions. The ultimate goal is for the children to become proficient at singing and moving simultaneously. This ability develops naturally and easily in time.

All the songs and games in this chapter involve an element of change, either in the words to be sung or in the movements to be made. In the first section of this chapter, no special arrangement of the group is necessary. All the activities, however, require some creative input, either for words, actions, or both. In the second section, the actions are described in the words of the songs, and a circle formation may be used for many of them. In the third section are songs and games with both specific movements and a special formation such as a circle, partners, a set, or a square. *Each section begins with material for the very young and ends with pieces that appeal to the interests and challenge the musical abilities of primary grade children.*

Songs for Informal Settings

The songs in this section are best learned and sung in an unstructured setting. The size of the group does not matter and the location can be indoors or out. When these songs are sung while sitting, standing, strolling, or lying under shady trees, they lend themselves to informal participation and to a wide range of creative input by children. The teacher should accept and incorporate the children's suggestions with the least amount of alteration. In fact, it is better to adapt the musical framework to accommodate a child's original words or actions than to alter her creation, implying that her offering needs adult editing to make it appropriate or acceptable.

WE'LL ALL CLAP HANDS TOGETHER

Key: F
Starting tone: C

Traditional

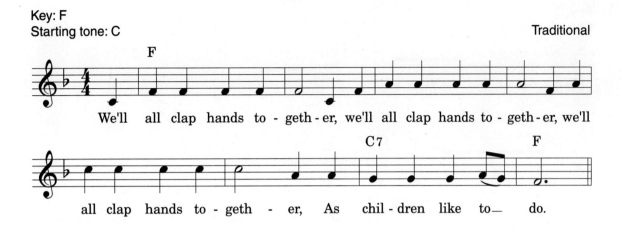

Other hand motions are suggested by teacher and children, and later movements of other body parts are substituted, such as "nod heads," "tap toes," "blink eyes," "stretch up," "turn around."

CLAP, CLAP, CLAP YOUR HANDS

Key: F
Starting tone: F

American Traditional

"Tap your head," "wave your hand," "point your toe," and many other actions can be suggested.

LET EV'RYONE CLAP HANDS LIKE ME

Key: C
Starting tone: G

American Traditional

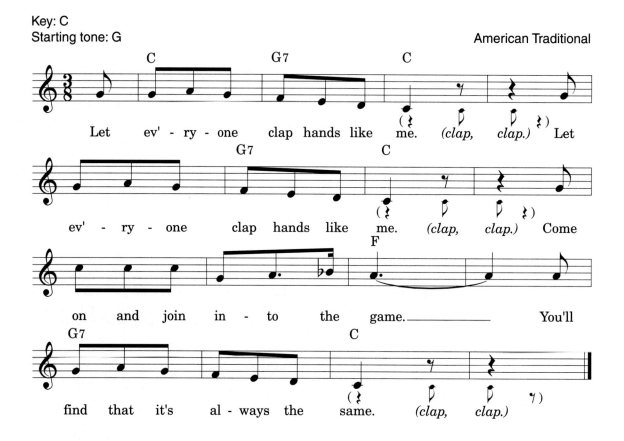

Let ev' - ry - one clap hands like me. *(clap, clap.)* Let

ev' - ry - one clap hands like me. *(clap, clap.)* Come

on and join in - to the game.——————— You'll

find that it's al - ways the same. *(clap, clap.)*

This song has endless possibilities. Whole categories of physical and vocal activity can be explored. Help the children to suggest novel movements such as "pull your ear," "rub your chin," "scratch your nose," "pat your elbow." This will extend their knowledge of body parts and of action verbs. Develop a sequence of human sounds such as yawn, sneeze, cough, hiccup, laugh, and cry. Then elicit animal names and appropriate sounds. This action song has proved to be very successful with non-English-speaking children. They recognize and identify with most of the suggestions made and willingly join in with the group.

TOMMY THUMB'S UP

Key: C
Starting tone: C

Traditional Rhyme
Melody: J. Haines

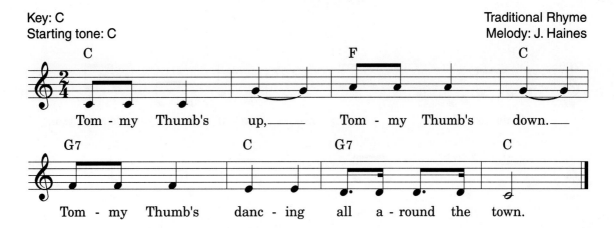

Tom - my Thumb's up,___ Tom - my Thumb's down.___

Tom - my Thumb's danc - ing all a - round the town.

This is an old finger play set to a simple tune. Whatever names the children know for the fingers can be incorporated. The fingers mentioned in the song point up first, then down, and then dance a jig around the lap of the child. A last verse involving all the fingers can be sung: "Finger Family's up, Finger Family's down. Finger Family's dancing all around the town."

◆ ─────────────────── ◆

No specific action is given for the next three songs. The teacher will need to initiate a movement as the verse, or possibly two or three, is sung, and then invite ideas from the children. The songs can be used for both fine and gross motor activities.

PENNY'S THE LEADER

Key: C pentatonic
Starting tone: G

Adapted: L. Gerber

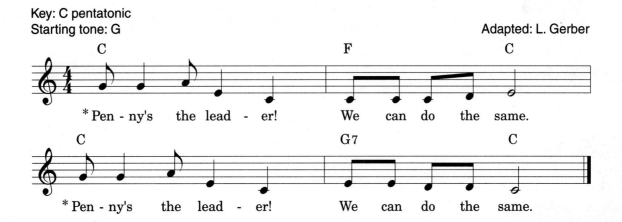

*Pen - ny's the lead - er! We can do the same.

*Pen - ny's the lead - er! We can do the same.

Use different children's names at asterisks.

THIS IS WHAT I CAN DO

Key: F
Starting tone: F

Traditional

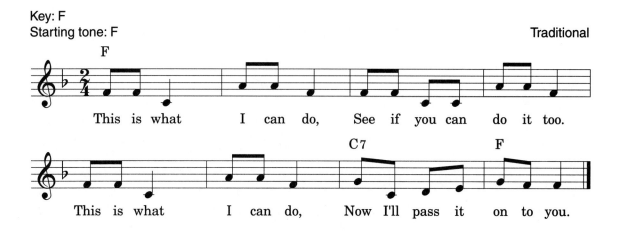

This is what I can do, See if you can do it too.

This is what I can do, Now I'll pass it on to you.

All join in with the leader as soon as the first two measures have been sung and the movement shown. During the last two measures the leader touches or points to a successor, who begins a new motion as soon as the song is repeated. Changing leaders and actions in this game requires more skill than is needed for "Penny's the Leader" (page 77).

WHAT SHALL WE DO?

Key: C
Starting tone: G

American Traditional

What shall we do when we all go out? All go out? All go out? What shall we do when we all go out? When we all go out to play?

This song is sung through once. Then children's suggestions are put into the song, with appropriate actions, to make up the answer verses, such as "We'll swing our arms when we all go out," "We'll march around . . . ," "We'll hop about . . . ," and so on.

The last five songs in this section can all be sung in an informal group. All give children the opportunity to contribute words that change the lyrics, and they may include motions also.

GOOD NEWS!

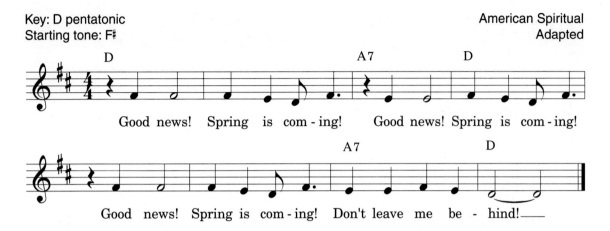

Key: D pentatonic
Starting tone: F♯

American Spiritual
Adapted

Word changes may be topical: "Santa's coming!" "Snow is falling!" "It's Jane's birthday!" They may imply action: "Hands are clapping!" "Drums are beating!" "Bells are ringing!" Or a change of mood may be reported: "Sad news! Rain is falling! We can't play outside!"

◆ ———————————————————————— ◆

The next two songs are sure to succeed with students and beginning teachers. At first, children may need help in creating new words. Questions such as "What day is today?" "Who has a birthday?" "What's the weather like?" will elicit responses, and soon children will begin to put their own news into both songs. If actions are wanted, one or two suggestions will start the ideas flowing, such as "Snap your fingers" or "Walk on tiptoe." In fact, a particular class of special needs children has incorporated "Toodala" into its vocabulary and regularly makes a group decision on "what we'll toodala today"!

HELLO EV'RYBODY, TOODALA!

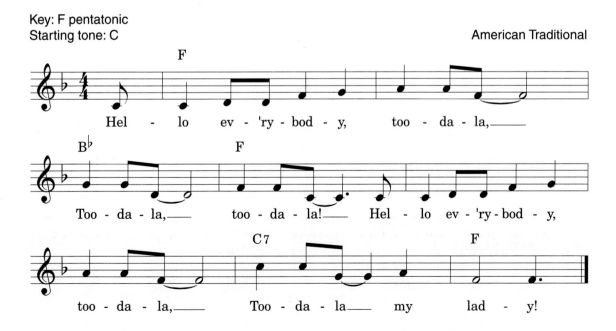

Key: F pentatonic
Starting tone: C

American Traditional

HELLO (LET'S SING HELLO TOGETHER)

Key: C
Starting tone: C

Edith Wax and Sydell Roth

Let's sing hel - lo to - geth - er, hel - lo, hel - lo, hel - lo.

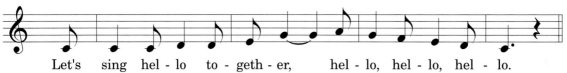

Let's sing hel - lo to - geth - er, hel - lo, hel - lo, hel - lo.

Ask the children to suggest motions for this song, such as "Let's tap our heads together" or "Let's shake our hands together." Use many different verbs and body parts.

◆ ———————————————— ◆

The next two songs invite new lyrics or rhythmic actions once they are familiar. They can also show a change of mood, tempo, or dynamics.

PUT A CLAP IN YOUR HANDS

Key: F
Startring tone: C

L. Gerber

Put a clap in your hands when you sing, "Hel - lo!" Put a

clap in your hands when you sing, "Hel - lo!"—— Put a

clap in your hands when you sing, "Hel - lo!"

Clap your hands—— when you sing, "Hel - lo!"

I'M GONNA SING

Key: G
Starting tone: D   American Spiritual

I'm gon - na   sing   when   the   spir - it   says

sing!_____   I'm gon - na   sing when   the   spir - it   says

sing!__   I'm gon - na   sing when   the   spir - it   says

sing,   And   o - bey   the spir - it of the   Lord!

For each repeat, add a new motion encouraging class participation and singing. Some examples are "I'm gonna shout when the spirit says shout!" "I'm gonna sleep . . . ," "I'm gonna rock . . . ," and so on.

Songs with Specific Motions

All the songs in this section are accompanied by specific rhythmic motions related to the words. The goal here is to develop and enjoy musical skills through participation. Accurate listening and singing are encouraged through melodies of small range built on chord tones, scalewise progressions, and simple phrases. Rhythmic sensitivity grows through response to a clear beat, strong accents, and repeated rhythmic patterns. All of these elements are brought together and internalized through the total involvement and activity of the child. The musically able teacher will find that the material in this section lays the foundations for vocal tone-matching and for the perception of rhythmic relationships needed in *solfège* (see Glossary under "Sol-fa") and music reading, which in turn lead to musical literacy. These skills hold the key to creative musical ability in later years.

Some of the selections that follow are best done with the children spread out informally, while others call for them to sit in a circle so that all may see and be seen. When an activity involves moving freely about the room, children should end it in the original formation: a place alone or a circle. Even very small children can learn to do this smoothly and with good inner control. This takes practice, however, and should be patiently established from the outset.

The action songs and games that follow are of increasing difficulty rhythmically or in the movements required. They all, however, have singable words and melodies lying within the range of an octave—with one exception ("Did You Feed My Cow?").

SEE, SEE SEE!

Key: D
Starting tone: D

Dutch Folk Song

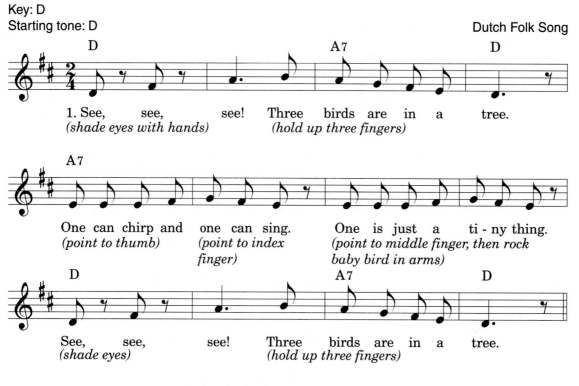

1. See, see, see! Three birds are in a tree.
(shade eyes with hands) (hold up three fingers)

One can chirp and one can sing. One is just a ti - ny thing.
(point to thumb) (point to index finger) (point to middle finger, then rock baby bird in arms)

See, see, see! Three birds are in a tree.
(shade eyes) (hold up three fingers)

2. Look, look, look!
Three ducks are in the brook.
One is white and one is brown.
One is swimming upside down.
Look, look, look!
Three ducks are in the brook.

Repeat the actions of verse 1, substituting a dip-and-dive motion of the hand to accompany "upside down."

ONE LITTLE DUCK

Key: F pentatonic
Starting tone: F

Words and Music: J. Haines

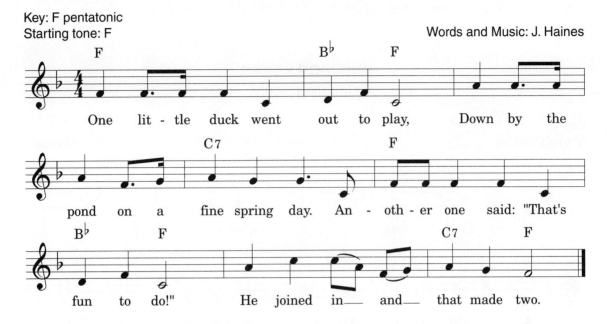

One lit - tle duck went out to play, Down by the

pond on a fine spring day. An - oth - er one said: "That's

fun to do!" He joined in— and— that made two.

Spoken: 1 little duck and 1 makes 2.

2. Two little ducks went out to play
   Down by the pond on a fine spring day.
   Another one said: " Hey wait for me!"
   She joined in and that made three.

Spoken: 2 little ducks and 1 makes 3.

3. Three little ducks went out to play,
   Down by the pond on a fine spring day.
   Another one peeked 'round the old barn door.
   He joined in and that made four.

Spoken: 3 little ducks and 1 makes 4.

4. Four little ducks went out to play,
   Down by the pond on a fine spring day.
   Another one saw them dip and dive.
   She joined in and that made five.

Spoken: 4 little ducks and 1 makes 5.

5. Five little ducks went out to play,
   Down by the pond on a fine spring day.
   The mother duck wished they would all come back.
   She called them home with a "quack, quack, quack!"

Teach the song using the fingers of one hand for the five little ducks and the index finger of the other for the mother duck. This game may be expanded into a mime or dramatization, and more verses may be created.

UNO, DOS Y TRES
(Counting Song)

Key: C
Starting tone: C   Mexican

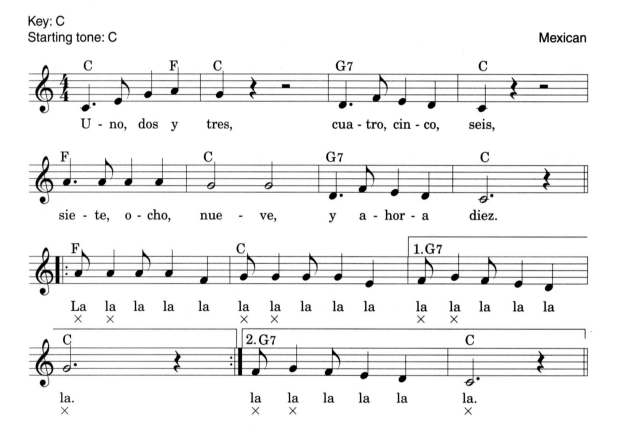

This song counts from one to ten in Spanish. Teach the song using the fingers of both hands. Clap as indicated by the *X*s.

ANIMALS LIVE IN THE FOREST

Key: F
Starting tone: A

Words and Music: J. Haines

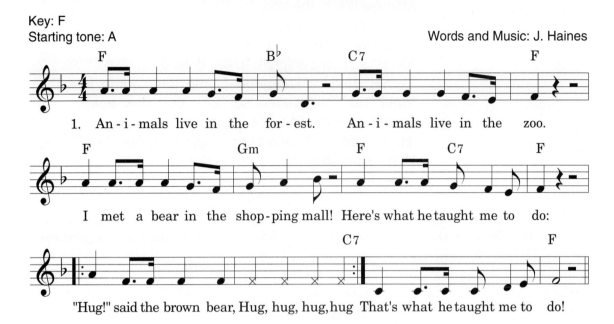

1. An-i-mals live in the for-est. An-i-mals live in the zoo.

I met a bear in the shop-ping mall! Here's what he taught me to do:

"Hug!" said the brown bear, Hug, hug, hug, hug That's what he taught me to do!

2. Animals live in the forest.
   Animals live in the zoo.
   I met a lion in the shopping mall!
   Here's what he taught me to do:
   "Roar!" said the lion, "Gr, gr, gr, gr!"
   "Hug!" said the brown bear.
   That's what they taught me to do!

3. Animals live in the forest.
   Animals live in the zoo.
   I met a mouse in the shopping mall!
   Here's what he taught me to do:
   "Eek!" said the little mouse, "Eek, eek, eek, eek!"
   "Roar!" said the lion, "Gr, gr, gr, gr!"
   "Hug!" said the brown bear.
   That's what they taught me to do!

4. Animals live in the forest.
   Animals live in the zoo.
   I met a kangaroo in the shopping mall!
   Here's what he taught me to do:
   "Jump!" said the kangaroo. "Jump, jump, jump, jump!"
   "Eek!" said the little mouse, "Eek, eek, eek, eek!"
   "Roar!" said the lion, "Gr, gr, gr, gr!"
   "Hug!" said the brown bear. "Hug, hug, hug, hug!"
   That's what they taught me to do!

5. Animals live in the forest.
    Animals live in the zoo.
    I met a dolphin in the shopping mall!
    Here's what he taught me to do:
    "Dive!" said the dolphin. "Dive, dive, dive, dive!"
    "Jump!" said the kangaroo. "Jump, jump, jump, jump!"
    "Eek!" said the little mouse, "Eek, eek, eek, eek!"
    "Roar!" said the lion, "Gr, gr, gr, gr!"
    "Hug!" said the brown bear. "Hug, hug, hug, hug!"
    That's what they taught me to do!

This is a cumulative song in which a new animal is added to each verse. Always sing the new addition first, and end with the four bear hugs. Add your and the children's suggestions for new verses.

THREE CROWS

Key: C
Starting tone:C´

Scottish Folk Song

Bend the left elbow at chest level so that the forearm represents the wall. Three fingers of the right hand peek out from behind the wall to represent the crows. Repeat the music with two, one, and no crows on the wall. Invent new lyrics with appropriate actions, such as "Three bees buzzed around a hive," "Three bears lived inside a cave," or "Three frogs jumped across a pond."

DID YOU FEED MY COW?

Key: F pentatonic
Starting tone: C

Music by Ella Jenkins
Words: Traditional

Did you feed my cow? Yes ma'm. Could you tell me how? Yes ma'm. What did you feed her?— Corn and hay. What did you feed her?— Corn and hay.

2. Did you milk her good? Yes, ma'm.
   Did you milk her like you should? Yes, ma'm.
   How did you milk her? ⎱ *Repeat*
   Squish, squish, squish. ⎰

3. Did my cow get sick? Yes, ma'm.
   Was she covered with tick? Yes, ma'm.
   How did she die? ⎱ *Repeat*
   Uh, uh, uh! ⎰

4. Did the buzzards come? Yes, ma'm.
   Did the buzzards come? Yes, ma'm.
   How did they come? ⎱ *Repeat*
   Flop, flop, flop. ⎰

This delightful song appeals to young children of all ages. An off-beat clap
(𝄽 ♩ 𝄽 ♩ :𝄆) makes an effective accompaniment. On "Squish,
squish, squish," mime milking the cow; on "Uh, uh, uh," bend backward three times with open
hands at shoulder level; and on "Flop, flop, flop," give three big, loose wing-flops. Groups of
primary grade children may be able to compose their own lyrics telling of other creatures.

SHE SAILED AWAY

Key: C
Starting tone: G

Camp Song

She sailed a - way on a bright and sun - ny day, On the
back of a croc - o - dile. "You see," said she, "He's as
tame as he can be! I'll float him down the Nile!" The
croc winked his eye as she waved them all good - bye,
Wear - ing a hap - py smile. At the end of the ride the
lad - y was in - side, And the smile on the croc - o - dile! (snap, snap)

Add motions to the song as follows:

- "She sailed away . . .": Put one hand flat on the back of the other. Rotate thumbs as hands sail back and forth in front of body.
- " 'You see,' said she . . .": Shake index finger; then stroke back of one hand with palm of the other.
- "The croc winked . . .": Wink, wave, and then outline a smiling mouth.
- "At the end . . .": Repeat sailing motion of line 1. Then slowly turn palms together, making the croc's mouth, ending with two snaps of the jaws.

JUMP DOWN, TURN AROUND

Key: F
Starting tone: A

African-American Folk Song

Jump down, turn a-round, pick a bale of cot - ton,

Jump down, turn a-round, pick a bale a day.

Oh, Lord - y! Pick a bale of cot - ton,——

Oh, Lord - y! Pick a bale a day.——————

This song needs a brisk, accented tempo and the ability to catch a quick breath. Suit the actions to the words, and include an upward flutter of both hands on "Oh, Lordy!" to help the voices follow the tune.

The next four action songs require very accurate movement and a high degree of muscular and vocal control. Young children like participating; older students enjoy working to meet the challenge.

A PIZZA HUT

Key: E♭
Starting tone: B♭

Adapted: J. Haines

2. When we were driving down the street,
   My mother asked me where I'd like to eat. (*Repeat*)

   Chorus

3. My dad said, "Please make up your mind,
   Or all the places will be left behind." (*Repeat*)

   Chorus

End the song by repeating verse 1. Use the following motions throughout:

♦ "A Pizza Hut": Raise arms; touch fingertips in a hut shape.
♦ "Kentucky Fried Chicken": Place hands on shoulders; flap arms against sides.
♦ "McDonald's": With hands draw arches outward from the waist.

Create your own motions for verses 2 and 3.

OLD MAN MOSIE

Key: C pentatonic
Starting tone: G

Traditional

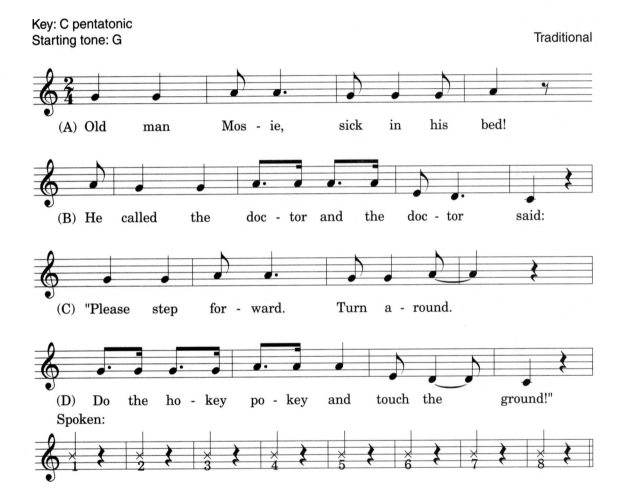

(A) Old man Mos - ie, sick in his bed!

(B) He called the doc - tor and the doc - tor said:

(C) "Please step for - ward. Turn a - round.

(D) Do the ho - key po - key and touch the ground!"
Spoken:

Motions:

A. Place both hands under left cheek, then both under right. Repeat.

B. Dial the phone; shake right forefinger.

C and D. Do what song indicates.

For the spoken phrase, perform any strong body movement to eight counts.

TONY CHESTNUT

Key: C
Starting tone: G

Camp Song

To-ny Chest-nut knows I love you, To-ny knows, To-ny knows,

To-ny Chest-nut knows I love you. That's what To-ny knows.

Teach the song by rote. Help the children discover the following motions, adding them to the song:

To-(toe)ny(knee) Chest-(chest)nut(head)

knows(nose) I(eye) love(self) you(point to another)

To challenge an older group of children, repeat the song eight times. Each time omit an additional sung word but keep the motion, until the song is silent except for "That's what." A good order for omitting the words is: (1) head, (2) chest, (3) knee, (4) toe, (5) point, (6) self, (7) eye, (8) nose. Young children may enjoy and be successful in omitting 1 through 4.

HEAD AND SHOULDERS, BABY

Key: F pentatonic

Starting tone: A

American Singing Game

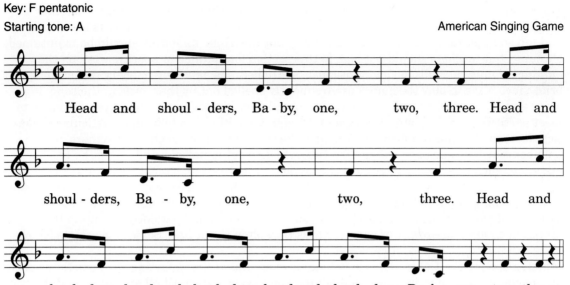

Head and shoul - ders, Ba - by, one, two, three. Head and

shoul - ders, Ba - by, one, two, three. Head and

shoul - ders, head and shoul - ders, head and shoul - ders, Ba-by, one, two, three.

Stand at ease for this song. Tap head and shoulders as indicated and clap-snap on "Baby, one, two, three"

$$\left(\begin{array}{c} \text{i.e., Baby , one , } \text{\rlap{/}?} \text{ , two , } \text{\rlap{/}?} \text{ , three} \\ \text{CLAP, SNAP, CLAP, SNAP, CLAP, SNAP} \end{array} \right).$$

Don't let the rhythm drag as the motions change. Add additional verses with the following suggested sequence:

Knees and ankles

Ankles and toes

Turn around

Shake a leg

Do a dance

Wave goodbye

If a sequence of body parts is developed, it may then be reversed and the tempo speeded up toward the end.

Songs with Formations

The songs in this section are designed to encourage participation, cooperation, and other social learning; coordination, rhythmic movement, and singing; and the elements of enjoyment and fun so important to music making throughout life. High standards should be maintained, of course, but teachers should not look to this section for detailed or specific work on the building of musical skills beyond those just mentioned. The teaching notes in this section are brief, since ways to play the games are frequently spelled out by the words in the song. Ingenuity and creativity by teachers and children will vary, simplify, and extend the activities to meet particular needs. Many singing games require the children to be in a particular formation, instead of grouped informally. Young children find it easier to choose partners, to remember which people have not yet had turns, to give out materials, and to see the teacher or other game leaders from the security of a circle or other predetermined formation.

In the early days of nursery school and kindergarten, children may have difficulty making a circle, forming a line behind a leader, or facing a partner in a space together. Practice these skills briefly and often, praising good effort and achievement and patiently repeating the process if children are rowdy or aggressive, as they often are at first. Some suggestions follow.

Making a Circle.   Calling children by name is helpful at first, starting with one for each of the teacher's left and right hands and adding one to each side until all are called and the last two join hands to complete the ring. The children will quickly learn each other's names and be able to take over the calling for themselves. Eventually even this will not be necessary. A command will suffice: "Make a circle, all holding hands."

Making a Line.   Initially, straight lines are formed by the teacher calling individuals to come and stand behind one or two leaders. A game for forming straight lines follows:

CHOO-KA-CHOO

Key: D
Starting tone: D   Words and Music: Ethel Crowninshield

The teacher starts by chugging around the circle of children like a lonely engine. At the end of the song, the teacher calls one name and that child joins the train. The game is repeated, and each new child added has a turn to call the next one to join. The last one is naturally the caboose. She rings the bell, and the engine starts a fast trip, doubling back and forth around the room with tiny, shuffling steps. If the train breaks and all fall down, this adds to the fun of this get-acquainted game.

Taking Partners.   Children standing together in free space may be assigned as partners in the beginning, or children may be asked one at a time to choose a partner. This will avoid competition over one particular child or neglect of another. If children are in a circle, walk quickly to your *left,* around the inside of the circle, holding up first one, then two fingers to each child as you go.

Each child, in turn, calls out the number of fingers you show him. If the last child is a one, you call "two" as you step into your place to his *left,* becoming his partner in the ensuing game. Now ask all ones to turn to their *left,* and check that this is done correctly. Next the twos turn to their *right.* You now have instant partners.

Singing Games

LOOK WHO'S STANDING IN THE CIRCLE

Key: D
Starting tone: D   Traditional

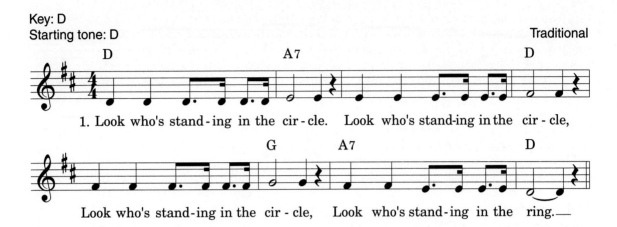

Start with the children in a circle. During verse 1 send a child to stand in the middle. All sing verse 2 using the chosen child's name, for instance:

2. Nancy's standing in the circle. (Nancy announces her motion and models it during the singing of verse 3.)

3. Nancy's hopping in the circle. (All do the motion while singing verse 4.)

4. We can hop the same way (We can hop the same). (During verse 5 Nancy chooses a new person and returns to the circle.)

5. Choose somebody special (Choose somebody new). (Repeat the game encouraging new actions.)

EL FLORÓN
(The Flower)

Key: C pentatonic
Starting tone: C

Argentinian

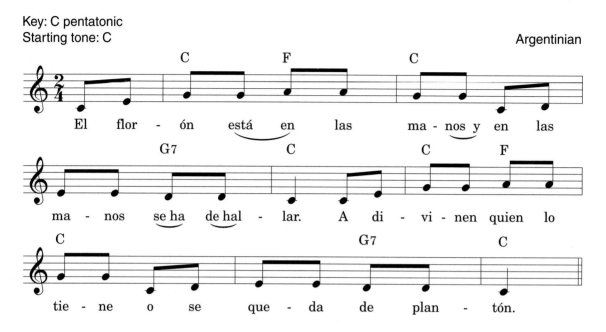

El flor - ón está en las ma - nos y en las
ma - nos se ha de hal - lar. A - di - vi - nen quien lo
tie - ne o se que - da de plan - tón.

Translation: A flower is hidden in the hands. Who can guess where it is?

This song accompanies a game. The children stand in a circle, facing the center, with their hands behind them. A leader walks around the outside of the circle as the song is sung. He holds a flower (or other object) which he slips into someone's hand during the song. At the end of the song he moves inside the circle. All try to guess who has the flower. The one who guesses correctly becomes the next leader.

BOW, BOW, O BELINDA

Key: F
Starting tone: F

American Singing Game

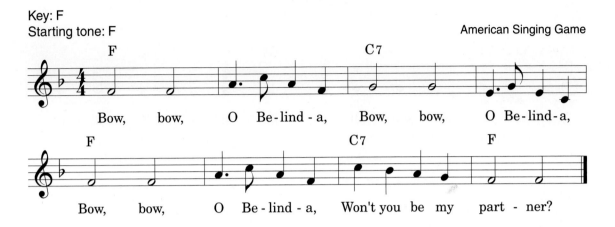

2. Right hands round.

3. Left hands round.

4. Both hands round.

5. Promenade the hall.

Children start by facing each other in pairs. The actions follow the words and on verse 5 the couples circle the room arm in arm. To conclude, verse 1 may be repeated, ending with "Thanks for being my partner."

HERE WE COME, ZUDIO

Key: C
Starting tone: C

Traditional Game

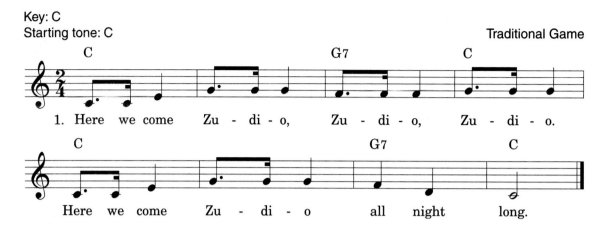

1. Here we come Zu - di - o, Zu - di - o, Zu - di - o.

Here we come Zu - di - o all night long.

```
    ×      ×      ×      ×
2. Back up Sal-ly, Sal-ly, Sal-ly.
   ×      ×      ×      ×
   Back up Sal-ly, all night long.
   ×          ×      ×       ×
3. Go-in' down the al-ley, the al-ley, the al-ley.
   ×           ×      ×      ×
   Go-in' down the al-ley, all night long.

4. Here we come Zudio, Zudio, Zudio.
   Here we come Zudio, all night long.
```

A dance accompanies this song.

Verse 1: Partners clasp each other's hands making a vigorous rhythmic sawing motion on the beat.

Verse 2: Partners back away from each other with small steps, clapping on the strong beats (Xs).

Verse 3: They come forward to meet again, clapping (or snapping) on the strong beats (Xs).

Verse 4: Repeat the motions in verse 1.

To effect a partner change, the teacher chants and claps rhythmically:

```
    X        X    X    X
Choose a new partner, partner, part-ner.
    X        X    X         X
Choose a new partner, different than before.
```

This may need to be repeated until all have new partners, when the dance begins again.

A LITTLE BLACK DOG

Key: G
Starting tone: D

American Singing Game

There are many variations of this favorite game—both in the words and the tune. Use a familiar version. One way to play the game follows:

A. Circle left holding hands.
B. Circle right.
C. Take four steps toward center.
D. Take four steps back.
E. Same as C.
F. Same as D.

I WANNA BE A FRIEND

Key: G pentatonic
Starting tone: D

Adapted: J. Haines

(A) I wan-na be a   friend of yours,   Mm, and a lit-tle bit

more.   (B) I   wan-na be   a   friend of   yours,

Mm, and a lit-tle bit   more!   (C) I   wan-na be   a

bum-ble   bee   buzz-in' round your   door,

(D) I   wan-na be   a   friend of yours, (E) Mm, and a lit-tle bit,

Mm, and a lit-tle bit,   Mm, and a lit-tle bit   more. Yea!

2. I wanna be a friend of yours, Mm, and a little bit more. (*2 times*)
    I wanna read a book with you, Maybe three or four.
    I wanna be a friend of yours, Mm, and a little bit (*3 times*) more.

3. *As above*
    I wanna take a walk with you, On the sandy shore.
    As above

4. *As above*
    I wanna share a snack with you, From the corner store.
    As above

Children stand in a circle, holding hands. The movements are as follows:

A. Circle left eight steps.
B. Circle right eight steps.
C. Take four steps to the center, four steps back.
D. Take four steps in place.
E. Patsch-clap three times, ending with a final patsch and "Yea!"

Two Ways to Play a Choosing Game

There are many traditional games that involve one child choosing a partner from the group. Each game is usually repeated several times, and it may be done in one of two ways. In the easier way, the leader takes the place of the child she chooses and the game is played again with a second child in her place. This pattern is continued until the desired number of children have each had a turn alone. This technique is useful when very young children are new to the setting. It helps them to get to know each other and the routines of group games. Many choosing games are best taught this way initially in the preschool.

The second, cumulative way to play these games is more complicated, though not too difficult for five-year-olds. After the leader has made his choice from the group, both children remain in the game. It is played again, and this time the two children both choose new players. Four children are thus active and the game can continue through to eight or sixteen participants. The sequence of numbers involved (1, 2, 4, 8, 16, 32) may be referred to at each increase. This reinforces the mathematical concept of doubling or "twice as many."

When children play a game in this way, some may not have a turn. The teacher should ensure that those not chosen in a particular game are immediately involved in another one in which they have an active role.

HERE WE COME A-WALKING

Key: D
Starting tone: D

American Singing Game

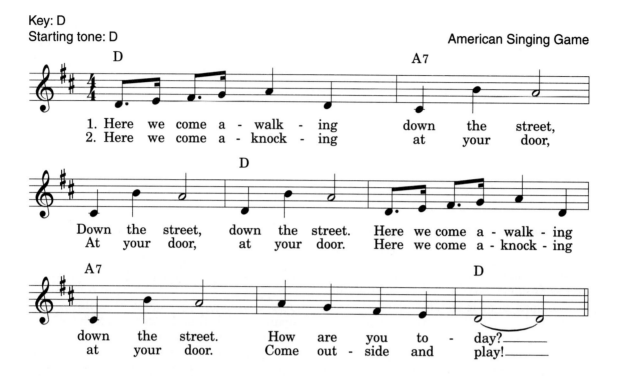

1. Here we come a - walk - ing down the street,
2. Here we come a - knock - ing at your door,

Down the street, down the street. Here we come a - walk - ing
At your door, at your door. Here we come a - knock - ing

down the street. How are you to - day?_____
at your door. Come out - side and play!_____

     Children sit in a circle with plenty of space between them. The leader walks around the outside of the circle as the first verse is sung. At the start of verse 2, the leader kneels behind the nearest child and taps on the floor, offering a hand to the child on "Come outside and play!" As described above, the game may now proceed in one of two ways—with the new child going round the circle alone or with both children "walking down the street." A number of the games that follow present the teacher with these two alternatives; circumstances will help determine which is the best way to play.

BLUEBIRD, BLUEBIRD

Key: C
Starting tone: G

American Singing Game

Standing in a well-spaced circle, the children hold hands, raising their arms high to form windows for verse 1. The chosen "bluebird" goes under the arches, in and out of the circle, standing behind the nearest child at the end of the verse. During verse 2, the bluebird taps lightly on the shoulder of the child he is near. The game is repeated, with the circle becoming smaller with each turn if played cumulatively. To end, partners may take hands and skip around the room to a repeat of verse 1.

I HAVE LOST MY LITTLE PARTNER

Key: G
Starting tone: G

Swedish Folk Tune

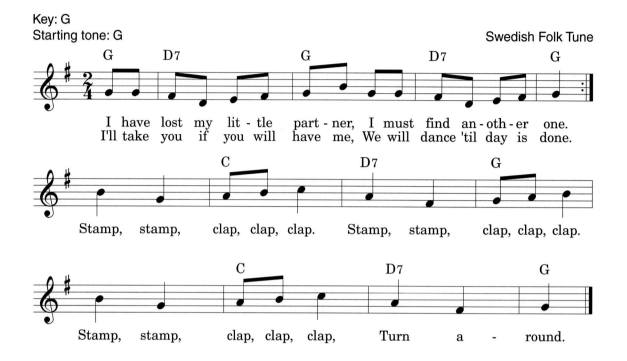

I have lost my lit - tle part - ner, I must find an - oth - er one.
I'll take you if you will have me, We will dance 'til day is done.

Stamp, stamp, clap, clap, clap. Stamp, stamp, clap, clap, clap.

Stamp, stamp, clap, clap, clap, Turn a - round.

Before playing the game, teach all the children standing in the circle the following rhythmic movements:

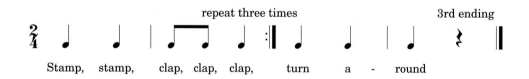

repeat three times   3rd ending

Stamp, stamp, clap, clap, clap, turn a - round

The leader walks freely around the circle to the first two phrases. By "day is done" she should be standing, facing a new partner. The pair now does the motions described and each partner takes off in a different direction, seeking a new partner as the song is sung again. When all have partners, children may walk around hand in hand, singing these words:

> I have found my little partner,
> I don't need another one.
> I'll keep you if you will have me,
> We will dance 'til day is done.

The game ends after the actions are repeated with the same partner.

ONE IN THE MIDDLE

Key: F pentatonic
Starting tone: F

American Singing Game

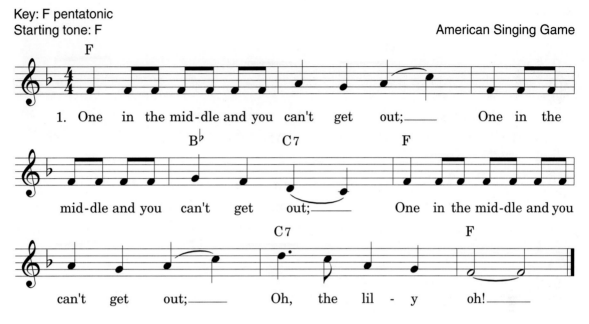

1. One in the mid-dle and you can't get out;⸺ One in the mid-dle and you can't get out;⸺ One in the mid-dle and you can't get out;⸺ Oh, the lil - y oh!⸺

2. Swing you another and another on in.

3. Two in the middle . . . .

The children hold hands in a circle and walk clockwise. One child in the middle, the leader, walks at random, pretending to look for a way out. On verse 2, the children stand still and clap the beat while the leader chooses a second child and draws her into the circle; then they swing each other around. On each repeat of the game, the last child chosen brings a new child in until as many are inside as the circle can contain. Then all drop hands and move around freely singing: "All in the middle and we dance about."

AS I LOOK INTO YOUR EYES

Key: G
Starting tone: D

American Play Party

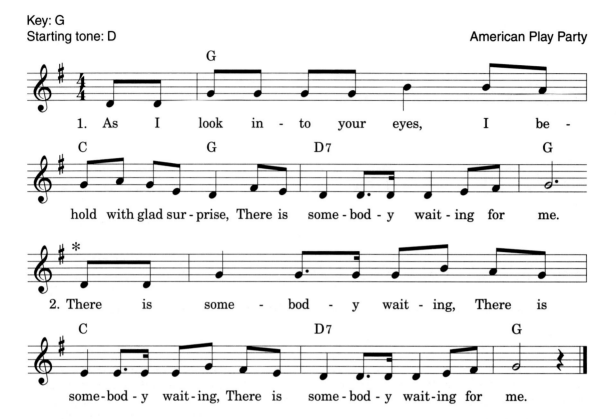

1. As I look in-to your eyes, I be-
hold with glad sur-prise, There is some-bod-y wait-ing for me.

2. There is some-bod-y wait-ing, There is
some-bod-y wait-ing, There is some-bod-y wait-ing for me.

*Verses 3 and 4 begin here.

3. Choose two, leave the others,
   Choose two, leave the others,
   Choose two, leave the others for me!

4. Swing one, leave the other,
   Swing one, leave the other,
   Swing one, leave the other for me!

Start with a circle of children holding hands and one child in the middle.

1. The circle walks one way, the center child the opposite way.
2. Reverse directions.
3. The center child chooses two children standing next to each other, brings them into the circle, and swings with them. The circle stands still and claps.
4. The center child swings *one* of the two chosen and the partners step back into the circle at the end of the verse. The extra child becomes the new leader and the game starts again.

CIRCLE ROUND YOUR ZERO

Key: D pentatonic
Starting tone: F♯

American Street Game

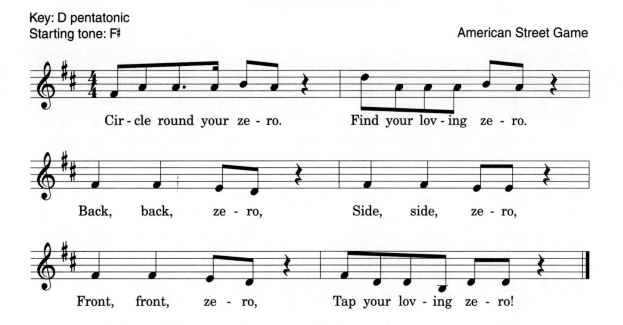

Cir - cle round your ze - ro.   Find your lov - ing   ze - ro.

Back,   back,   ze - ro,   Side,   side,   ze - ro,

Front,   front,   ze - ro,   Tap your lov - ing   ze - ro!

     The circle of children does a patsch-clap motion throughout this game. A leader moves around the outside of the group for the first two measures, stopping behind a child on "your loving zero." Back to back, the children bump twice on "Back, back"; on "Side, side" they bump hips. Then, facing each other on "Front, front," they clap each other's hands twice. On "Tap" the leader taps his zero's shoulder and takes her place.

NGO WAK TŌ WAL-LAH YAH
(Seal Hunt Chant)

Key: A pentatonic   Eskimo
Starting tone: E   Ben Snowball

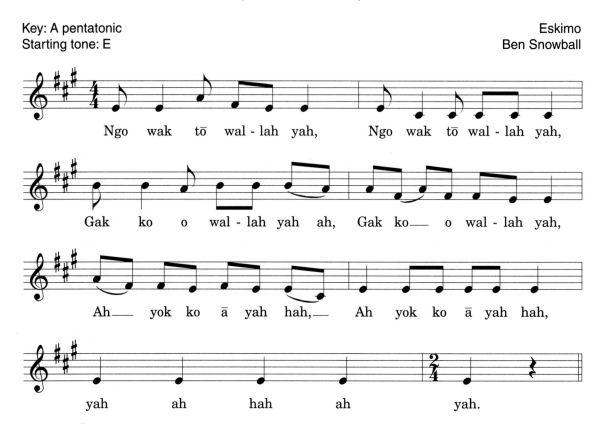

This Alaskan Eskimo chant and dance is accompanied with a steady drum beat and a rhythmic bounce of the knees. The words are pronounced phonetically, as written, and elided into each other. The first phrase tells about paddling the kayak, the second about looking around for signs of seals. The last four measures are a refrain.

Measure 1: Three paddle strokes to the left, rest.

Measure 2: Three paddle strokes to the right, rest.

Measure 3: Right hand over eyes, scan right to left.

Measure 4: Left hand over eyes, scan left to right.

Measure 5: (To left of body, starting low, moving up) Right, then left, hands forward, wave motion.

Measure 6: Repeat to the right side.

Measure 7: Right/left wave motion to front of body twice.

Measure 8: Both hands down on left side.

DOWN AND CLICK YOUR PARTNER'S STICK

Key: B♭
Starting tone: D

Betty Barlow

Down and click your part - ner's stick (Repeat)‒‒‒‒‒‒‒‒‒‒‒‒‒‒‒‒‒‒‒‒
  1   2   3   4   1   2   3   4

That's   the   way   to   play   the   stick   game.
  1   2   3   4   1   2   3   4

Down and click your part - ner's stick   (Repeat)‒‒‒‒‒‒‒‒‒‒‒‒‒‒‒
  1   2   3   4   1   2   3   4

That's   the   way   to   play   the   stick   game.
  1   2   3   4   1   2   3   4

Partners sit on the floor facing each other with rhythm sticks upright. In each measure they do the following:

1. Tap sticks on the floor.
2. Click own sticks together.
3. Tap partner's sticks.
4. Click own sticks together.

After the last repeat ending with "game," each child raises his sticks in the air.

MA KOOAY
(Stick Song)

Key: D   Native American
Starting tone: A   (North West)

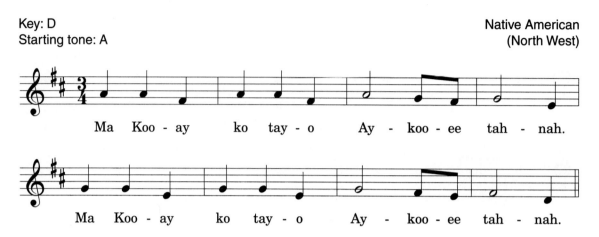

Ma Koo - ay   ko tay - o   Ay - koo - ee   tah - nah.

Ma Koo - ay   ko tay - o   Ay - koo - ee   tah - nah.

Teach the song, with a three-beat ostinato: patsch, clap, clap. When this is secure, seat the children in pairs, facing each other. Now practice: patsch, clap, touch left hands, patsch, clap, touch right hands. Sing the song with this new ostinato.

Finally, add the sticks. They should be held vertically and in the middle. Tap the following pattern:

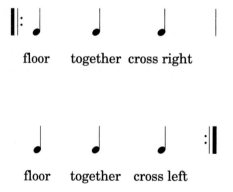

floor   together cross right

floor   together   cross left

As children become proficient, create new three-beat patterns.

KAPULU KANE
(Puili Game)

Key: F pentatonic
Starting tone: C

Hawaiian

A. Ka - pu - lu, pu - lu Ka - ne, Ka - pu - lu, pu - lu Ka - ne,

B. Ka - pu - lu, pu - lu Ka - ne ku - ka - na - lu - a.

C. Ka - pu - lu, pu - lu Ka - ne, Ka - pu - lu, pu - lu Ka - ne,

D. Ka - pu - lu, pu - lu Ka - ne ku - ka - na - lu - a.

Puili are bamboo sticks with one end cut like a fringe. They make a light, rhythmic sound when tapped, as in this game. Teach the song, patsching the beat. When secure, give out the puili (or rhythm sticks) and keep the beat on the floor while singing. Seat the children in pairs, facing each other, and teach them the following puili sequence:

Phrase A:

Measure 1: a. Tap floor
           b. Tap together
           c. Tap floor
           d. Tap together

Measure 2: a. Tap partner's left shoulder with right puili
           b. Tap partner's right shoulder with left puili
           c. Tap own shoulders
           d. Tap overhead

This pattern is repeated for phrases B, C, and D.

The three games that follow are done in line formation with partners as in the Virginia reel folk dance.

WHERE, OH WHERE

Key: F
Starting tone: F   American Traditional Game

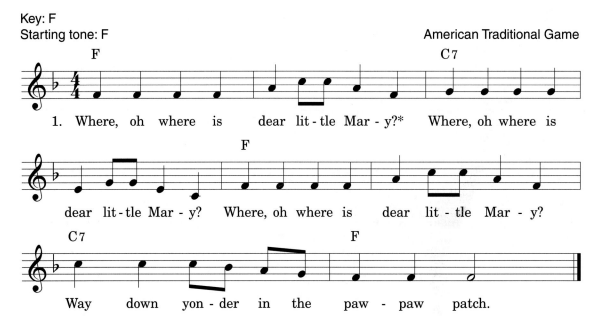

1. Where, oh where is dear lit-tle Mar-y?* Where, oh where is dear lit-tle Mar-y? Where, oh where is dear lit-tle Mar-y? Way down yon-der in the paw - paw patch.

*Change the name as appropriate.

2. Come on boys, let's go find her! (*Repeat 3 times*)
   Way down yonder in the paw-paw patch.

3. Pickin' up paw-paws, puttin' 'em in her pocket, (*Repeat 3 times*)
   Way down yonder in the paw-paw patch.

Boys stand in one line, girls in another, facing forward and in pairs. A set may consist of any convenient numbers of pairs; four to six are enough with primary children. The following motions accompany each verse:

1. Girl 1 turns away from the set and skips around the set to return to her place during the singing of the verse.

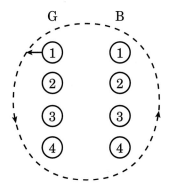

2. Boy 1 repeats girl 1's actions, followed immediately by the rest of the boys in order. Each circles the set once, ending in his own place.

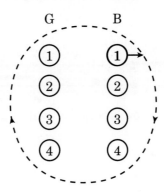

3. Girl 1 and boy 1 turn away from the set and skip toward each other at the rear of the set, each followed by a line of children. This is known as "casting off." When the two meet, they make an archway with their arms under which the other children pass in pairs. At the end of verse 3, the set is ready for a repeat with couple 2 as leaders.

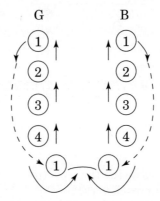

Here is a Spanish version of this song. The game is played in exactly the same manner.

DÓNDE
(Where, Oh Where)

Spanish Lyric: Martha Garcia Ririe

1. Dón-de es-ta la ni-ña mí-a, (*3 times*)
   Vi-si-tan-do a su tí-a ia.

2. Ven-gan ni-ñi-tos a mi ca-sa, (*3 times*)
   Y los lle-vo con mi tí-a, ia.

3. Dón-de es-ta la prin-ce-si-ta, (*3 times*)
   Vi-si-tan-do a su tí-a, ia.

THIS WAY YOU WILLOWBEE

Key: C pentatonic
Starting tone: C

American Traditional Game

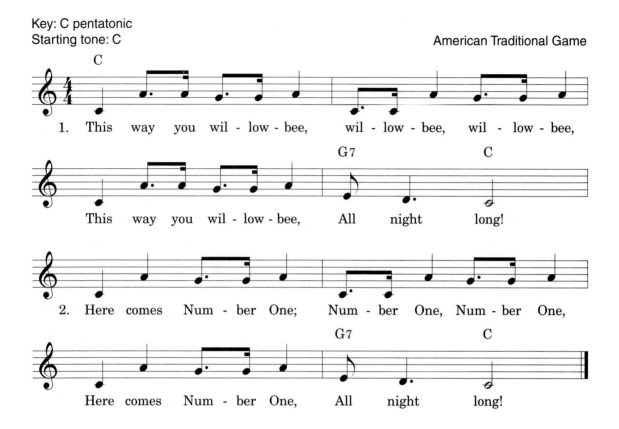

1. This way you wil - low - bee, wil - low - bee, wil - low - bee,
   This way you wil - low - bee, All night long!

2. Here comes Num - ber One; Num - ber One, Num - ber One,
   Here comes Num - ber One, All night long!

The children stand in two lines facing their partners, with a sizable space between them. The following motions go with each verse:

1. With hands on hips, alternate feet are pointed forward on the beat, with a slight swing and dip of the hip.
2. The set stands and claps the beat. Number 1 moves in any fashion down the set to the diagonal space next to number 6.

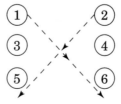

Repeat verse 2, changing the words to "Number Two." The second child follows, using a different motion. Continue in this fashion until each child has had a chance to move.

Each child moving down the set should be encouraged to find a unique way to move. As the game progresses, the set should move up the room to allow space for those who move down as their number is sung. The game ends with a repeat of the first verse when all are in their original places.

LA RASPA

Key: G
Starting tone: D

Mexican

La   ras - pa yo bai - lé   al de - re - cho y al re - vés.   Sí

quie - res tú   bai - lar,   em - pie - za a mo - ver   los pies

Brin - ca, brin - ca, brin - ca tam - bién, mue - ve, mue-ve mu-cho los pies. Que la

ras - pa ras a bai - lar   al de - re - cho y al re - vés.

Partners face each other, hands on hips.

A. Repeat the following twice:

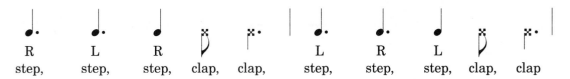

R   L   R   L   R   L

step,   step,   step, clap, clap,   step,   step,   step, clap, clap

B. Repeat the following twice:
   Link right arms, skip around once.
   Link left arms, skip around once.
C. Repeat part A.

I HEARD, I HEARD AN OLD MAN

Key: E
Starting tone: A   Traditional Game

Children take partners and stand in two concentric circles, facing their partners. The outer circle (the 1s) faces inward; the inner circle (the 2s) faces outward. The movements are as follows:

A. The 1s (outer circle) do-si-do right around the 2s (inner circle).
B. On "John," stamp feet.
   On "Kanaka naka," slap knees in rhythm.
   On "Toola," clap own hands twice.
   On "ay," clap partner's hands once.
C. Repeat do-si-do left.
D. Repeat movements for B.
E. The 1s step to the left and face new 2s.
F. Repeat movements for B.

The game is repeated with new partners.

RELATED ACTIVITIES FOR STUDENTS

1. From your own childhood, recall several popular singing games and action songs that you have not found in this chapter. Tape each song along with clear directions on how to play the game or move to the song. Share the activities with your classmates.

2. Extend your repertoire by locating several new games and songs. For sources consider your curriculum library, student teaching, lab school, local day or church schools, and day-care centers. Write out the songs and actions carefully.

3. For one of the following, create a new verse with accompanying motions.

   "See, See, See!" (page 82)
   "Did you Feed My Cow?" (page 87)

4. For one of the following familiar songs, create a sequence of circle movements, one for each phrase of the melody.

   "Yankee Doodle"
   "Skip to My Lou"
   "Jimmy Crack Corn"

5. Create a new movement sequence to one of the following stick games:

   Down and Click Your Partner's Stick (page 109)
   Ma Kooay (page 110)
   Kapulu Kane (page 111)

   Try out your sequence with your classmates.

Chapter 6

Songs for Singing

In Chapter 1 we emphasized the important basic principles underlying singing, active listening, and creative musical experiences during the years of early childhood. The ages and stages discussed in Chapter 1 also include references to the development of the ability to sing a tune. (It will be helpful to the reader to review this material before moving into Chapter 6.) In the first part of this chapter we deal with specific techniques, materials, and activities that will develop accurate listening skills and singing that is in tune and of good tone quality and rhythm. In the second part there are criteria for choosing songs, techniques for teaching them, and—SONGS!

Part I: Learning to Sing

Vocal Range

Young children usually have a limited vocal range, often consisting of only the tones between C and A:

As the singing voice develops, the range expands, and many eight-year-olds sing comfortably in the range B to D' or E':

Some children may be able to sing only a few tones at first. Sing many songs in the C to A range, expanding it gradually with new material.

Listening and Tone Matching

Incidental teaching is an important factor in helping children acquire the ability to sing. Hence, the singing games and action songs already presented help the young child to sing rhythmically and in tune. In addition, most children benefit from daily activities that focus their attention on singing and matching tones.

There are two tones that are particularly easy for children to sing accurately. In fact the descending minor third (*sol-mi,* or the fifth and third tones of the major scale) is probably the earliest interval sung spontaneously by children of many cultures including our own. This interval often forms a little two-tone melody for calling to others in the home or outdoors at play. The tones may be pitched quite low, near the level of the speaking voice, but mastery of this two-tone melody lays the foundation for singing in tune. In school, the singing of *sol-mi* pitches should be encouraged and reinforced both in groups and on an individual basis by echo or call-and-response singing.

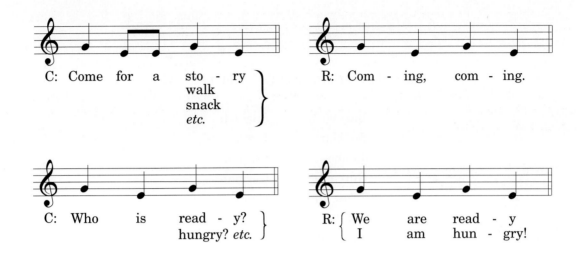

Since teachers keep a record of the daily attendance of their children, one of the most useful means of doing this and helping individual singers is the following:

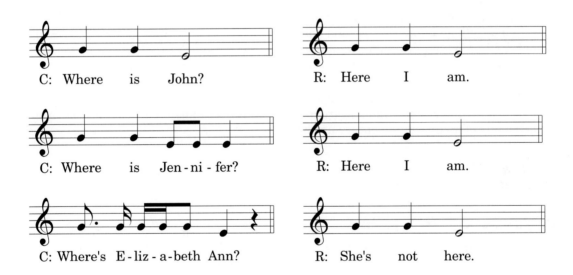

Call a few children's names each day so that over two or three days' time all have a chance to participate. In addition to singing, silence, gestures, and spoken answers may be forthcoming at first. Most children, however, soon join in. The shy child who doesn't speak should always be included. A comment such as "I see you're here, Sarah! One day we'll hear your voice" offers acceptance and encouragement. Several children may respond with an accurate *sol-mi* interval, starting on a different pitch, usually lower. This is progress! On occasion repeat the call on the two tones the child has used. In responding the child has the physiological and aural experience of matching what she has just heard. These feelings are also enhanced when a child responds to a greeting in her "home" language. In our experience most children enjoy singing in other languages.

Buenos dias	Spanish
Bonjour	French
Jambo	Swahili
Guten tag	German
Ts'ow ahn	Chinese
Boh-ker tov	Hebrew
Ya at tay	Navajo

Many nursery rhymes may be sung on the tones of the minor third. Look for them in Mother Goose and primary anthologies. "See-Saw, Margery Daw," "Peter, Peter, Pumpkin Eater," "Jack-Be-Nimble," "A Dillar, A Dollar," and "Christmas is Coming" are a few of the rhymes that could be used.

One more suggestion for the use of this beginner's tune is to use it in informal conversation during the day. While children wait for the schoolbus or a parent, serve and eat lunch, or work at independent activities in the classroom, gym, or outdoors, the teacher can make comments, ask questions, or offer praise and encouragement by singing them on this interval, fitting the rhythm to the words. Many children will reply in like manner and will be increasingly creative and musical in their replies. Some will enjoy a long dialogue and often initiate such singing-talk with adults and peers.

Additional singing tones soon appear in the young child's repertoire; often *la*, the sixth tone of the scale, comes next. The playground is a good place to listen for a three-tone song that is usually of an uncomplimentary nature:

Bring this melody into school and a new range of songs is available, built on the three tones *la, sol, mi* and extending into five tones, or the *pentatonic scale*. The pentatonic scale, comprised of *do, re, mi, sol, la,* is discussed further in Chapter 8, in the section "Introducing Melody Instruments."

If a child has difficulty matching the pitch given by the teacher, ask the child's name, singing the question on a descending minor third (*sol, mi*) in the middle range:

The child may well respond by singing his name to a similar interval, but starting on a different pitch:

Take the child's initial pitch for the starting tone of the song. This will enable him to sing his name while matching your tonality:

The experience of matching a tone interval given by the adult model, even though the tones themselves are originated by the child, physiologically and psychologically reinforces the child's ability and confidence and frequently helps her to lift her singing voice out of "the basement" and quite rapidly match the teacher's initial pitch. The alert teacher will use this technique often, first matching the child's pitch level and then offering different levels (usually higher) as the child gains in confidence and the ability to concentrate her singing voice. Shaping the rise or fall of the melody with hands and arms also helps the child to focus and direct her voice more accurately.

Songs to Develop In-Tune Singing

STARLIGHT, STARBRIGHT

RAIN, RAIN

Key: C pentatonic
Starting tone: G

Traditional Melody

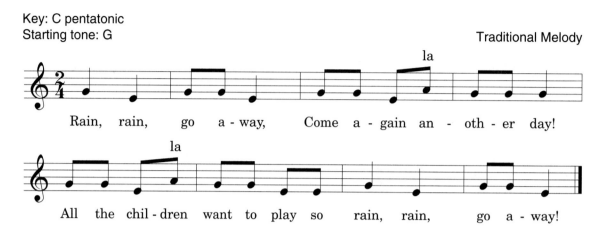

Rain, rain, go a - way, Come a - gain an - oth - er day!

All the chil - dren want to play so rain, rain, go a - way!

Feel free to change these words. After a spring planting, for example, sing: "Rain, rain, come along, Nights are short and days are long! Help our seeds grow big and strong, so rain, rain, come along!"

BOUNCE HIGH, BOUNCE LOW

Key: C pentatonic
Starting tone: G

Traditional

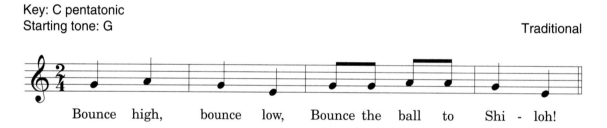

Bounce high, bounce low, Bounce the ball to Shi - loh!

Suggested game: Children stand in a circle. The teacher stands in the middle and bounces the ball on the first beat of each measure as all sing. On the last word of the song the teacher bounces the ball to one child who sings the song and then bounces the ball back to the teacher. Older children can bounce the ball and sing at the same time.

RING AROUND THE ROSIE

Key: C pentatonic
Starting tone: G

Traditional Melody

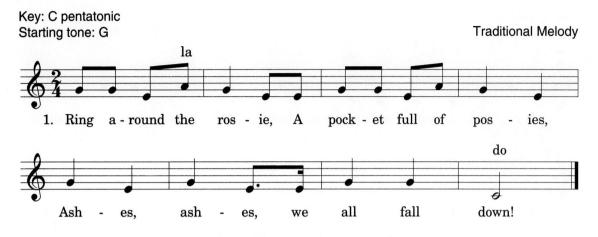

1. Ring a - round the ros - ie, A pock - et full of pos - ies,

Ash - es, ash - es, we all fall down!

2. The King has sent his daughter
To fetch a pail of water.
Ashes, ashes we all fall down!

Notice that "Ring Around the Rosie" includes *do* at the end of the tune. Now four of the five pentatonic tones are in use, in a natural and easy sequence.

AS I LOOKED OUT MY WINDOW

Key: C pentatonic
Starting tone: G

Words and Music: M. Burnett

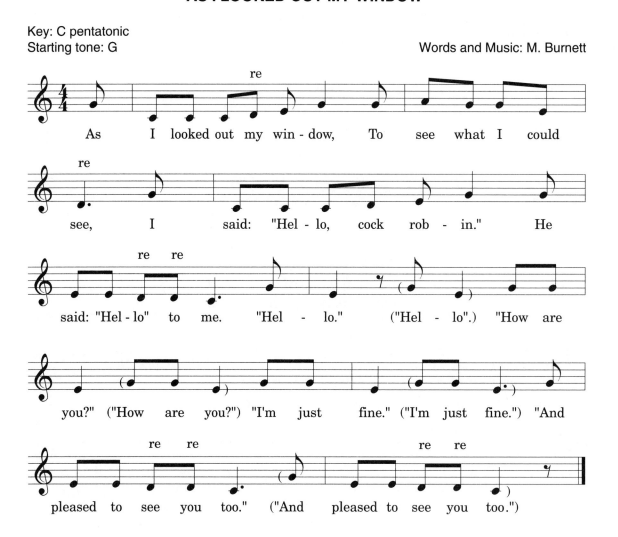

This charming song gives groups and individuals call-and-response practice and intro-duces *re,* the tone that completes the pentatonic scale. Change "cock robin" to the names of other birds, animals, and people in the children's lives. Accept a variety of suggestions and adjust the rhythm as needed.

Echo Songs

Direct echo singing helps young singers to sustain both pitch and tone quality. To teach these songs, simply say "Sing what I sing" and begin!

CHI-CHI-PA-PA

Key: F pentatonic   Japanese
Starting tone: F   (adapted)

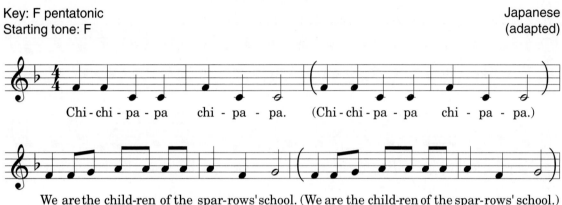

Chi - chi - pa - pa   chi - pa - pa.   (Chi - chi - pa - pa   chi - pa - pa.)

We are the child-ren of the spar-rows' school. (We are the child-ren of the spar-rows' school.)

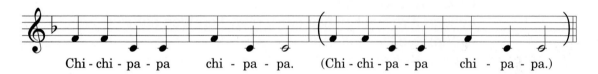

We can sing a song and sing it ve-ry well. (We can sing a song and sing it ver-y well.)

Chi - chi - pa - pa   chi - pa - pa.   (Chi - chi - pa - pa   chi - pa - pa.)

Many more pentatonic songs appear in this book in other keys. See the index to augment the examples given here.

Consistent use of the pentatonic material will ensure teaching success with very young singers. Tone matching and pentatonic songs should be part of the daily singing activities of young children, in groups as well as individually. These activities help to develop accurate listening and tuneful singing. We believe, in addition, that many songs in the diatonic major and minor scales should be included in the repertoire, just as they are in everyday life. Adults and children alike listen to and participate in the full range of melody making, and ear, voice, intellect, and emotions all benefit from such experiences.

The concluding songs in this section are in the diatonic scale, using *fa* and *ti*.

KYE KYE KULE

Key: C
Starting tone: G

African

Kye kye ku-le. (Kye kye ku-le.) Kye kye ko-fi nsa. (Kye kye ko-fi nsa.)

Ko-fi nsa lan-ga. (Ko-fi nsa lan-ga.) Ka-ka shi lan-ga. (Ka-ka shi lan-ga.)

All

Kum a-den-de. (Kum a-den-de.) Kum a-den-de, Hey!

Leader: Kye kye kule (chay chay koo-lay)
Group: Kye kye kule
Leader: Kye kye kofi nsa (chay chay koh-feen sah)
Group: Kye kye kofi nsa
Leader: Kofi nsa langa (koh-feen sah lahn-gah)
Group: Kofi nsa langa
Leader: Kaka shi langa (kah-kah shee lahn-gah)
Group: Kaka shi langa
Leader: Kum adende (koom ah-dehn-day)
Group: Kum adende
Leader and group: Kum adende, hey!

This echo song comes from Ghana; it is also found elsewhere in Africa. The words are vocables, without specific meaning.

HELLO, THERE!

Key: C
Starting tone: G

Traditional

Hel - lo, there! (Hel - lo, there!) How are you? (How are you?)

It's so good (It's so good) to see you. (to see you.)

We'll sing and (We'll sing and) be hap - py. (be hap - py.)

We're all here to - geth - er a - gain!

I HAVE A SONG
(Yo Canto Hoy)

Key: C
Starting tone: E

Words and Music: M. Rudd

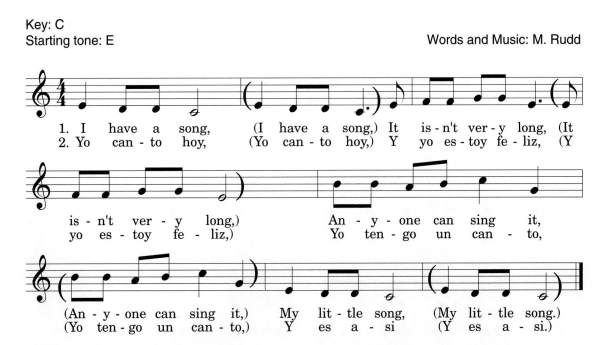

1. I have a song, (I have a song,) It is - n't ver - y long, (It
2. Yo can - to hoy, (Yo can - to hoy,) Y yo es - toy fe - liz, (Y

is - n't ver - y long,) An - y - one can sing it,
yo es - toy fe - liz,) Yo ten - go un can - to,

(An - y - one can sing it,) My lit - tle song, (My lit - tle song.)
(Yo ten - go un can - to,) Y es a - si (Y es a - si.)

Out-of-Tune Singers

Some people, both children and adults, have difficulty matching their voices to the pitches heard, even though their speaking voices have expressive inflections and their hearing is normal. We sometimes refer to them as "out-of-tune" singers. The cause of this is often lack of concentration. We have found two techniques to deal with this problem at age levels from early childhood to adult: physical contact and eye contact between teacher and learner. Either one may help and both together provide strong reinforcement.

Hold both hands of the uncertain singer with a firm, confident grasp as you sit or stand directly in front of her. Tell her to look at you, and hold her gaze by concentrating fully on her—her eyes and the feel of her hands in yours. Now sing to her a two-tone call such as "Here I am" or "It's a sunny day." Holding your hands, the learner responds to the call you offer her. Repeat the call several times, encouraging each effort on her part and intoning "Listen," "Try again, higher," or whatever seems appropriate. If the learner more nearly matches your pitch at any point, praise her achievement and repeat the echo several times before moving on.

In a supportive and trusting environment, little children will not feel embarrassed or inferior during these individual tone-matching games. Keep the games short and do them with others in the group in a good-humored manner. In our experience, uncertain singers of any age find it easier to come close to accurate tone matching when the teacher uses strong physical and visual contact.

A further problem with out-of-tune singers of all ages may be de-energized singing. This is characterized by minimal articulation and diction, hardly any use of the lips, the teeth, or the tip of the tongue, and either superficial breaths that cannot produce more than two or three tones or full breaths that are exhaled in the first few seconds of singing. Both of these breathing methods result in what we call "breathy singing" that lacks tone quality and support and produces the need to inhale after every three or four syllables. The solution to this problem comes through focusing the voice. Use such instructions as "Make the words clearer," "Stand taller," "Pull in your tummy," "Sing to people farther away," or "Sing all this . . . without breathing again." Be sure to model each direction as you give it. You may actually desire somewhat louder singing. It is, however, detrimental to good singing to ask for more volume without couching the request in other terms, since shouting will result.

Remember that in-tune singing is built on clear, focused speech. Diction, articulation, and inflection should be the intent of every syllable spoken. To achieve this, include a wide range of speech activities at all developmental levels. Children enjoy repetition, especially if it is rhythmic and has humor or a dramatic touch, as do many nonsense nursery rhymes. Be sure that each repetition improves on the speech qualities of the previous one. Some examples follow.

TWO LITTLE SAUSAGES

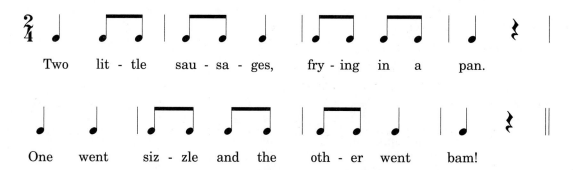

BUBBLE GUM

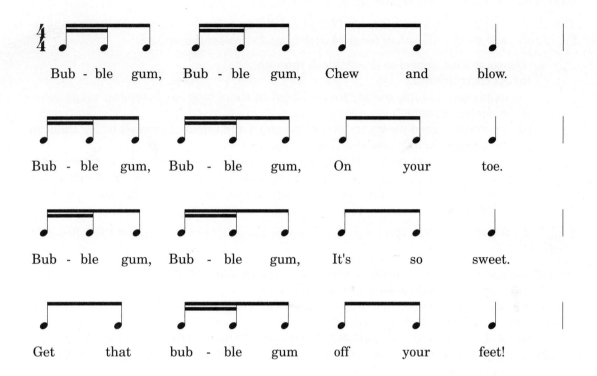

GREGORY GRIGGS

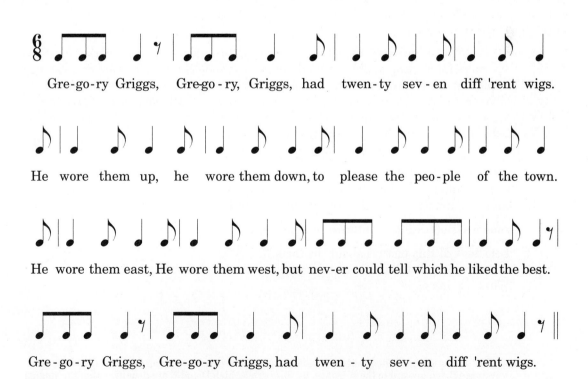

For additional chants, see Chapter 4.

Part 2: Building a Song Repertoire

Criteria for Choosing a Song

The ability to choose good song material for young children is an important skill. The following criteria are always necessary for good choices and successful teaching.

1. The song must appeal to the children through:
   (a) its clear rhythm.
   (b) its pleasing, simple melody that is based on chord tones and stepwise progressions.
   (c) its singable range.*
   (d) its content (good poetry, natural word order, and topics of interest to the children).
2. It must be well known and well liked by the teacher.
3. It must have a close relationship between words and the melody. The meaning of the words should be reflected in the style of the music. The phrasing of the words and the melody line should coincide. The words and the melody should fit together like a hand in a glove.

Songs for little children that can easily be memorized often contain several of the following attributes:

4. They may be short or divided into several verses and a chorus.
5. They may contain verbal or melodic repetition.
6. They may suggest physical activity or instrumental accompaniment.
7. They may deal with the familiar.
8. They may stimulate the mind and imagination to new interests and knowledge.
9. They may correlate with other areas of subject matter. (Or they may not—in fact, a song can be pure nonsense!)

When you choose a song, be sure it meets the first three criteria. Some of the criteria in 4 through 9 will further influence your choice. Often the true test of a good song for young children is that it seems to teach itself after one or two hearings.

Teaching a New Song

No one method fits all situations for teaching a new song to children. Using a varied approach provides for a more interesting and diversified program. A song chosen on sound criteria may relate to a topic of current interest or may involve the use of a particular music concept or activity, or both—or it may seem to happen just for fun! Of course, each song should give the children pleasure and contribute, however incidentally, to the development of musical skill.

To teach a new song successfully, the teacher should:

1. Like the song.
2. Know and sing it well.
3. Have in mind the reasons for teaching it, including a musical purpose.
4. Plan its introduction and the steps to be used in teaching it.

Here are some ways of initiating interest in a new song:

1. "Let's look at this picture about the farm."
2. "Susan's going to tell us about the hat from Mexico she's brought."
3. "What a rainy day!"

---

*Very young singers do best in the limited range of middle C up to A. As accurate singing develops, the range is expanded downward to B and upward to the B′ octave. By third grade, high D and E are usually within the singing range.

4. "When's the first day of spring?"
5. "Who knows what happens a week from today?"
6. "Listen . . ." (Don't overuse this one.)
7. "Shut your eyes. Listen and see a picture inside your head."
8. "I'm going to play a record of someone singing the song we're going to learn. Listen and see what it's about."
9. "Who can find the silly words in this song?"
10. "When I touch you on the head, go and stand in a circle (with a partner, by yourself) in a space that you like."
11. "Do you remember this book we read the other day?"
12. "Today I have a poem for you to listen to and a song to go with it."
13. "Join with me in a finger play and see what I do next!"
14. "Today we're going to learn a song from Israel. Moishe will help us with the Hebrew words."

A variety of approaches should be used from day to day. Remember, the object is not to develop a fifteen-minute discussion but to get into the song itself while interest is at its peak.

Once you have introduced the song by singing it all the way through, find reasons for repeating it until the children begin to join in. During this process you may notice parts of the song where the children are not matching your model. Take those phrases singly and have the children "echo sing" them with you to improve their accuracy. In this way the song is learned quickly and as a whole. Interesting and involving repetition is the secret of success in rote teaching. To lead into the repetition of a new song, you can:

1. Ask a question answered in the words at the end, in the middle, or at the beginning of the song.
2. Add motions to the song.
3. Ask children to find like parts in the tune or the words.
4. Clap or play on instruments the beat or pulse of the song.
5. Add one or more instruments to the singing.
6. Listen to a recording of the song.
7. Hum the tune.
8. Find the words that rhyme.
9. Move to the phrases.
10. Dramatize the words of the song, if appropriate.
11. Play an instrumental accompaniment.
12. Play a chord accompaniment on autoharp or resonator bells.

Several of these techniques may be used in any order. Encourage the children to join in when they feel ready. Often they will join in uninvited, especially in singing or chanting. There is no need to feel a whole song must be taught at one sitting. Part of a song may be enough: "That was a good start! We'll sing it again tomorrow." A familiar and well-loved song should be included before ending the singing time.

Three Ways to Start a Song

1. Identify the starting tone from the written music. Then sound the tone on any tuned instrument, such as piano, resonator bells, metallophone, recorder, or pitch pipe.

2. Start the song and sing it through. If the pitch seems too high or too low for the singers, start over by using a little higher or lower tone. This trial-and-error method leads to increasing skill and accuracy. The tendency is usually to pitch a song too low. Beware of it!

3. Ask a reliable, tuneful singer in the group to start a familiar song. A comfortable range is usually achieved. This is another skill that will grow.

Songs for Every Day

Two groups of songs follow. Those in the first group are pentatonic and have an asterisk in the index. Those in the second group are *diatonic*, in either major or minor mode. Easier songs begin each group.

Note that these songs are samples of suitable material for young children and not exhaustive lists. Many excellent songs are omitted since they appear in so many current collections and music series and are either easily accessible or very familiar. Some of the songs included here are less well-known, but all of them have proved to be both enjoyable and conducive to good in-tune singing. When choosing songs from other sources, you will find it helpful to review the criteria discussed earlier in this chapter.

Pentatonic Songs

TEN IN THE BED

Key: G pentatonic
Starting tone: D

American Folk Song

Count down to one. In the final verse, sing: "There was one in the bed, and the little one said, (*whisper*) 'Good night'."

RIDING IN THE BUGGY

Key: C pentatonic
Starting tone: C

American Folk Song

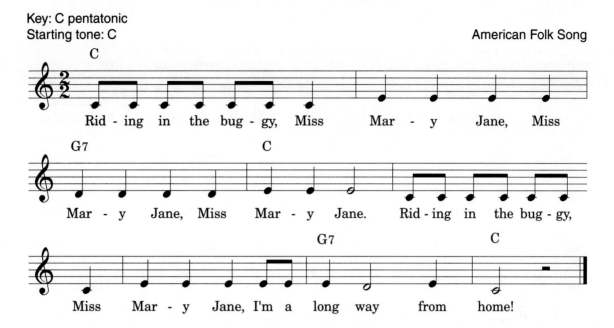

2. Sally has a house in Baltimore, in Baltimore, in Baltimore.
   Sally has a house in Baltimore, three stories high!

3. Sally has a house in Baltimore, in Baltimore, in Baltimore.
   Sally has a house in Baltimore, full of good pie!

Substitute a child's name for Sally. Have him tell where his house is and what kind of pie he would like in his house. Then sing for him and for others in the group. End the activity by having everyone sing his or her own particular verse at the same time!

DUERME PRONTO
(Go to Sleep)

Key: F pentatonic
Starting tone: F

Spanish

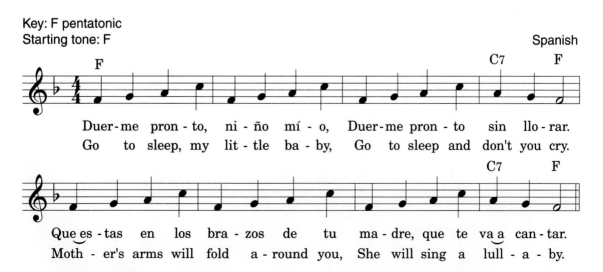

OVER MY HEAD

Key: F pentatonic
Starting pitch: F

American Spiritual
(adapted)

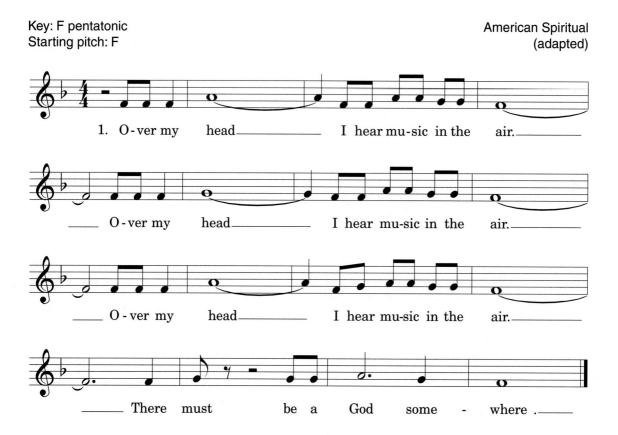

1. O-ver my head I hear mu-sic in the air.

O-ver my head I hear mu-sic in the air.

O-ver my head I hear mu-sic in the air.

There must be a God some - where.

Add additional verses such as:

> Clapping my hands, I hear music in the air
> Singing my song, I hear music in the air
> Holding your hand, I hear music in the air

End with "There must be a God somewhere."

COOKIE

Key: D pentatonic
Starting tone: A

African-American Folk Song

Cook - ie, you sure no - bod - y passed here?_____

(No, my friend.)_____ Cook - ie, you sure no - bod - y

passed here?___ (No, my friend.) Well! One of my

dump - lin's gone! (Don't tell me so!) One of my dump - lin's

gone! (Don't tell me so!) One of my dump - lin's gone! (Aw!)

Other verses may include different numbers of missed objects or other objects such as jelly beans, apple pies, or pizzas.

WHEN THE TRAIN COMES ALONG

Key: C pentatonic
Starting tone: C

African American Song

When the train comes a - long,____ When the
train comes a - long,____ I'll meet you at the
sta - tion when the train comes a - long.
It may be snow - ing, It
may be cold, But I'll meet you in the
sta - tion when the train comes a - long.

THIS TRAIN

Key: F pentatonic
Starting tone: F

African American Song

Create other verses such as "This train is going to the farm to see the animals in the barn," or "This train is going to the park. We'll get home before it's dark."

THERE'S A LITTLE WHEEL

Key: D pentatonic
Starting tone: D

African-American

1. There's a lit-tle wheel— a-turn-in' in my heart.

There's a lit-tle wheel— a-turn-in' in my heart.

In my heart,_____ in my heart,_____

There's a lit-tle wheel— a-turn-in' in my heart.

2. There's a little bell a-ringin' in my heart.

3. There's a little drum a-beatin' in my heart.

4. There's a little song a-singin' in my heart.

FROG WENT A COURTING

Key: F pentatonic
Starting tone: F

American Folk Song

Frog went a-court-ing and he did ride,

King Kong Kit-chie Kit-chie Ki - me - o. Sword and a pis - tol

by his side, King Kong Kit-chie Kit-chie Ki - me - o.

Ki - mo Ke - mo Ki - mo Kee, way down yon-der in a

hol - low tree, an owl and a bat and a

bum - ble - bee. King Kong Kit-chie Kit-chie Ki - me - o

2. Rode 'till he came to Miss Mousie's door,
   King Kong etc. . . . .
   There he knelt down on the floor,
   King Kong etc. . . . .

3. Said "Miss Mouse, will you marry me?"
   King Kong etc. . . . .
   Said Miss Mouse "Most certainly!"
   King Kong etc. . . . .

THIS IS THE TIME

Key: C pentatonic
Starting tone: C´

Words and Music: J. Haines

This is the time to make some mu-sic, This is the
time to sing and play. This is the time to
be to-geth-er, We're going to have a hap-py day!

2. This is the time to talk things over,
This is the time we like to share,
This is the time we look and listen,
So many ways to show we care.

3. We're very glad to be together,
We're very glad we came this way,
We're very glad we woke this morning,
Isn't it great today's today?

To encourage in-tune singing, use songs that emphasize descending intervals, like "This Is the Time," "Three Crows," "Jump Down, Turn Around," "Oh My, No More Pie," and "Bluebird, Bluebird." These require a higher degree of energy than those with ascending melodic patterns.

◆ ——————————————— ◆

In addition to being easy to sing, pentatonic songs lend themselves to the accompaniment of melodic ostinati—fragments of the tune repeated over and over as accompaniments to the singing. A variety of tuned instruments may be used: piano, resonator bells, glockenspiels, xylophones, metallophones. See the section "Melodic Ostinati" in Chapter 8. For easy accessibility all pentatonic songs appear in the index with an asterisk.

Diatonic Songs

TODAY IS MONDAY
(Hoy, Hoy Es Lunes)

Key: F
Starting tone: C

J. Haines
Spanish Lyric: Martha Garcia Ririe

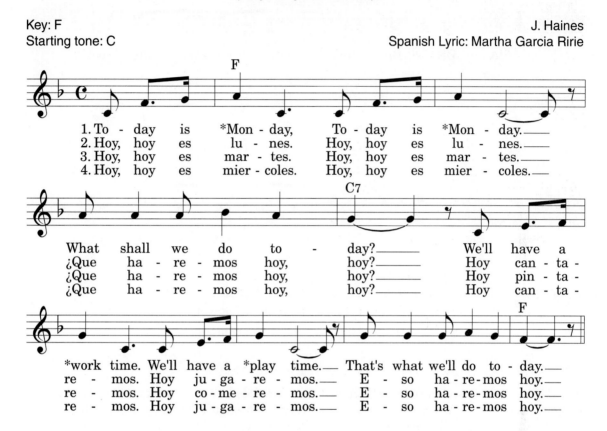

1. To - day   is   *Mon - day,   To - day   is   *Mon - day.___
2. Hoy, hoy   es   lu - nes.   Hoy, hoy   es   lu - nes.___
3. Hoy, hoy   es   mar - tes.   Hoy, hoy   es   mar - tes.___
4. Hoy, hoy   es   mier - coles. Hoy, hoy   es   mier - coles.___

What shall we   do   to - day?___   We'll   have   a
¿Que ha - re - mos hoy, hoy?___   Hoy   can - ta -
¿Que ha - re - mos hoy, hoy?___   Hoy   pin - ta -
¿Que ha - re - mos hoy, hoy?___   Hoy   can - ta -

*work time. We'll have a *play time.___ That's what we'll do to - day.___
re - mos. Hoy ju - ga - re - mos.___ E - so ha - re - mos hoy.___
re - mos. Hoy co - me - re - mos.___ E - so ha - re - mos hoy.___
re - mos. Hoy ju - ga - re - mos.___ E - so ha - re - mos hoy.___

Change the days and activities as appropriate at the asterisks. For extended activities in English see page 249. Spanish verses for the rest of the week appear below.

4. Hoy, hoy es jue-ves.
   Hoy, hoy es jue-ves.
   ¿Que ha-re-mos hoy, hoy?
   Hoy bai-la-re-mos.
   Hoy brin-ca-re-mos.
   E-so ha-re-mos hoy.

5. Hoy, hoy es vier-nes.
   Hoy, hoy es vier-nes.
   ¿Que ha-re-mos hoy, hoy?
   Hoy gui-sa-re-mos.
   Hoy co-me-re-mos.
   E-so ha-re-mos hoy.

6. Hoy, hoy es sá-bado
   Hoy, hoy es sá-bado
   ¿Que ha-re-mos hoy, hoy?
   Hoy na-da-re-mos.
   Hoy co-rre-re-mos.
   E-so ha-re-mos hoy.

7. Hoy, es do-min-go.
   Hoy, hoy es do-min-go.
   ¿Que ha-re-mos hoy, hoy?
   Hoy dor-mi-re-mos.
   Hoy so-ña-re-mos.
   E-so ha-re-mos hoy.

BA-BE-BI-BO-BU

Key: E♭
Starting tone: G

Words and Music: J. Haines
Spanish Lyric: Martha Garcia Ririe

This song is based on the vowels *A, E, I, O, U,* preceded by consonants and worked into vocables. Create new verses by substituting different consonants for the initial *B.* The initials of first names always stimulate interest and the discovery that more than one person may be featured in the same verse. Teachers and parents of auditorily impaired preschoolers have found this song helpful in speech therapy. Spanish words are included.

COME, COME AND PLAY WITH ME

Key: E♭
Starting tone: E♭

Anonymous

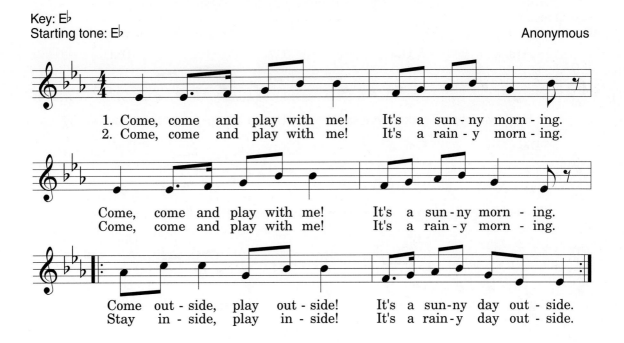

1. Come, come and play with me! It's a sun - ny morn - ing.
2. Come, come and play with me! It's a rain - y morn - ing.

Come, come and play with me! It's a sun - ny morn - ing.
Come, come and play with me! It's a rain - y morn - ing.

Come out - side, play out - side! It's a sun - ny day out - side.
Stay in - side, play in - side! It's a rain - y day out - side.

MON PAPA

Key: G
Starting tone: D

French Canadian

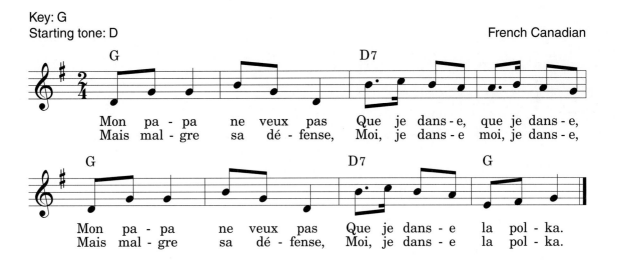

Mon pa - pa ne veux pas Que je dans - e, que je dans - e,
Mais mal - gre sa dé - fense, Moi, je dans - e moi, je dans - e,

Mon pa - pa ne veux pas Que je dans - e la pol - ka.
Mais mal - gre sa dé - fense, Moi, je dans - e la pol - ka.

Father has forbidden the singer to dance the polka, but in spite of this, the dance goes on!

HUSH YOU BYE

Key: D minor
Starting tone: D

American Folk Song

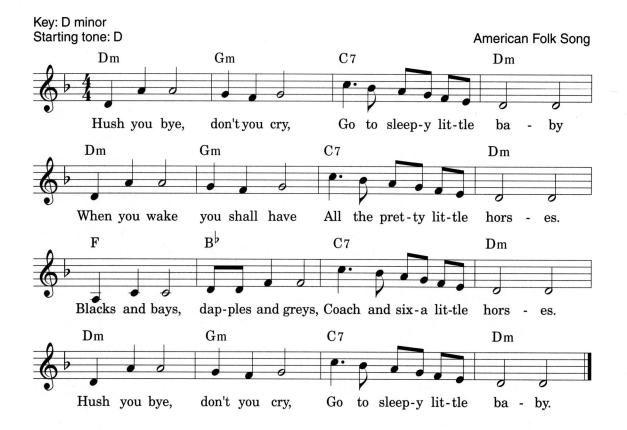

Hush you bye,   don't you cry,   Go to sleep-y lit-tle   ba - by

When you wake   you shall have   All the pret-ty lit-tle   hors - es.

Blacks and bays,   dap-ples and greys, Coach and six-a lit-tle   hors - es.

Hush you bye,   don't you cry,   Go to sleep-y lit-tle   ba - by.

EV'RYBODY OUGHT TO SING
(Todos Debemos Cantar)

Key: F
Starting tone: A

L. Gerber and J. Haines
Spanish Lyrics: Martha Garcia Ririe

Ev - 'ry - bod - y ought to sing!____ Ev - 'ry - bod - y ought to
To - dos de - be - mos can - tar!____ To - dos de - be - mos bai -

smile!____ Hap - py fac - es all a - round, Make each day worth-
lar!____ Y fe - li - ces se - re mos, el sol bri - lla -

while.____ Ev - 'ry - bod - y ought to sing!____
rá.____ To - dos de - be - mos can - tar!____

Wheth - er skies are gray or blue!____ Learn our song and
To - dos de - be - mos bai - lar!____ A - pren - de nues -

sing a - long, And let the mer - ry sun shine through!____
tra can - cion y con - ten to tu es - ta - rás.____

JOIN HANDS ALL AROUND THE WORLD

Key: A
Starting tone: C♯

J. Haines and L. Gerber

Join hands all a-round the world, Join hands
Make friends all a-round the world, Make friends

all a-round the world,_____ Join hands
all a-round the world,_____ Make friends

all a-round the world, It's good for you and me!_____
all a-round the world, That's how it's meant to be!_____

3. Spread joy all around the world,
   Spread joy all around the world,
   Spread joy all around the world,
   And let God's love be free!

4. Glory, glory, hallelu,
   Glory, glory, hallelu,
   Glory, glory, hallelu,
   That's how it's meant to be!

Encourage your children to make up new verses. It doesn't matter if they do not rhyme.

TAKE A BITE OF MUSIC

Key: D
Starting tone: D

Mary Ann Hall*

*Music for Children Productions, P.O. Box 3457,
Westport, CT 00880.

HEY LIDEE, LIDEE, LIDEE!

Key: D
Starting tone: A

From a Calypso

Hey Li-dee, Li-dee Li - dee!   Hey Li-dee, Li-dee - lo!—

Hey Li-dee, Li-dee, Li - dee!   Hey Li-dee, Li-dee - lo!—

2. We can sing it all the time.
   Hey Lidee, Lidee-lo!
   Feel the beat and hear the rhyme.
   Hey Lidee, Lidee-lo!

3. With our voices and our feet,
   Hey Lidee, Lidee-lo!
   Hear the rhyme and feel the beat.
   Hey Lidee, Lidee-lo!

4. Join us in our little song.
   Hey Lidee, Lidee-lo!
   Not too short and not too long!
   Hey Lidee, Lidee-lo!

To celebrate Earth Day, use the following words to the above tune.

2. Sing a song in praise of Earth Day.
   Hey Lidee, Lidee-lo!
   Celebrate our planet's birthday.
   Hey Lidee, Lidee-lo!

3. Ev'ry son and ev'ry daughter
   Hey Lidee, Lidee-lo!
   Needs fresh air and sparkling water.
   Hey Lidee, Lidee-lo!

4. Take a stand! Do something drastic!
   Hey Lidee, Lidee-lo!
   Don't use styrofoam or plastic.
   Hey Lidee, Lidee-lo!

5. Stop the use of fossil fuel.
   Hey Lidee, Lidee-lo!
   Chemicals and sprays are cruel.
   Hey Lidee, Lidee-lo!

6. Sing in praise of Earth, our mother.
   Hey Lidee, Lidee-lo!
   We will serve her and each other.
   Hey Lidee, Lidee-lo!

Words copyright © 1990 by B. Joan E. Haines.

LOVE GROWS ONE BY ONE

Key: C
Starting tone: G

Carol A. Johnson*

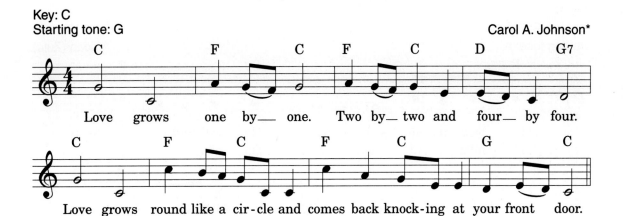

Children enjoy "signing" this song. Authentic sign language may be used, or motions, such as the following, created:

Love: closed hands crossed over heart.

Grows: right hand comes up through left hand C-shape, then opens.

Sign numbers with fingers, first one hand, then the other.

Round: draw a circle high in the air with right forefinger.

Comes: knock on imaginary door, in front of face.

Your front door: open both hands toward group, then turn palms outward, close together, in front of chest.

Sing about other qualities too—peace, joy, hope—and add new gestures.

Older classes may learn the following verse by Carol A. Johnson and sing it between two repeats of the chorus.

Carol A. Johnson*

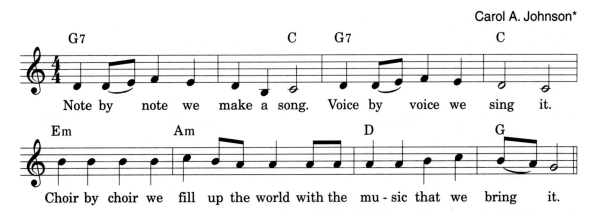

*Carol Johnson Recordings, P.O. Box 6351, Grand Rapids, Mi 49506.

GO WELL AND GO SAFELY
(Hambani Kahle)

Key: F
Starting tone: A

African (Zulu)

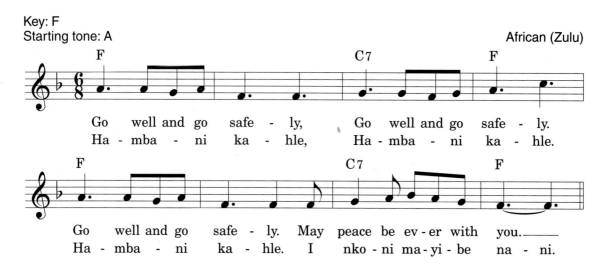

Go well and go safe - ly, Go well and go safe - ly.
Ha - mba - ni ka - hle, Ha - mba - ni ka - hle.

Go well and go safe - ly. May peace be ev - er with you.
Ha - mba - ni ka - hle. I nko - ni ma - yi - be na - ni.

Songs for Special Times

This group of songs can be used throughout the year to enhance the various seasons and celebrate special occasions.

RED LEAVES AND YELLOW

Key: G
Starting tone: D

B. Beament and J. Haines

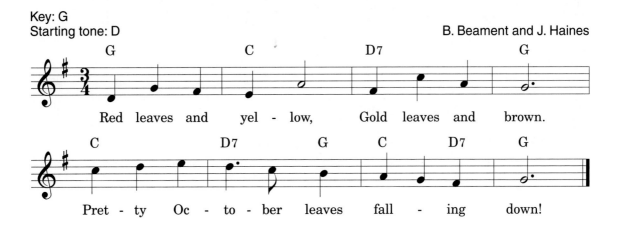

Red leaves and yel - low, Gold leaves and brown.

Pret - ty Oc - to - ber leaves fall - ing down!

ONE LITTLE SKELETON

Key: G minor
Starting tone: G

Lucille Wood

One lit - tle skel - e - ton hop-ping up and down, hop - ping up and down,

hop - ping up and down. One lit - tle skel - e - ton

hop - ping up and down,___ For this is Hal - low - e'en.

2. Two little witches flying through the air.

3. Three little pumpkins walking in a row.

4. Four little goblins skipping down the street.

5. Five little children playing trick or treat.

OLD MRS. WITCH

Key: C minor
Starting tone: C

Lucille Wood

Old   Mrs. —— Witch,   Old   Mrs. —— Witch,

Tell   me how   you fly,   Tell me how you fly,   I

fly—— on a broom - stick—— up through the sky.

2. Old Mrs. Witch, Old Mrs. Witch,
   Tell me what you see, Tell me what you see.
   I see a little Jack-O'-Lantern looking at me.

3. Old Mrs. Witch, Old Mrs. Witch,
   Tell me what you'll do, Tell me what you'll do.
   I'll ride on a broomstick and I'll scare you.

HALLOWEEN, HALLOWEEN, TRICK OR TREAT

Key: F minor
Starting tone: F

L. Gerber and J. Haines

Hal - low - een, Hal - low - een! Trick or treat!

Hear the sound of a spook - y beat.

Clap your hands and tap your feet.

Hal - low - een, Hal - low - een, Trick or treat!

2. Halloween, Halloween! Trick or treat!
   A witch in a hat and a ghost in a sheet—
   All dressed up and you look real neat!
   Halloween, Halloween! Trick or treat!

3. Halloween, Halloween! Trick or treat!
   Put on your mask! Walk down the street!
   Scare all the people that you happen to meet!
   Halloween, Halloween! Trick or treat! BOO!

The lyrics to the above song make an effective chant. Establish an easy rap beat, with claps and/or foot taps, patschen, or snaps—whatever your children can do—and keep up throughout.

GRINDING CORN

Key: F pentatonic
Starting tone: C

Hopi

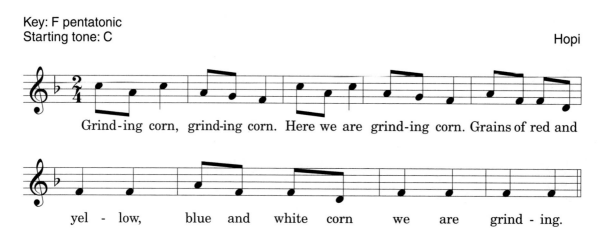

OH, GREAT SPIRIT

Key: C minor
Starting tone: C´

Yuma Indian Chant

2. Oh, Great Spirit, Send us rain clouds. (2) A-wah. (4)

3. Oh, Great Spirit, Rain is falling. (2) A-wah. (4)

THANKSGIVING DAY

Key: F
Starting tone: A

J. Haines

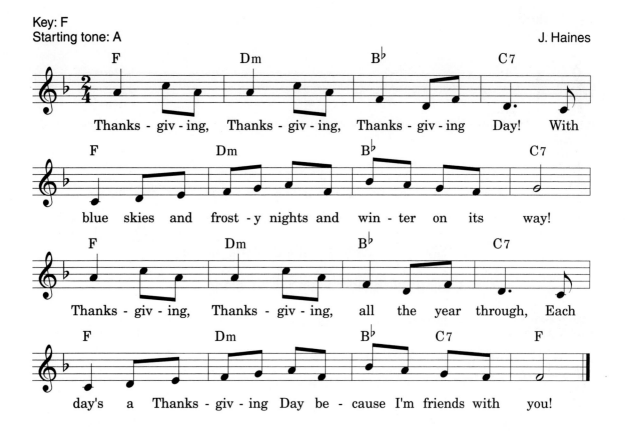

Thanks - giv - ing, Thanks - giv - ing, Thanks - giv - ing Day! With

blue skies and frost - y nights and win - ter on its way!

Thanks - giv - ing, Thanks - giv - ing, all the year through, Each

day's a Thanks - giv - ing Day be - cause I'm friends with you!

BURN LITTLE CANDLES

Key: D minor
Starting tone: D

Hebrew

2. Shine little candles, shine, shine, shine.

3. Sing little children, sing, sing, sing.

4. Dance little children, dance, dance, dance.

HANUKKAH!

Key: C
Starting tone: G

Jewish Folk Song

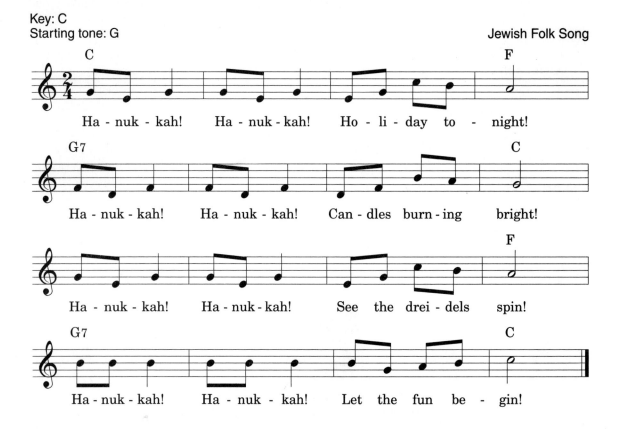

CHRISTMAS BELLS ARE RINGING

Key: C
Starting tone: C

E. Crowninshield

Christ - mas bells are ring - ing. Ding, Dong, Ding. Ev - 'ry - one can hear the

song they sing. Christ - mas bells are ring - ing. Hear them call!

"Mer - ry, Mer - ry Christ - mas to you all!"

LITTLE LAMB

Key: G
Starting tone: D

Roberta McLaughlin

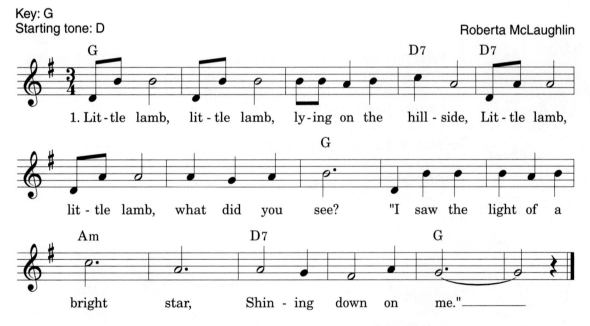

1. Lit - tle lamb, lit - tle lamb, ly - ing on the hill - side, Lit - tle lamb,

lit - tle lamb, what did you see? "I saw the light of a

bright star, Shin - ing down on me."_____

2. Little lamb, little lamb, lying on the hillside,
   Little lamb, little lamb, what did you hear?
   "I heard the voice of the angels,
   Singing sweet and clear."

3. Little lamb, little lamb, lying on the hillside,
   Little lamb, little lamb, where did you go?
   "I went to see the dear Baby,
   Born so long ago."

WHO IS COMING ON CHRISTMAS NIGHT?

Key: G
Starting tone: G

Claire Senior Burke

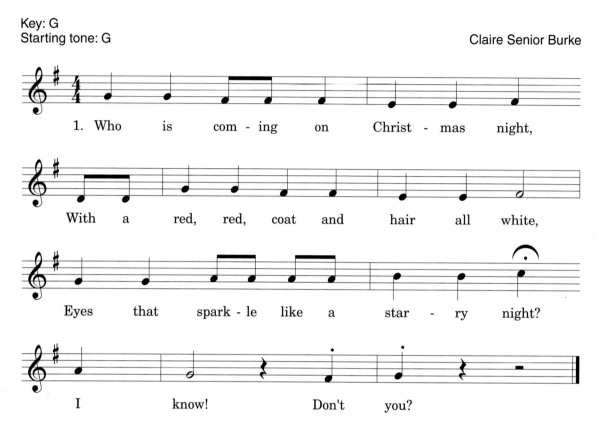

1. Who is com - ing on Christ - mas night,

With a red, red, coat and hair all white,

Eyes that spark - le like a star - ry night?

I know! Don't you?

2. Who has a sack all filled with toys,
   And wonderful things for the girls and boys,
   And a beautiful sleigh that makes no noise?
   I know! Don't you?

3. Who is it knows what the children do,
   And if they're very good or naughty too?
   And who has a book about me and you?
   I know! Don't you?

THE GROUND HOG

Key: D minor
Starting tone: D

J. Haines

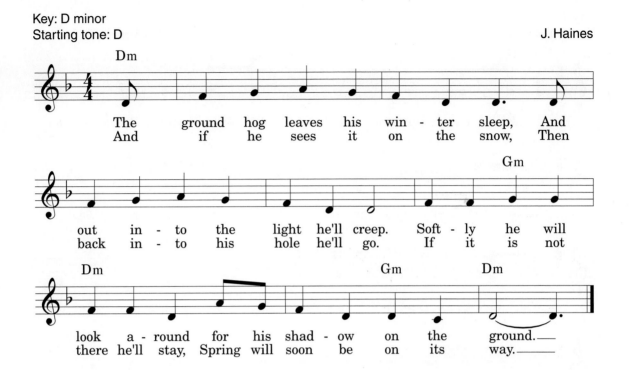

The ground hog leaves his win - ter sleep, And
And if he sees it on the snow, Then

out in - to the light he'll creep. Soft - ly he will
back in - to his hole he'll go. If it is not

look a - round for his shad - ow on the ground.—
there he'll stay, Spring will soon be on its way.—

VALENTINE'S DAY

Key: G
Starting tone: G

Words & music: J. Haines

Val - en - tine's Day! Val - en - tine's Day! You make a pret - ty card and you give it a - way! Val - en - tine's Day! Val - en - tine's Day! Red hearts are ev' - ry - where. On that morn - ing, rain or shine, I'll be yours and you'll be mine. I'll give you my Val - en - tine, To show you that I care.

Many kindergarten and first grade classes celebrate the one hundredth day of school, which usually comes in March. They will enjoy singing these lyrics to the previous melody:

THE HUNDREDTH DAY OF SCHOOL

A wonderful day! A wonderful day!
A wonderful day is on its way!
A wonderful day! A wonderful day!
The hundredth day of school!

On that day, come rain or shine,
We'll add one to ninety-nine;
Celebrate the number line;
The hundredth day of school!

On the ninety-ninth day, sing:

Tomorrow is the day! Tomorrow is the day! etc.

On THE DAY itself, sing:

Today is the day! Today is the day!
A wonderful day has come our way!
Today is the day! Today is the day!
The hundredth day of school!

Count your blessings! I'll count mine.
We'll add one to ninety-nine;
Celebrate the number line;
The hundredth day of school!

THIS IS A SONG FOR ST. PATRICK'S DAY

Key: G
Starting tone: G

Melody: Mulberry Bush
Words: J. Haines

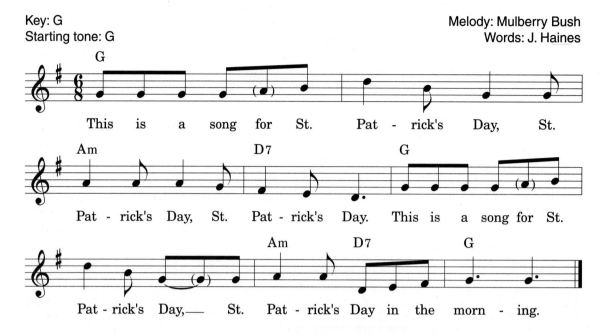

This is a song for St. Pat - rick's Day, St. Pat - rick's Day, St. Pat - rick's Day. This is a song for St. Pat - rick's Day,— St. Pat - rick's Day in the morn - ing.

2. People are wearing the shamrock green,
   Shamrock green, shamrock green.
   People are wearing the shamrock green
   On St. Patrick's Day in the morning.

3. People will dance the Irish jig,
   Irish jig, Irish jig.
   People will dance . . . etc.

4. Corned beef and cabbage we love to eat,
   Love to eat, love . . . etc.

5. Top o' the mornin's the way we greet,
   Way we greet, way . . . etc.

"Erin go braugh" may be sung in the last verse.

Adding Songs to Stories

Young children love spontaneous, dramatic play. Clothes and accessories for dressing up and a few props add to the realism and enjoyment.

Acting out familiar stories and poems brings drama into a group setting and adds structure to it. There are many nursery rhymes and tales with four or five characters and a lot of repetition in the dialogue that can be acted out. Add to these a song or two, with simple words and a familiar tune, and everyone can participate. The resulting plays still have a spontaneous quality yet are predictable enough to be shared with another class or group of parents, or occasionally presented at a school assembly.

Here is a sequence of steps for blending songs with acted-out stories:

1. Help the group to choose a story and decide on the story line. A wall chart of the events is helpful, as there may be several versions of the same story. Even with non-readers the chart helps keep the plot on track.
2. Choose the characters and, if appropriate, a narrator and a sound-effects person. At first the teacher should take the narrator's role.
3. Teach the songs to the whole group so that they can be the chorus and join in.
4. Use the narrator to tell the ongoing parts of the story or let the characters themselves carry the action.
5. The characters create and speak their own lines and act out the story in movement.
6. The sound-effects person may add to the drama with instruments or vocal rhythmic patterns.
7. Help the chorus to bring in their songs at the right moments. End with a song if at all possible. This gives a sense of closure, which young children often find difficult to create.
8. Repeat these little plays from time to time, with different actors and narrators. Add props and costumes, but be sure to keep them simple so that they do not hinder spontaneous movement or speech.

Four dramatic stories with songs added* are included in this section, one based on a nursery rhyme and three on familiar stories. There are two verses for each one, sung to well-known tunes. Once the inventive teacher is familiar with these examples, the skill of creating new ones will quickly develop. The following can be used as a theme song to introduce and end stories with songs, as well as story-rhythms (page 191), song swaps (page 231), or mini-concerts (page 231).

STORIES AND SONGS

Key: F
Starting tone: F

Words and Music: J. Haines

Stor - ies and songs— the kind we like to list - en to!

Mus - ic and words— to sing and— say!—

Stor - ies and songs— the kind we sing and whis - tle to!

That's what we've got— to share to— day!

♫ ACTIVITY 1: THE THREE LITTLE KITTENS _____

Characters: The Mother Cat and Three Little Kittens

Story line: Use the two best-known verses of this old rhyme as the basis for the dramatization. A narrator may speak the first two lines of each stanza.

> Three little kittens, they lost their mittens
> And they began to cry:
> "Oh Mother dear, see here, see here!
> Our mittens we have lost!"
> "Lost your mittens, you bad little kittens,
> Then you shall have no pie!"
> "Miaow, miaow! We shall have no pie!"
>
> Three little kittens, they found their mittens
> And they began to cry:
> "Oh Mother dear, see here, see here!
> Our mittens we have found!"
> "Found your mittens, you good little kittens,
> Then you shall have some pie!"
> "Prr-rr, prr-rr! We shall have some pie!"

Song: After the first verse, the group may sing (to the tune of "Are You Sleeping?"):

> Lost their mittens, lost their mittens,
> Oh dear me! Oh dear me!
> Mother's very angry, Mother's very angry,
> We can see. We can see.

End with this short verse (to the tune of "Hot Cross Buns"):

> Home-made pie! Home-made pie!
> For the kittens wearing mittens—
> Home-made pie!

♫ ACTIVITY 2: THE GINGERBREAD BOY _____

Characters: A Little Old Woman, the Gingerbread Boy, a Cow, a Horse, and a Fox (a Little Old Man may be included)

Story line: Review the story, which usually ends with the Fox gobbling up the Gingerbread Boy. There is a version in which he escapes and runs home to the Little Old Woman.

Song: Each time the Gingerbread Boy runs away, the group sings (to the tune of "This Old Man"):

> Run away, run away!
> Run by night and run by day.
> If you're gingerbread, never take a rest—
> Ginger cookies taste the best!

As the Fox gets the Gingerbread Boy to sit on his nose, you can sing this (to the tune of "Old MacDonald"):

> Ginger cookies taste so good!
> They're the very best.
> We would eat them if we could,
> Just like all the rest.
> With a moo, moo here,
> And a neigh, neigh there!
> Here a snap, there a snap,
> Everywhere a snip-snap!
> Ginger cookies taste so good!
> They're the very best.

ACTIVITY 3: THE THREE LITTLE PIGS

Characters: A Mother Pig, her three Little Pigs, a Big, Bad Wolf, and a Man with a bundle (Three Men with bundles may be chosen if the group is large)

Story line: The story, which begins with the Mother Pig seeing off her first Little Pig to seek his fortune, has one problem that needs to be settled at the outset: the fate of the first two Little Pigs. Are they eaten up by the Wolf, or do they escape to the safety of their brother's brick house to share his victory over the Big, Bad Wolf? Children will discuss how they want their version to end. They may want to play out the story twice, once for each ending, with a change of cast also.

Song: When the first Little Pig is given straw by the Man with the bundle, have the group sing (to the tune of "Row, Row, Row Your Boat"):

> Pig, Pig, build a house,
> Quickly as you may.
> Hurry up, hurry up, hurry up, hurry up!
> Wolf is on his way!

Repeat the song when the second Little Pig receives his sticks and the third, his bricks.

If the story ends with the Wolf falling down the chimney, sing (to the tune of "Farmer in the Dell"):

> The Wolf is in the pot!
> The Wolf is in the pot!
> We'll all be safe tonight,
> The Wolf is in the pot!

If he escapes, sing these words:

> The Wolf has run away!
> The Wolf has run away!
> We'll all be safe tonight!
> The Wolf has run away!

ACTIVITY 4: THE THREE BEARS _____

Characters: Poppa Bear, Momma Bear, Baby Bear, and Goldilocks (and her Mother, if desired)

Story line: Review the story, deciding on how it will end. Goldilocks may jump out of the window in a fright as the Bears watch in surprise. Or she may run down the stairs, out the door, and home to Mother, promising her never to go to the Bears' cottage again.

Song: Each time Goldilocks tries something new, the group sings (to the tune of "Farmer in the Dell"):

> There's nobody at home!
> There's nobody at home!
> You can do just what you like—
> There's nobody at home!

As the story ends, sing (to the tune of "Twinkle, Twinkle"):

> When the bears were not at home,
> Goldilocks had chanced to roam.
> Chair was broken, porridge gone,
> She was sleeping on and on!
> When the Bears came home that day,
> Goldilocks soon ran away!

Rhythms for Story Songs   The preceding two songs may be added to the movement version of "The Three Bears" (see Story-Rhythms, page 193).

"The Billy Goats Gruff," another story-rhythm (page 192), may be expanded by adding the following verses (to the tune of "The Mulberry Bush"):

> The Ugly Old Troll let the first Goat pass,
> First Goat pass, first Goat pass.
> He's over the bridge in the nice green grass.
> The Ugly Old Troll is still hungry!

Repeat this verse for the second Billy Goat. Conclude with this chorus (to the tune of "John Brown Had a Little Indian"):

> The third Billy Goat pushed the Old Troll over!
> The third Billy Goat pushed the Old Troll over!
> The three Billy Goats are in fields of clover—
> Hurray for the Billy Goats Gruff!

See also "The Three Bears' Jive" (page 59), "The Little Pigs' Jive" (page 62), "The Red Hen Rap" (page 64), and "The Famous Four of Bremen Town" (page 259).

RELATED ACTIVITIES FOR STUDENTS

1. Select from additional sources an appropriate song for each of the following groups of children: four-year-olds, six-year-olds, eight-year-olds. Justify each choice using the criteria for choosing songs presented in this chapter (page 132).

2. Form a group of three or four children from your neighborhood or local school. Spend fifteen minutes with them singing songs they know and new ones you teach them. Following this session, write an anecdotal record for each child, commenting on (a) tunefulness, (b) vocal range, (c) quality of voice, (d) participation in singing, and (e) attitude.

3. From this chapter choose five songs that you especially like and would enjoy teaching to children. Learn the songs thoroughly, memorizing both words and melody. Practice singing each song using the key and starting tone given. Tape-record your songs and exchange tapes with a classmate. Evaluate each other's performance for (a) tunefulness, (b) diction, (c) tempo, (d) voice quality, and (e) appropriate mood. Extend your repertoire by learning any unfamiliar songs on your partner's tape.

4. Choose three of the songs you learned in question 3. Write a short plan for teaching each. Indicate the age and size of the group and the procedures for teaching the song. For assistance, see the lesson plan section in Chapter 2, sample plans in Appendix A, and the section on teaching a new song in this chapter (page 132).

5. Choose a familiar story or rhyme with a story line that is easy to act out. Then select two well-known tunes. Make up a verse for each of them: one to be sung in the middle of the story and one at the end. Use rhyming words that really rhyme to the ear and words that readily fit the rhythms of the melodies chosen.

Chapter 7

Movement to Music

Much has been written about the role of movement in the growth of young children, and there is no doubt that it is basic to their early learning processes. Movement is a fundamental attribute of music. Music moves tonally, from one pitch to another; it moves rhythmically, with varied patterns and beats; and it moves through changing tempi, moods, and intensities. The young child should learn about the art of movement in sound through his own mode of movement in space, experiencing through his physical being music that reaches him initially through his listening ear. This chapter contains activities designed to give children physical experiences of music appropriate to their abilities and interests.

To increase creative expression and interpretation, we believe that children need to develop accurate listening skills, minds that perceive what is heard, and bodies that respond to what is known and felt. The child thus acquires a store of listening and movement experiences and learns to use them as a basic repertoire in creating her own responses to the music she hears.

Music and movement are linked in early childhood education in other ways. One approach leads toward dance. This may be a structured approach in which the focus is on particular body skills, movements, and steps. Such dance sequences are more or less closely related to music, often to a specific composition. They may be taught and practiced in small bite-sized pieces and put together into a whole as mastery is achieved. Sometimes the total musical experience is added at that time.

In another approach music and movement lead toward drama. Here music is used to suggest a tempo, rhythm, or mood. Children are then encouraged to take off from this stimulus and let their responses grow as their own impetus carries them forward. Or, movement may come first, in response to some descriptive words or directions by the teacher. As children begin to move, expressing the ideas the adult has initiated, music may be added as an accompaniment. In this case, the music may relate to the activities of only a few of the children. It will, however, foster concentration by reducing verbalization, helping to control the use of the body in time and space, and filling the silence as the children concentrate on developing their ideas. This silence often seems embarrassing to adults; children sense this and quickly become self-conscious in the same way. Children will even ask for music, saying they feel silly moving without it. We believe this is a learned and unchildlike attitude that inhibits the natural creative and dramatic movement of the child.

While both approaches have their place in movement education, this chapter discusses movement to music. All the activities are directed toward developing in children the ability to listen accurately and attentively to music and sound and to respond quickly and creatively. Our goal is for children to move with growing spontaneity and skill and increasing consonance and unity with music throughout its duration. Elements of dance (especially interpretive dance) and of drama (especially mime) are present in our approach, but our goal is to lead the child into a closer relationship with music itself.

Auditory Awareness and Sound Localization

One of the first abilities to develop is auditory awareness of the presence or absence of sound. The following sequence of activities develops this skill and extends it to include sound localization and directionality. Closed eyes help children focus on active listening in many of the games that follow.

ACTIVITY 1: LISTEN TO THE SILENCE

While sitting in an informal group, ask the children to be silent—"not to make a sound." Then quietly identify for them the sounds in the environment outside the room, for example, a plane overhead, a truck passing, a distant police car siren, a bird's song, the wind in the trees, or the custodian running the floor polisher.

Next focus the listening inside the room: the buzz of an insect, the hum of an electric clock, a dripping tap, the noise of a drinking fountain or radiator, the scrabble of the gerbil in its cage, and so on.

Lastly, bring attention to the sounds of living people such as a cough or yawn, a sigh or sniffle, or the sound of a shoe on tile or rug.

The game may be played frequently and the children asked to name what they hear as the group grows quiet. The last segment may be replaced by asking the children to close their eyes and listen for one more sound, a specific sound such as a piano chord, triangle, resonator bell, or gong. Also use tape recordings of other sounds such as animal and bird calls and sounds in the home.

♪ ACTIVITY 2: HOW LONG DOES IT LAST?

During listening time, show the children a triangle, gong, or resonator bell. Let them hear the sound and draw attention to how the sound lasts after the instrument has been struck and gradually fades away into silence.

Tell the children to close their eyes, listen again, and raise both arms high when they no longer hear the sound. (Notice the different times at which the arms go up.) Repeat this several times, shortening the sound sometimes by damping the instrument with the hand.

On another day, use a different sound that resonates or a body sound such as humming or blowing. Start the game sometimes with the children standing tall with their arms already raised. Ask them to lower their arms gradually as the sound softens, ending with their hands by their sides as silence returns.

Play arpeggios (spread chords) on the piano or play a tape of same. Ask the children already standing to move about the room lightly as the music is played and to sink down gradually as it fades, so that they are lying at rest by the last sound of the music.

Notice how this game leads from the simplest task to one involving creative and individual responses. It gives excellent preparation in listening for closing cadences and ending phrases, which will be encountered later in creative movement to music.

After introducing some experiences with the presence and absence of sound, develop with the children an awareness of the location of the source of sound or the direction from which it comes.

♪ ACTIVITY 3: WHERE IS THE SOUND?

Seat children together on the floor with the teacher (and later, child leader) on a chair a little apart from the group.

Tell the children to point to where the sound is being made as the leader claps high in the air, close to the floor, and in a middle position in front, to the side, or in back.

Now repeat the game, having the children close their eyes. Vary the game by making the sounds from different points in relation to the group. Move far away, stand on a table, or step into the cloakroom or closet. Each time, tell the children to respond by arm movements or body turns toward the source of the sound. Change the sound itself from time to time. Whistle, snap your fingers, patsch, and then move on to sounds made with familiar objects such as pencils, crayons, blocks, or toys. Finally, play musical instruments including sticks, drums, maracas, bells, wood or sandpaper blocks, and resonator bells.

As these variations are introduced, ask for different responses, leading the children to explore the space around them. For example, while the children are standing in open spaces with eyes closed, tiptoe toward the door and tap out a clear rhythm on a wood block. Move quickly and silently to another part of the room, hiding the wood block from sight. When you say, "Open your eyes and walk toward what you heard," the children do just that from wherever they may be standing. High, medium, and low sounds may be added to this game and shown by arm gestures as the children walk. Music from a small cassette or transistor radio can also be used in this game.

Another challenging variation is to work with only three or four children standing with their eyes closed in an open space. The others sit in a group to observe. Sing or hum a melody and walk silently and slowly around the space. The children move as the sound moves, still with their eyes closed. They may turn and walk toward it or walk sideways or backwards, as they wish. Remember that little children do not have the inhibitions about moving blindfolded or backwards that we see in adults who have been conditioned always to look where they are going.

Two games conclude this segment on auditory perception. One involves active movement for all; the other, more quiet listening and less vigorous movements.

♪ ACTIVITY 4: MUSICAL BUMPS _____

While the auditory and movement goals of Musical Bumps are the same as for Musical Chairs, this version is preferred. Musical Chairs can be dangerous; the game often becomes highly competitive, rowdy, and very unmusical.

The children walk freely and lightly about the room to a rhythmic or musical accompaniment. (Later they may run or skip.) When this stops, they drop to the floor, squatting, kneeling, or sitting, as they choose. The accompaniment begins again, and the children get up and continue moving until the next stop. After several practices, explain that the last person to go down will sit out, being joined by others as the game is repeated. Try to stop the accompaniment at unexpected times, sometimes after a long stretch, sometimes after a short one. During the game, if two children are the last down, call them both. Play until two or three children remain and declare them winners. Older children are more competitive and may wish to play to the end, but younger ones are happy to have several victors. The children will enjoy watching and will receive ear training at the same time. At first it may be difficult to spot the last person down with a large group. Try letting your eyes range just above the heads of the moving children, rather than focusing on faces. (We do not recommend asking those sitting out to help decide who is last. Let the umpire's decision be final!) Begin this game with a rhythmic accompaniment only: sticks, wood block, or a hand drum. Then play improvised pentatonic melodies on the resonator bells or keyboard. Finally, use full piano accompaniment or a recording of clearly rhythmic music. Do not establish a pattern of stopping the music at the end of a phrase or the children will quickly memorize the pattern and lose the need to listen.

♪ ACTIVITY 5: MOTHER CAT AND HER KITTENS _____

This is an old well-loved game that, like many others, can be adapted to offer increasing challenges as children grow. It is described here for the youngest ones.

Seat the children in a well-spaced circle. In the center sits Mother Cat. She chooses four kittens to sit with her. Then she falls asleep. Very quietly the kittens creep away and each hides in a different place in the room. When she wakes up Mother Cat calls for her kittens by name: "Kitten Robin, meow, meow." Robin replies from her hiding place: "Meow, meow, here I am." Mother Cat tries to find her and the others one by one by listening for the source of the sound and going toward it. Anytime she needs to, she repeats her call and the kitten replies. She should make the fewest calls she can and use her ears rather than look with her eyes. When all kittens have returned, the last one may become Mother Cat and choose four new players to repeat the game.

Sometimes the teacher may blindfold Mother Cat first and then choose the kittens from the circle to hide, assigning each one a number orally. Now Mother Cat calls by number only and must locate her offspring and name each one before they return. If the blindfold is removed before the kittens are called, disguised voices will offset the clues Mother Cat may pick up from observing who is missing from the circle.

The creative and inventive teacher may extend all these awareness activities in many ways. Use them in other settings, such as the playground and the gymnasium. Use other kinds of sounds or music. Ask for the answers to match the tones of the questions. Remember to ask the children to take on the leadership of the activity as it becomes well known and to choose the materials and rules for playing these listen-and-move games.

Auditory Discrimination

In the last version of Mother Cat and Her Kittens, a new skill is required: identifying a child by the tone quality of his voice. This task introduces a new skill: auditory discrimination, or the ability to distinguish between qualities or kinds of sound. Mothers' voices sound very different from fathers' and teachers' from peers', but it requires more listening skill to tell the difference between the voices of two classmates, especially when they are out of sight.

Moving in response to a sound aids listening if the activity is quiet. It helps the child to concentrate, to focus attention consciously and actively. It is sometimes helpful to talk about the experience afterward to reinforce and internalize it. This also extends language skills and imaginative thinking.

ACTIVITY 1

Seat the children in the middle of the room. Demonstrate *two* sounds they are going to hear. They may be body sounds (patsch, clap, whistle, blow, rub hands) or single instrument sounds (drums, sticks, resonator bell, maraca). Stay in front of the children and ask them (with their eyes closed) to raise both arms above their heads when they hear a chosen sound.

ACTIVITY 2

Add sound localization to activity 1 by asking the children (with eyes closed) to follow the chosen sound by pointing in the direction from which it comes. Walk softly around the outside of the group, making the sound at intervals. Sometimes make it high above the children's heads and sometimes near the ground as it moves from place to place.

ACTIVITY 3

With the children's eyes closed, add more and different sounds as skill develops, using instruments and familiar objects as well as body sounds. After a movement response, pointing or turning, ask the children to identify what they heard. Occasionally ask an individual to duplicate the sound she heard by selecting the right source from those being used.

ACTIVITY 4

Demonstrate two well-contrasted sounds such as jingle bells and bongo drums. Ask the children to stand in a space (with eyes open) and move in a way that "goes with" the sound. At first it may be helpful to suggest some movements, such as arms and hands moving to the bells and legs and feet to the drum. Quickly the children will initiate their own movements to show the contrasting sounds heard.

ACTIVITY 5 _____

Ask the children to move about the room as they respond to a series of short, sharp sounds on the tone block or long, resonant sounds on the gong or cymbals. (Note: The piano may be used for activities 5 and 6. Arpeggios and glissandos contrast well with a series of staccato single tones or chromatic tone clusters.)

ACTIVITY 6 _____

Stand in a place where the children cannot see your hands. Play a specific tone (middle C, for example) and sing to it "Johnny One-Note" with the children echoing to confirm the tonality. Now play the tone and sing on that note, "Johnny One-Note says," following it with a spoken direction such as "Raise your arms," "Turn around," or "Stamp your foot." Warn the children that if Johnny One-Note's song sounds different from the first note they must not obey him. While using the original pitch most frequently, sing some commands on another pitch much different from the original one. Play the game rather slowly at first, always using the same "wrong song" until the original tonality is well established. Do not send children out of this game; rather, ask them all to say "Johnny Wrong-Note" when they hear the different song. The game may be speeded up and more than one wrong song added, nearer in pitch to the original one, as skill and quick responses grow.

Auditory Sequencing

Auditory sequencing is the ability to reproduce a sequence of sounds in the order heard. The development of this listening and remembering skill is crucial not only to musicianship but to the acquisition of language and literacy skills.

Echoing activities, such as echo singing, tone matching, and echo clapping, provide a foundation for the development of this skill. Peek-a-boo and pat-a-cake are early examples of echoing activities. So are cumulative songs and games such as "Old MacDonald" and "I Know an Old Lady Who Swallowed a Fly." Mirroring and other follow-the-leader movement activities add another dimension to the understanding of the ordering of sound.

ACTIVITY 1 _____

Clapping a steady beat, sing the following words to the familiar tune "Are You Sleeping?"

> Can you copy? (Can you copy?) One, two, three. (One, two, three.)
> Copy what I show you. (Copy what I show you,)
> Just like me! (Just like me!)

Repeat, asking the children to echo each phrase exactly with hands or voices, or both, according to ability. Change the actions often, asking the children for their movement suggestions and giving them the leadership role.

 **ACTIVITY 2** _____

THIS IS WHAT I CAN DO

Key: F Pentatonic
Starting tone: F

J. Haines

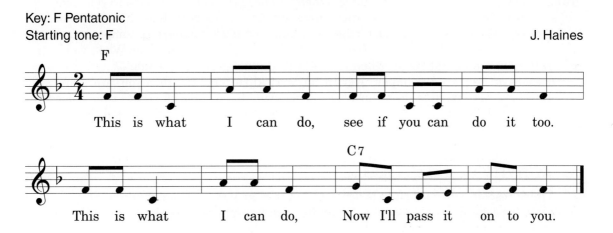

Teach this simple song. Each time the song is sung, a different child is the leader who shows what it is that she can do. Things to be done include marching, snapping fingers, rowing boats, swinging arms, and so on. All children join in the game and follow the leader.

ACTIVITY 3 _____

Pattern echoing is an important musical skill involving sequence memorization. Start by giving out simple clapping patterns based on children's names such as:

You can also use familiar phrases, such as "Please tidy up," "Time for gym," and "See you tomorrow," for echo clapping. Patsch, stamp, jump, and snap other short patterns without words. Distribute instruments such as sticks, tone blocks, drums, and single resonator bells and develop the activity further. Children enjoy dictating patterns to other individuals or the whole group. This game should also be used with vocal patterns, spoken and sung.

The next two movement activities involve remembering a sequence of aural clues.

♫ ACTIVITY 4

With the youngest child, give two activities to remember, as follows: "While I play the drum, you march around inside the circle. When you hear the bell(s), go back to your place and sit down." Do many of these activities, changing the actions as well as the sound clues. Build these skills, extending the challenge according to different children's competencies. Here is a simple example: "Esther, when you hear maracas, walk to the door. When you hear the drum, skip around the room. When you hear your name, run here to me."

Here is an advanced example: "Martin, on 'one' skip around the room, on 'two' stand still and clap, on 'three' march in place, on 'four' kneel down." Sequences like these can be used with groups of children as well as individuals. The clues may also be given in a different order, once the response is memorized.

♫ ACTIVITY 5

Quick response to aural clues is developed in this activity for older children. Seat the children cross-legged in a circle, near enough to reach a neighbor's knee on both sides. Teach simple patterns using clap, snap, and patsch and shoulder and head taps done with one, both, or alternate hands. Choose two patterns and choose sound clues for them. Here is an example:

Patsch, clap, patsch, clap . . . (clue: three quick maraca shakes)

Tap head, tap shoulders, tap head, tap shoulders . . . (clue: one bell tone)

The group repeats the activities, switching from one to the other as the teacher (or a child) plays the sound clue. Older children enjoy working out new patterns involving patsching right or left (moving each hand to a neighbor's knee):

(Patsch) own, right, own, right . . .

(Patsch) own, left, own, left . . .

Devise interesting and challenging routines, choosing appropriate sound clues for each movement and changing back and forth appropriately. Be sure to keep a steady beat during the activity. Use a drum or chant a verse or a repeated phrase.

Relaxation

In all music activities, the aim is to capture the child's enthusiasm and interest as well as develop his concentration and musical skills. It is important to avoid tension, both mental and physical, for this interferes with enjoyment and learning. Change the pace and kind of activity often, avoid competition and comparison between children, and know the difference between useful practice of skills and tedious drill. This will help to keep the atmosphere relaxed. Also plan some specific activities to develop children's ability to unwind deliberately and to sense the difference between a tense and a relaxed body.

Speak the verses of the first two activities on a very steady, regular beat. They should be almost chanted, with clear accents.

ACTIVITY 1 _____

1. Standing with feet apart, the children flop forward limply from the waist. Heads and hands hang loosely toward the floor, and a slow, slight swing from side to side or a small bouncing motion of the back accompanies the beat of the verse spoken very slowly:

> Raggedy Andy, Raggedy Andy, Raggedy Andy, Raggedy Ann.
> Flop right over, flop right over, flop right over, if you can.

2. Change to a brisk, marching tempo on the next verse. The children straighten up, stiffen arms and legs, and march in exaggerated fashion to the new beat:

> Soldier brave, sailor true,
> See if we can march like you.
> Arms are stiff, legs are straight,
> March along, it's getting late.

Repeat the first verse to heighten awareness of relaxation.

 ACTIVITY 2 _____

The children stand freely with plenty of space around them for wide arm movement. Their actions match the words of the verse, which starts with fingers or hands and travels throughout the whole body. Increasingly large movements are involved until the whole body is shaken out. Since there is a silent beat in the rhythm of the verse, it is notated rhythmically. Establish a strong inner beat before beginning.

Shake your fin - gers, shake your fin - gers, shake 'em nice and   loose!

Shake 'em, shake 'em, shake 'em like a   —— Moth - er   Goose!

Continue with wrists, arms, head, shoulders, back, leg, and other body parts, concluding with "Shake your body" to elicit a complete relaxed wiggle.

Basic Movement

Locomotor movements are those that move the whole body from one place to another. Babies roll over, crawl, and creep on all fours; older children somersault and cartwheel. Many children invent quite complex steps as they move about. The basic movements used in the activities that follow are common to many young children, from the three-year-old on, and are very useful in promoting and reinforcing important musical learning.

♪ **ACTIVITY 1** _____

Ask several children how they came to school today. Invite a child to show how she walked from home. Let those who wish join in the walking and encourage the free use of the floor space rather than a circle with an unused area in the middle. Comment as the children walk: "Mark looks as if he is marching along. Can we march like him?" Or, "Joanie is just strolling so easily. We'll stroll, too." As you speak of the different speeds and styles you see, take your drum (or a woodblock or pair of sticks) and play on it evenly at the tempo of the different children you mention. This aural stimulus will help the group to find a common beat and to march briskly with Mark or stroll more slowly with Joanie.

Walking rhythm:

The basic rhythm should be varied to match those of individuals and also to provide the basis for group activity. Always start with what comes from the children.

Discuss other ways of coming to school, going to the store, and so on. Let individual children show how they run and skip. Pick up these rhythms on the drum also, first matching your tempo to the child's and then giving it to the group.

Running:

Skipping:

When these basic rhythms have been identified and experienced, ask the children to identify them as you play different ones on your drum. As you vary the tempo, they will soon be able to identify rhythms such as a fast run, a slow skip, a tiptoe walk, a giant stride, and so on.

♪ **ACTIVITY 2** _____

Continue to use the basic movements described in activity 1 and extend them by encouraging the children to discover other ways to move about. You will be sure to encounter the following basic locomotor movements:

Step-bend (a slow walk with knee bend after the step, on the second beat of the two-beat notes):

Sliding, gliding, or skating:

Galloping (an uneven movement, like skipping, but with the same foot moving forward each time):

Jumping with feet together or hopping on one foot:

This rhythm is played steadily as in walking but with very short, detached, staccato taps on the drum or other instrument.

As the children suggest and move in rhythmic ways, develop in them an awareness of the repeated sound pattern made by each mode of locomotion. Clap the pattern or use a percussion instrument, the piano, or resonator bells. Give the children many opportunities both to move and to play these rhythms. Encourage free use of space and remind the children to move in different directions, traveling backwards, sideways, or around and around. Suggest that they stretch up high or crouch down low to the floor to explore different levels and planes as they move. Talk, rather than demonstrate, so the children will create their own ways of moving.

The activity of following the music is appropriate to begin and end a movement period and may be done with no verbal instruction.

ACTIVITY 3

Play varied sequences of basic rhythms on drum, bells, or keyboard. If your pianistic skill is limited, improvise pentatonic melodies on the black keys in the various rhythms, or simply chant the patterns to *la* or *loo*. The changing rhythms, which may also be played by a child, should elicit quick and increasingly sensitive responses from the group involving free use of space. Avoid using familiar tunes or set pieces for these activities, since the goal is for children to respond to basic rhythms rather than to recognize a particular melody.

ACTIVITY 4

Make oaktag flash cards of the basic rhythms and use these as clues for movement and later for instrument playing.

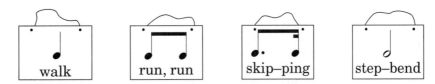

Hang the cards on hooks accessible to the children, so that they may use them for improvisation and other informal and creative activities.

Note: *Nonlocomotor* or *axial movements* are those performed in place. The above locomotor activities can be transferred to axial movement by hand clapping and playing percussion instruments. However, in our view, it is very important that the basic rhythms be experienced **first** in total body movement.

Moving to Musical Elements

The Phrase

Just as spoken language has units of meaning that we call sentences, exclamations, questions, and phrases, so there is a unit of thought in music that is called the phrase. Melodies acquire meaning for us as we hear them in segments, rather than in one continuous flow of sound. To understand this, try the following experiment.

Use the familiar melody that follows. Omit the words, as they detract from the meaning of the melody itself.

1. Sing the whole tune to *la* without a pause for breath.
2. Sing it again, breathing as indicated by this sign:'
3. Sing it again, breathing any time, but *not* at a breath sign.

Even without the words, your ear will tell you that the second version makes the most musical sense, and the third version the least. Version 2 is correct because you have breathed at the end of each small musical idea or phrase.

Phrasing is characteristic of all melodies and is what makes them intelligible to us. Phrases may be long or short, equal or unequal. The end of a phrase may be marked by a longer tone, as in many children's songs and nursery rhymes. This is not always the case, however. Sing "My Country 'Tis of Thee" to *la,* and discover where the phrase endings are. Certainly there are no long tones to indicate them.

We cover phrasing fully here for we find that it is often neither understood nor taught. This is a regrettable omission since phrase awareness is easily acquired by young children, adding greatly to their musicianship both in creating and interpreting. Here are some activities to develop phrasing skills.

ACTIVITY 1 _____

In an informal setting, sing a familiar song such as "Twinkle, Twinkle, Little Star." Help the children to identify when you took a breath in the song. Repeat this, using *la* and somewhat emphasizing the breathing places. Discuss how we breathe when the music finishes saying one thing and gets ready to say something else. Avoid talking about the end of the line as this refers to text rather than the phrases of a melody.

ACTIVITY 2 _____

Repeat activity 1 with other familiar tunes, leaving out the words. Now ask the children to lift their arms high, bow their heads, or bend way forward when they hear the end of a phrase. Introduce the word *phrase* for the musical thought or idea and use "the end of the *phrase.*" Don't talk about "when the music stops." This is not what happens until the melody is over.

ACTIVITY 3

As soon as the children show a grasp of this listening-moving activity, space them around the room and introduce different ways to show phrasing. Have children walk, changing direction on each phrase; stand and clap one phrase, walk the next; or kneel on one knee and rise up on each phrase ending. Or divide the children into groups and have one group at a time move in response to each phrase.

Accompany these activities by singing familiar melodies, changing to tunes the children do not know as their competence grows. Improvise or make up unfamiliar music using your voice, the resonator bells, or the piano, using the pentatonic scale. It is important to increase the listening challenge as the skills grow. In time, recorded music may be used, such as simple pieces for piano and other instruments. Remember that identifying phrases in the thicker texture of instrumental music is more difficult than in the simple melodic line of voice or bells. We like to use flute or recorder music because its tone is clear and its phrasing is related to the player's breathing. Introduce music with unequal phrases, too, for children will quickly memorize the length of equal phrases and respond automatically without listening.

ACTIVITY 4

Group conducting is a creative activity calling for movement to phrases. Have a group of six to eight children stand together at one end of the available floor space. Stand in the middle and by arm gestures move the group in different directions: beckon them toward you, send them away, move them to the right and to the left, move them in a circle around you, raise them on their toes, and lower them to the ground. Do this preparatory activity in silence, trying to think in phrases as you conduct. It is helpful to have a familiar tune inside your head, such as "Where Oh Where Is Dear Little Mary?"

ACTIVITY 5

Repeat activity 4 to recorded music that you have studied. Choose a short selection of moderate speed. Be sure you know where the phrase endings are. As the music plays, move your group as before. Now make the change in your gesture each time a phrase ends, so the children move differently to each phrase. Repeat this activity with another group of children. (Remember that watching children are learning children.)

ACTIVITY 6

Two groups may now work together, and you may move them on alternate phrases or for several phrases at a time. Use different areas of the room for each group, seating one group with a gesture and bringing the other to its feet as the phrases unfold.

ACTIVITY 7

Prepare more selections, choosing different tempi and rhythmic styles as the children grow more skillful. Give the group one hearing before they move, and also discuss the tempo and mood of the music.

ACTIVITY 8

Now pass the conductor's role to the children. At first choose children who you feel confident will succeed and give them simple activities without music. Then give individuals the opportunity to lead in group conducting, using some recorded pieces you have already used. Ultimately, your child conductors will be able to do this activity to unfamiliar music. If they have acquired confidence, good listening skills, and responsive bodies, the results will be both musical and creative as children draw on their growing repertoire of basic movement skills.

The movements of all will show increasing awareness of the mood and structure of the music. You will, of course, be singing and using instruments at other times in your daily program while these movement activities are going on. The transfer of the skills developed here will soon appear in the children's singing and playing. A growing sensitivity to the phrasing of music may well earn for the young children the tribute "They cannot do an unmusical thing!"

Tempo and Duration

By the time children are ready to join a group setting, even at age two, most will have had some experience with speed, rate, or tempo. "Hurry up!" "Be quick!" "Eat it slowly!" "Don't run so fast!" "Take your time!" "Hustle, you little slowpoke!" Such phrases and many others are familiar to every child, both at home and elsewhere. It must seem to him that whatever tempo he chooses is the wrong one for the adults in his life.

As you explored basic locomotor movement with your group, you paid attention to fast and slow movements in response to rhythmic patterns, melodies, and instrumental music. Extend this awareness and focus attention on different tempi and on changing speeds (*accelerando* and *ritardando*) by using the activities that follow.

ACTIVITY 1 _____

Focus the children's attention on their inner rhythms by asking them to find their own pulses, in the neck, wrist, or chest. Have them express the tempi of these inner rhythms by clapping or chanting the beats.

ACTIVITY 2 _____

Play different tempi on the drum. Discuss these and have individual children show in movement what they hear.

ACTIVITY 3 _____

A freight, a passenger, and an express train are formed from three groups of children. Each group stands in single file holding hands behind an "engineer." A train moves when it hears its own tempo played on the drum. It weaves its way around the stationary trains and under bridges and tunnels formed by pairs of children at different points on the way. When a new tempo is heard it stops in its tracks and the appropriate train takes over. Children listen for tempo changes, recognize their own, and move in a group at a regular pace.

ACTIVITY 4 _____

Play the train game as before, but include a speeding up and a slowing down for each train. As the *ritardando* begins, the moving train should begin to slow down while heading back to its original spot. Ideally, it will arrive there and come to a halt as the drum beat or music slows to a halt. The listening skill and physical response are more advanced in this version. Either of the songs "When the Train Comes Along" or "This Train" may be sung between each train trip when these games are first taught, to separate the different tempi. Later they can be used at the beginning and end of the whole activity.

ACTIVITY 5 _____

With children sitting in a circle, start a steady walking-beat hand clap. The children join in. Gradually accelerate and slow down the tempo, with the children staying right on the beat as they clap along. Keep this activity soft and encourage careful listening and absolute unison in clapping. Do not clap so fast that the children lose control or slow down so much that the inner feeling of a steady beat is lost. It is more difficult to do this well than it first appears. Give children turns as leaders.

ACTIVITY 6 _____

While standing in free formation, the children "echo" by clapping or walking, four beats ♩ ♩ ♩ ♩ played on the drum. When the beats are played at a different speed, the children's movements vary appropriately.

ACTIVITY 7 _____

"Follow the Music" is a good opening or closing activity for a movement period. Music is played at changing speeds on a drum, resonator bells, or piano. The children follow the music with appropriate movements. They may walk, run, skip, or do whatever is suggested by the speed and rhythmic pattern the teacher plays.

ACTIVITY 8 _____

Divide the class into two groups. Give one group a fast tempo to follow and the other a slow tempo. Each group moves appropriately as it hears its tempo played. Include *accelerando* and *ritardando* in this activity.

ACTIVITY 9 _____

"A Bar Behind" is a game that requires sound knowledge of the basic movement rhythms before it is played. Children should be skillful at matching these movements to the music:

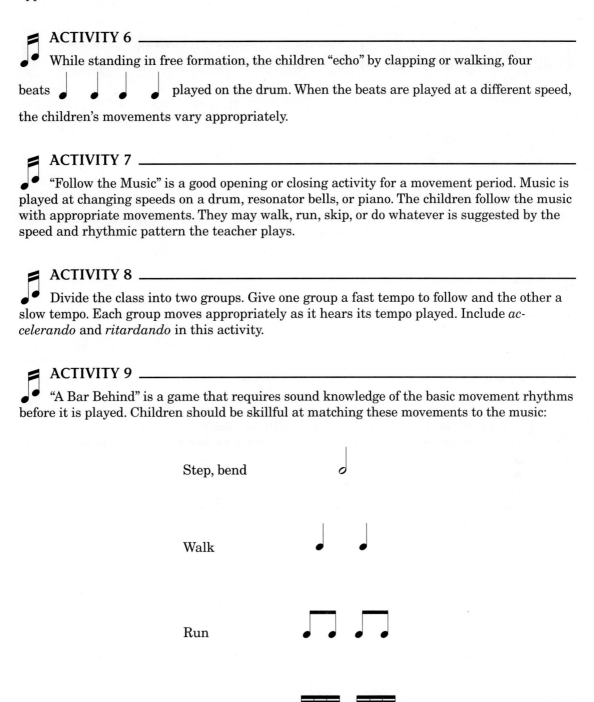

Before teaching this game, practice playing the following sequence on the drum with a steady underlying beat:

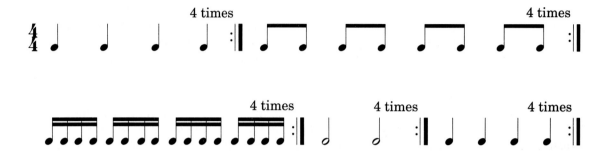

Children move *after* listening to the first bar. Movement is therefore always one measure behind sound. The child moves to the last repeat of a pattern while listening to the first part of a new pattern. Obviously, the game finishes with unaccompanied movement.

Dynamics

Dynamics is the musical term that describes the volume of sound, the loudness or softness, and changes from one to the other. These changes do not always sound across a wide range. Sometimes the gradations are subtle ones, from soft to almost inaudible or from loud to thunderous. At other times they are sudden and dramatic: a burst of sound following a softer passage, such as raindrops followed by a clap of thunder. Here again we find that the beginner at school, however young, has some experiences with this set of concepts: "Sh! The baby's sleeping!" "Please be quiet, I'm on the phone!" "Speak up, I can't hear you!" "Turn the volume down on the TV please; it's too loud!" "Just whisper it softly, you don't need to shout!" Every child knows what such comments mean, and most have a remarkable degree of control over the volume of sounds they make vocally and physically. Infants and toddlers seem to have a high degree of tolerance for the loud sounds they make themselves. They love to bang objects and doors and to shout and stomp about. Conversely, they are easily startled by much softer sounds made by others. The doorbell or a sneeze causes a baby to jump and even shiver; a car backfiring or an unexpected hand clap can cause a three- or four-year-old to turn pale or blush, to cover his ears, or even to cry. It is not difficult, therefore, to lead children to understand and use the dynamic component of music.

ACTIVITY 1 ———————————————————————————————————

Say familiar rhymes and sing well-liked songs, using a variety of dynamic levels.
Use the volume control on the tape or CD player to demonstrate different sound levels. Discuss and try out the size of the voices of familiar characters, such as the Three Bears or the Billy Goats Gruff.

ACTIVITY 2 ———————————————————————————————————

The children choose to be different kinds of plants that grow in the ground. They may be flower or vegetable seeds, nuts, or bulbs. The time of year may influence their choice. While you drum softly or improvise a pentatonic melody on piano or bells or in song, the children make themselves as small as possible, curled up in the ground as if planted there. As the music grows gradually louder in a crescendo, each child begins to grow, uncurling and stretching, standing and reaching up toward the sun. At the peak of the music, all will have grown as much as possible. (A light dancing rhythm or melody may be played as the plants bloom in sun or rain. Someone may mime the gardener gathering flowers, fruit, or vegetables to an appropriate rhythm.) Finally, the music begins to grow softer in a decrescendo, and as it fades into silence the children sink down to the floor, planting themselves again, ready for another season. Waking and sleeping animals or people may be enacted, waking to work and play and going to sleep again at the end of the day. The teacher may talk the children through this kind of activity at first, accompanying it appropriately. As the imagination and ear gain skill, just an idea followed by the changing dynamics of the music may be sufficient stimulus.

◆ ———————————————— ◆

Children should be able to express dynamic change in a variety of ways. The tendency for many people is to think of big or high movements as expressing loudness and small, low motions as meaning softness. Avoid teaching this stereotyped and inaccurate notion. It is the quality of the movement—its relative strength or weakness, its firmness or gentleness—that equates more appropriately with the dynamic range from loud (*forte*) to soft (*piano*).

♪ ACTIVITY 3 _____

As the children stand freely, ask them to stretch up in as soft a way as possible. Suggest or use floating feathers or ribbon streamers. Play a soft accompaniment. As the sound grows, describe each child as growing firmer and stronger, moving toward the ground with flexed muscles, taking up smaller space but using more energy. Finally, each one is thrusting downward into the ground with the whole body compact and tensed for powerful action. End with an invitation to relax, such as "Roll over and relax for a minute." Similar activities may be done with movements away from the body gaining in strength and scope as the music grows, or in reverse, with the peripheral motions being the softest. Sometimes begin with the loud sound and movement, and at other times begin softly.

♪ ACTIVITY 4 _____

Have the children stand in a circle holding hands. Ask them to show the changes in the music by making their circle larger or smaller. Drum a crescendo to start with if the circle is small, then a decrescendo to bring it back from the edges of the space. Reverse this and move out gently to the decrescendo and stomp in with raised arms on the crescendo. Another time ask the children to keep the circle the same size but to show the dynamic changes by growing downward as the sound softens and upward as it increases. Again, be sure to reverse these directions occasionally to avoid the stereotyped response. Older children can move the circle around, still holding hands, as they enact dynamic changes. As skill with these gross motor activities grows, challenge the children to show dynamics with smaller fine motor actions: fingers only, heads and shoulders, elbows, and so on. While they are lying on the floor, have them explore other ways to represent changes in volume.

♪ ACTIVITY 5 _____

Emile Jaques-Dalcroze was a Swiss educator whose work in eurhythmics has contributed much to our teaching of movement to music. Dictée, or dictation, was always included in his classes in some form, to develop accurate listening and sensitive responding. Activities 5 and 6 are variations of this activity, using dynamic changes.

The younger children sit in a large circle with the teacher. Dictate by clapping very short, simple patterns at different dynamic levels. Each pattern is echoed once by the group. Remember to use the floor and the space above, beside, and behind you.

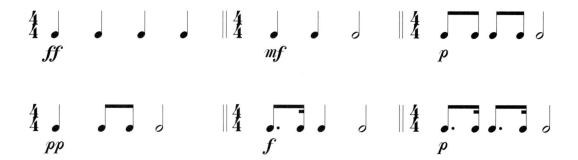

Create many more simple patterns using ♩ , ♫ ♩ , ♩. ♪ , and ♩ . As the group becomes confident and proficient, give patterns to each child clockwise around the circle.
Ultimately, dictate to individuals at random. Extend this activity by repeating each pattern
at a different dynamic level.

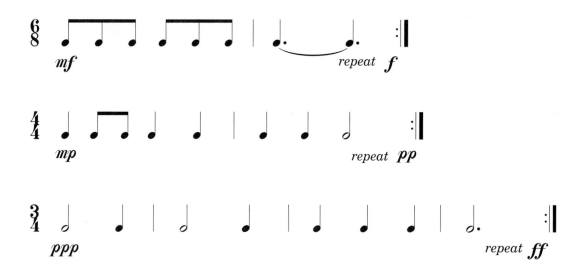

Once the children have facility with clapping responses, have them stand and make their dynamic echoes with their feet, in place. Start with the simplest pattern based on ♩ , ♫ ♩ ,
and ♩ Encourage free axial movements of arms and legs, in place, to express the differences
in volume. The skipping rhythm is difficult to do in one place, so use it cautiously.

♪ ACTIVITY 6 _____

Primary age children who have become skillful at echoing dynamic changes in the way just described will enjoy a more challenging version of dynamic dictation. The children stand in free formation. The teacher calls a name and claps out a dynamic pattern. The child responds first by clapping the pattern accurately and then by moving it forward in space, matching the size and strength of her movements to the dynamics given. For instance, the teacher claps, then the child repeats:

The child then moves forward strongly:

Repeat this pattern with several children before going on to a new one. The activity may be extended by giving a second pattern to a child as the first one is completed. The teacher claps, then the child repeats:

The child then moves gently. (Notice that skipping is now included.) On completing this movement pattern, the teacher continues, without breaking the rhythmic pattern:

The child then continues with the second pattern. Create new patterns in different meters to extend the child's musicality even further.

Pitch

Children associate the words *high* and *low* and *up* and *down* with position and place. The following activities will help them relate these words to the concept of musical pitch.

♪ ACTIVITY 1

Review "Freight Train, Freight Train" (p. 45) and "The Three Bears' Jive" (p. 59) for pitch awareness.

♪ ACTIVITY 2: THE APPLE TREE

Tell the following story, acting it out with hand motions. Repeat the activity immediately, asking the children to show with their hands the climb up and down the tree and the fall of the apple. Another time retell the story, acting it out with larger body movements.

"Once there was an apple tree. All the apples had been picked except a big red one way up at the top of the tree. Bobby said,

Key: C
Starting tone: C

Ethel Crowninshield

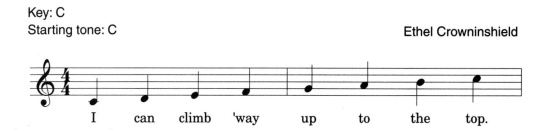

I   can   climb   'way   up   to   the   top.

So he climbed way up, and just as he reached the big red apple, it fell down to the ground. Then Bobby carefully climbed down, singing,

Down,   down,   down,   down,   down,   down,   down,   down.

And he picked up the big red apple and ate it."

♪ ACTIVITY 3

Tell a story about a field trip to an apple orchard where children walk among the trees with shopping bags, gathering windfalls from down on the ground and other apples from up in the trees. Dramatize the story by retelling it using three pitches or levels of sound: middle range tones for the walk, high sounds for picking apples from the trees, and low sounds for picking them up from the ground. Make the pitches with the voice, or on the piano or resonator bells, using only one or two tones from the middle, high, and low ranges. Refer to Chapter 2, page 24.

♪ ACTIVITY 4

Stand a set of step bells on a low table in front of a group of children, with the high tones to their right and the low tones to their left. Play on the bells to show the children both visually and aurally how the pitches go up or down or remain the same depending on which bell is struck. Improvise sequences and let the group show the rise, fall, and repetition of pitches with arm and hand movements. Give individual children the leadership role. Repeat these activities with the step bells lying flat.

ACTIVITY 5

Seat the children where they can see the piano keyboard or resonator bells, ensuring that the high tones are to their right and the low to their left. Play a simple sequence to a steady beat in the middle range. Ask the children to clap. They will do so at a midbody level. Play the sequence again on the high tones and lead the children to clap above their heads. Finally, play in the low register, on the left side of the instrument. Have the children clap near the ground. At another time, repeat this activity with the children's eyes closed or with your hands concealed, removing the visual clue. When children can distinguish these three pitch levels aurally, use pitches that are closer together for them to judge. Play an ascending or descending sequence and ask them to show the direction in which the music is moving with their hands and arms. Repeated tones should be shown by a gesture at the same level. This skill is useful later in teaching new songs by rote. The teacher may reinforce the rise and fall of a tune by shaping the melody line with arm gestures or even on the chalkboard. Children may do this themselves to confirm the direction of their singing voices.

ACTIVITY 6

High, middle, and low pitches may also be dramatized using scarves as extensions of the arms. This activity not only heightens an awareness of pitch but provides another interesting medium for practicing the same skill.

ACTIVITY 7

Play simple melodies on the piano or resonator bells, keeping a strict tempo. The children walk forward when the melody ascends and backward when the melody descends. If the melody stands still, the children mark time in place.

◆ ———————————————————— ◆

Note: Remember that all movement activities must be based on many and frequent experiences, gradual progressions, and very small daily increases in the complexity of the listening and responding required. This is particularly true of work in dynamic expression since it requires much control of the body and awareness of the quality, intensity, and vigor of movement. The movement of the body through time and space should always reflect the nature of the musical sounds that initiate and sustain it.

◆ ———————————————————— ◆

Story-Rhythms

Story-rhythms take the expressive process one step further, synthesizing the elements of music, expressing them in basic and creative movement, and adding the emotional and dramatic content of a simple story line.

Telling a story in movement has already been encountered in the description of plants growing in the ground (page 186), gathering apples in the orchard (page 190), and Bobby's adventure up the tree (page 190). These examples illustrate incidental teaching, exploration of changes in pitch, and the experiencing of crescendo and decrescendo. Familiar stories also lend themselves to this treatment.

ACTIVITIES 1 AND 2

For the following two activities, have the children well spaced around the room. Use a hand drum and other nonpitched instruments or melodic improvisations on bells or keyboard as accompaniment. Tell the story, pausing in the narration for the children to move to your rhythmic playing as indicated in parentheses. Give musical clues for both basic locomotor movements and mime appropriate to the story line. Keep it short to hold the children's concentration, even if you must break the story into installments covering two or three days. *All* the children participate in every action and represent each character in turn. *Save the allocating of individual roles for creative dramatics, or for special occasions such as a school program.*

THE BILLY GOATS GRUFF

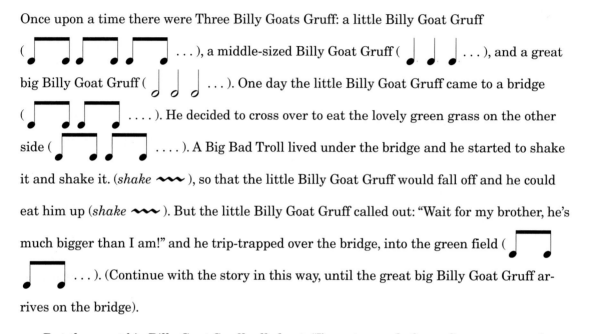

Once upon a time there were Three Billy Goats Gruff: a little Billy Goat Gruff

([♩♪♩♪♩♪] . . .), a middle-sized Billy Goat Gruff (♩ ♩ ♩ . . .), and a great

big Billy Goat Gruff (♩ ♩ ♩ . . .). One day the little Billy Goat Gruff came to a bridge

([♩♪♩♪] . . . .). He decided to cross over to eat the lovely green grass on the other

side ([♩♩♩♩] . . . .). A Big Bad Troll lived under the bridge and he started to shake

it and shake it. (*shake* ∿), so that the little Billy Goat Gruff would fall off and he could

eat him up (*shake* ∿). But the little Billy Goat Gruff called out: "Wait for my brother, he's

much bigger than I am!" and he trip-trapped over the bridge, into the green field ([♩♩]

[♩♩] . . .). (Continue with the story in this way, until the great big Billy Goat Gruff ar-

rives on the bridge).

But the great big Billy Goat Gruff called out: "I'm not scared of *you*. Come on up and get

me!" And the Big Bad Troll jumped onto the bridge (♩). No sooner was he there than the

great big Billy Goat Gruff gave him a great big push (♩) and off he went, down the river and

out of sight! Soon the great big Billy Goat Gruff was over the bridge and with his brothers

(♩ ♩ ♩ . . .), and they all three went on their way to eat the lovely green grass: The little

Billy Goat Gruff ([♩♩♩♩] . . . .), the middle-sized Billy Goat Gruff (♩ ♩ ♩ . . .),

and the great big Billy Goat Gruff (♩ ♩ ♩ . . .)!

THE THREE BEARS

Once upon a time there were three bears: a great big Poppa Bear (𝅗𝅥 𝅗𝅥 𝅗𝅥 . . .), a middle-sized Mamma Bear (♩ ♩ ♩ . . .), and a teeny weeny Baby Bear (♫ ♫ ♫ . . .). They all lived together in a house in the woods. One day Mamma Bear made porridge for breakfast. It was too hot to eat, so the family went for a walk to let it cool. Out through the woods went Poppa Bear (𝅗𝅥 𝅗𝅥 𝅗𝅥 . . .) and Mamma Bear beside him (♩ ♩ ♩ . . .). Baby Bear went along, sometimes in front and sometimes behind them (♫ ♫ ♫ . . .).

While they were gone, a little fair-haired girl called Goldilocks came through the woods (♩. ♩. ♩. . . .). When she came to the Bears' house she knocked on the door (♩ 𝄽 ♩ 𝄽 ♩ 𝄽) and listened (▭ 𝅝)—no answer. She knocked again (♩ 𝄽 ♩ 𝄽 ♩ 𝄽), and listened (▭ 𝅝); still no answer. So Goldilocks opened the door and tiptoed inside (♩ ♩ ♩ . . .). No one was there. When she saw the porridge bowls, Goldilocks felt very hungry. She tasted Poppa Bear's great big bowl (𝅗𝅥 𝅗𝅥 𝅗𝅥 . . .), but it was too hot.

(Develop the rest of the familiar story in similar fashion.)

RELATED ACTIVITIES FOR STUDENTS

1. Create a listening game to develop auditory awareness that can be played outside in either a rural or an urban setting. Take a group of children or classmates outdoors and tape-record your playing of the game.

2. Design an auditory discrimination game based on the following rhyme:

   A. Who's that ringing my front door bell?
   B. I'm a little kittycat and I'm not very well.
   A. Go and rub your nose with a bit of mutton fat,
      That's the best thing for a little kittycat!
   B. Meow, meow, meow.

   Test your game in a group setting.

3. Develop a three-part sequence of activities for seven- or eight-year-olds to contrast relaxation and tension similar to relaxation activity 1 on page 179. Write your own two rhymes to accompany the activity.

4. Make up and teach a game using a hand drum and cards showing ♩ , ♩ , and ♫ .

   Base your game on the movement patterns of three flying machines (e.g., hot air balloon, helicopter, jet) or three animals (e.g., turtle, duck, mouse), creating a little story around them and their movements.

5. Tape-record a piano piece with smooth, clearcut phrases. Work with a group of children to express these phrases first using locomotor movement, then axial movement with chiffon scarves.

6. Choose a familiar nursery tale. Edit it carefully to include maximum opportunities for movement and minimum narration (but enough to keep the mood of the story alive). Add to your version the appropriate basic rhythmic notations, as in the examples in the text. Test your story in class, discussing and modifying it before taking it into the children's setting.

7. When you become confident working with familiar stories in this way, create one of your own or use a favorite story of the children's choice.

Chapter 8

Playing Instruments

Throughout Part Two of this book, we have referred frequently to the use of musical instruments by both children and teacher. We have already introduced them to accompany and enrich chanting, singing, and playing games. They have been used in movement activities to stimulate, sustain, and vary physical responses and to help children experience, internalize, and express the elements of music: rhythm, melody, and dynamics. In this chapter, we focus on the instruments themselves to help children discover their qualities and capacities and learn to use them in varied and musical ways.

Among music educators, opinions vary as to the values and limitations of classroom instruments. Some prefer to use only those with the purest tone, to develop in the child the most sensitive and discriminating musical ear possible from the very beginning. Others believe that young children should experiment with simple homemade or environmental musical sounds, progressing to more refined or sophisticated instruments as they develop. Our eclectic approach includes all sources of musical sound in the belief that how an instrument is used determines its value.

Classroom instruments fall into four main categories: home and found instruments; those available, often in sets, from rhythm band manufacturers; the Orff instruments, often called the Orff Instrumentarium; and melody and chording instruments used chiefly by the teacher but to some extent by children.

The sequence of activities that follows is designed for use in the classroom where standard percussion (pitched or unpitched) instruments are available. The instruments used should be of the best quality affordable: broken instruments should be discarded. Instruments should be handled carefully and have an assigned storage space. They should never be dumped indiscriminately into a cardboard carton or piled in a basket or on a shelf. This is not good for the instruments or for the attitudes of children toward them. Attractive, accessible storage that allows the children to use instruments independently should be provided.

Instrument Storage Ideas

1. Add appropriately sized hangers and cans to a peg board.
2. Salvage an unused book shelf and add hooks and cans.
3. Take the rods and beads off an old-fashioned bead-counting frame. Add cup hooks on top and cans and boxes along the bottom.
4. Look in catalogs for other ideas you can adapt. Be inventive!

Percussion Instruments

Rhythm Sticks. Wooden sticks, one smooth, one serrated. Play by tapping one on the other or rubbing the smooth one over the serrated one.

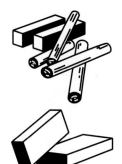

Claves. Short, polished hardwood sticks. Place one lightly across one palm and strike it with the other. Hold both loosely to produce a clear, vibrant tone.

Wood Blocks. Hollow cylinders that produce one or two tones when struck. Strike lightly with a wooden-tipped striker. If the blocks are serrated, they may also be rubbed together. Also called tone blocks.

Sandpaper Blocks.   Wooden blocks covered with sandpaper and mounted with a knob to hold. Rub them back and forth across each other rhythmically. The sandpaper is replaceable.

Jingle Clog.   Wooden paddle with one or more pairs of metal jingles that move freely. Hold the handle and strike the wooden back of the clog lightly and rhythmically against the palm of the other hand, or shake the clog in the air to produce a longer-lasting sound.

Triangle.   Steel rod formed into a triangle with one corner open; the triangle is suspended from a holder so that it hangs freely. Tap lightly with a metal striker on the bottom bar or tap from side to side on the inside near the top of the triangle. A steady hand and gentle playing are essential.

Maracas.   Gourds—real, wooden, or plastic—with seeds or rattlers inside them and a handle. Hold one or a pair at shoulder height and shake sharply, as if they were hitting against a firm surface, to produce a clear rhythm, or shake continuously for a sustained sound.

Wrist or Jingle Stick Bells.   Small sleigh-type bells on a plastic or canvas strap formed into a bracelet or fastened to a wooden handle. Hold them firmly and shake rhythmically. (They can also be worn on the wrists or ankles during free movement activity.)

Hand Cymbals.   Slightly hollowed brass plates with holding knobs or straps. Hold them without touching the metal and strike one against the other with an up-and-down motion so that the sound may ring. (When cymbals are struck in a clapping motion, the sound clashes and is immediately damped.) One cymbal alone may be held hanging down and struck on the edge with a stick or padded mallet.

Finger Cymbals.   Slightly hollowed, very small brass plates with elastic loops. Hold a loop between the thumb and index finger of each hand and strike the edge of one cymbal against the other. The tone is bell-like and resonant. Older children may slip one loop over the thumb and another over the middle finger of the same hand and "ching" the cymbals lightly against each other.

Tambourine.   Circular wooden frame with a plastic or skin drumhead and several pairs of jingles mounted in cut-out spaces around the frame. Hold the tambourine steady at shoulder height with one hand and rap it lightly with the fingertips or knuckles of the other. Tap it against knees, elbows, or head, or shake it continuously to obtain different sounds.

Drums.   *Side drums* have two drumheads and a bright tone and may be struck with one or two wooden drumsticks using a crisp staccato touch. *Tomtoms* often have softer heads. One or sometimes two may be played with fingers, hands, or a padded or felt drumstick.

Bongo drums may be in sets of two or more and may be of different sizes. They have single heads of different tones and are played by hand. *Single-headed hand drums* of different sizes and pitches resemble tambourines without the jingles; they are held and played either with a felt drumstick or with the fingers or hand. *Tub and barrel drums* are large and deep toned, usually single headed and shaped as their names suggest. They may be played by hand or with a drumstick. All drums should be played with a light, bouncy, resilient touch to allow the drumheads to reverberate and give a clear sound. Tell the children, "Play the drum as if it were hot and you can't get your fingers or your drumstick away from it fast enough."

Introducing Percussion Instruments: A Discovery Approach

ACTIVITY 1

Have an easily accessible table that the children know contains materials for experiment and investigation during self-directed activity. Early in the school year, put out one or two pairs of rhythm sticks, smooth and serrated, and a wood block and mallet. Encourage the children to play with these, finding out different ways to use them and the different sounds they make. After you have observed a number of children doing this, introduce these instruments during a group time or class meeting (see activity 2). As the sticks and blocks become familiar, replace them on the table with a sequence of new instruments such as those listed above. At first you might put out just one kind of instrument and then add two contrasting instruments. Make a point of interacting with children as they try them out, leading them to discover new possibilities through questions and clues rather than by demonstration. In this way it is possible for the entire group to have access to all the instruments listed in an informal, experimental way over a few-week period and for the teacher to introduce each one in a group setting during the same period of time.

ACTIVITY 2

When a number of children have experimented with the sticks and wood blocks, bring several sets of these instruments to a group circle. The children will talk about and demonstrate what they have discovered about them. Distribute sticks to half the group, and after a few moments of free tapping and rubbing of the smooth against the serrated, pick up a steady beat on the drum, piano, or bells, or chant rhythmically verses from "Freight Train" or "Hickory Dickory Dock" or a repeated phrase such as "We can play the sticks" or "Tap the beat! Tap the beat!" Some children will join in immediately on the beat. After a short time, ask the players to give their sticks to someone else, and repeat the activity until all have had a turn. If attention and interest are high, have the children lay down their sticks and repeat the activity with the wood blocks.

ACTIVITY 3

Repeat activity 2 with other pairs of instruments, using different rhymes, chants, and songs with a clear beat, until you have worked with all the instruments the children can handle competently.

♪ **ACTIVITY 4** _____

If you do not play the piano, use a recording of a familiar nursery rhyme or song. Be sure it has steady, clear rhythm and phrasing to help the children know when to take their turns. Arrange the students in two groups, and give one kind of instrument to each group. Explain that you will tell the groups when to take turns by the movement of your arms and that they will need to listen to each other and watch you. When you conduct, stand in the space between the groups, using a strong up-and-down beat with your right arm in front of the group you wish to play. Keep your ear attuned to the music and change groups with the song's phrasing. Make your beat clear and use both arms together when you wish both groups to play at once. Make your cutoff or finish clear by moving your arm out from the body instead of up and down. If you are conducting from the piano, only small hand motions will be possible. Spoken directions and facial expressions will ensure that children begin and end with the musical phrase. This activity is referred to as *phrase-wise playing*.

◆ ———————————————————————————— ◆

Repeat these activities until the children have all had a chance to play most of the instruments. During these sessions, establish ground rules for distributing and collecting the instruments and handling them carefully and with control.

Managing the Instruments

When you introduce playing instruments as a group, give out and take in the instruments yourself. At a later time, this task can be done by children to a musical accompaniment. Very young children find it difficult at first not to pick and play their instruments when it is someone else's turn. If playing out of turn is a problem, tell the children, paraphrasing to suit your own teaching style: "You know, children, some of these instruments have a hard time taking turns. Even when they are on the floor in front of you, they seem to find their way back into people's hands and start playing. Are you good bosses? I hope so! It's really a help if you can be the boss of your instrument today. When you put it down, shake your finger at it and say: 'Now, you stay there until I pick you up and give you a turn to play again!' If your instrument has a hard time doing what you say, just you let me know and we'll put it away for a rest." Follow through on this in a friendly, objective way. The children will be intrigued and will gain control quickly.

New Learning with Instruments

With procedures and simple ground rules established and your whole music program moving forward, especially in singing and movement, your children will now be ready for new learning with the percussion instruments. As much as possible, try to allow the children to choose which instrument they would like to play from day to day. Most classrooms have many small instruments, such as sticks and wood blocks, and few large ones, such as cymbals and drums. While this restricts the children's freedom of choice somewhat, it also keeps a balance in the tone quality and volume within the playing group. Give children frequent opportunities to play and ensure that the more popular instruments such as maracas, triangles, and drums are shared fairly among all the children from day to day.

Orchestration.   When the class comes together to play, seat those playing the same instrument or type of instrument together, with a small space between each group. Figure 1 shows a suggested arrangement for twenty children that will give a balanced sound (the numbers in parentheses are for a group of ten children).

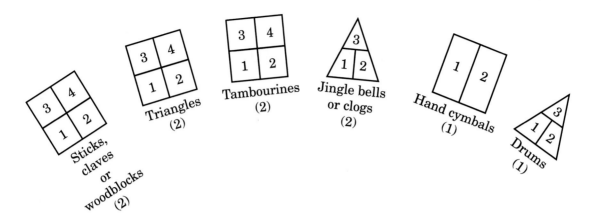

Figure 1 ◆ Class Arrangement for Instrument Playing

　　With preschool, kindergarten, and beginning first graders, have a group of ten children as the orchestra or band. Use the rest as a singing group or choir. With the children, select a short familiar song for which you create an accompaniment. Have the singing group sing the song through phrase by phrase, trying out with the players different instruments for individual phrases. Point out to the children that more than one group may play a phrase and that occasionally they may enjoy the sound of the whole orchestra or band at one time. After experimenting, help the group decide on an arrangement that they would like to learn. Since the song is short, the arrangement will be memorized quickly and performed by rote in the future. Be sure to exchange playing and singing roles frequently.

Musical Experience Charts.　When a repertoire of three or four such orchestrations has been created, introduce the idea of writing the arrangements on a musical experience chart. Put a large sheet of newsprint on the easel or chalkboard, head it with the title of the song, and indicate by a sketch or symbol the phrase order in which the instruments are to play. Two examples are shown.

GOOD MORNING TO YOU
(Tune: Happy Birthday)

(sticks)

(drums)

(tambourines)

(cymbals)

This song is sung and accompanied in four phrases.

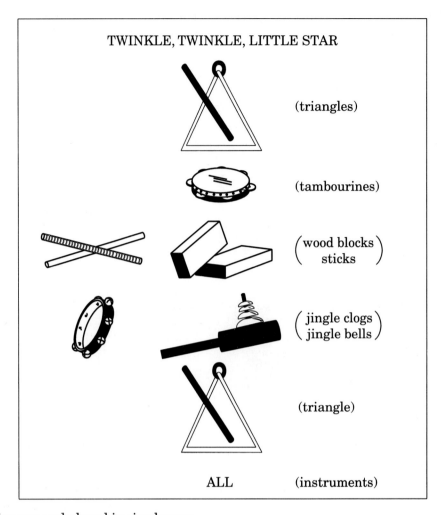

This song is sung and played in six phrases.

Beat, Pattern, and Accent

Throughout these activities, most of the children will be clapping and playing the beat of the music with a clear rhythm. A few may falter at times, but if the movement activities and singing games are being continued, this will happen only occasionally and should be ignored. One or two children may use a more complex-sounding pattern that matches the rhythmic pattern of the words of the song. A few others may play a regular but much slower-sounding beat than the majority. Since participation is the *initial* goal in music making, all these responses are appropriate. A group able to create and use the visual symbols and simple scores, however, is also ready to understand what is happening and use all three of these rhythms.

Following are three ways in which children may clap or play the first phrase of "Baa, Baa, Black Sheep."

1. **Beat.** The *beat* is the ongoing pulse of the music. It is constant and regular and is always perceived or "heard" by the inner ear whether or not it is being sung or played.

2. **Pattern.** The *rhythmic pattern* of the melody changes with the varying length of the tones that make up the tune. In many songs, the rhythmic pattern of the melody matches that of the words, so that children are able to clap or play for each word or syllable they sing.

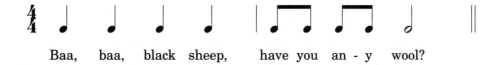

3. **Accent.** The *accent* is the strong beat in each measure. Usually the first beat after each bar line, it receives more stress or emphasis than the others, whether the meter is 2/4, 3/4, or 4/4. This accent strengthens the rhythm and vitality of the music and seems to urge it forward in time.

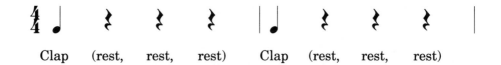

Before going on to more complex playing skills, you should explore these three aspects of rhythm with primary age children. If you have observed these patterns being used, have different children demonstrate how they are responding to the same music. Teach the correct term for each of the three rhythmic responses, and have all the children clap and play the beat, rhythmic pattern, and accent to familiar songs. At first do each one singly while the whole song is sung. Stay with clapping until the children are competent, then transfer these skills to instruments. Ask the class to give the beat while you take the pattern. Then reverse roles. Do the same with accent and beat and then accent and pattern. Work on this a little at a time, both clapping and playing in small groups, until the children have grasped and internalized the concept and can use all three responses interchangeably and with skill.

If, as sometimes happens, your children all have been playing on the beat during the instrumental activities in this chapter, beat, rhythmic pattern, and accent should now be taught. This may be done through a song such as the following, which contains three identical rhythmic patterns.

WE CAN SING

Key: C
Starting tone: G   Folk Tune

1. Teach the simple folk tune "We Can Sing" by rote.
2. Have the children clap with you a steady quarter-note beat to accompany the song. Discuss what was clapped and teach its name: the *beat* of the music.
3. Ask the children to listen for something different in your clapping and repeat the song alone as you clap the rhythmic *pattern*. Follow this with discussion and participation. Next clap the *pattern*

and ask which words fit the pattern you have just clapped. "We can sing, listen to our singing" should be suggested. Develop and clarify the concept that the rhythmic patterns in the first three phrases (1, 2, and 3) are all the same.

4. Transfer the pattern to percussion instruments, playing it for each of the three phrases as the song is sung.
5. Now help the class to discover how the fourth phrase (4) differs by one note.
6. Create a simple, four-phrase orchestration. Guide the children to discover which instruments are most suitable for each type of rhythm, such as triangles, tambourines, and bells for beat, sticks, jingle clogs, or wood blocks for pattern, and cymbals, gong, and drum for *accent*.
7. Sing and play many familiar songs with repeated rhythmic patterns. From this book, use the following:

"Clap, Clap, Clap Your Hands" (page 75)
"Good News!" (page 79)
"I Wanna Be a Friend" (page 100)
"Where, Oh Where" (page 112)

Extended Percussion Activities

Children who are competent in the skills described; who have internalized the concepts of beat, pattern, and accent; and who are concurrently developing reading skills in the primary grades enjoy composing and playing from their own blank rhythm scores and also sight-reading from scores you prepare for them. This involves the use of visual symbols. Some simple ones already have been used in the movement program (see the activities on page 181).

♫ ACTIVITY 1 _____

Review and extend knowledge of music symbols by transferring them from locomotor movement to clapping and then to playing. Display flash cards of note values or put them on the chalkboard:

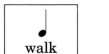

Establish a walking (quarter-note) beat on a drum. It is important to keep this going steadily throughout the activity. Point to the ♩ flash card, asking the children to clap what they see to your beat. After a few measures, and with your beat still going, point to the ♫ note value, asking the children to clap these notes. Continue with the ♪. ♪ which will be uneven in sound. Half-note clapping—point to ♩ —will sound twice as slow as the walking beat and can be shown by a throw-away gesture of the hand on the sustained second beat of each note. Use this activity as a game, not a drill, and play it for several days.

♫ ACTIVITY 2 _____

Substitute groups of instruments for the clapping and repeat the game, assigning a symbol to each group, such as:

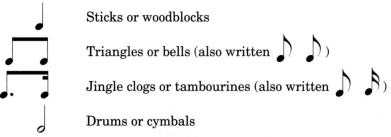

Sticks or woodblocks

Triangles or bells (also written ♪ ♪)

Jingle clogs or tambourines (also written ♪ ♪)

Drums or cymbals

Omit the action words from the flash cards as soon as the symbols are known and the activity is transferred from moving to playing.

ACTIVITY 3

Write simple blank rhythms on the board for the children to clap as they read the movement words under the notes. To establish the tempo, chant, "One, two, ready, clap":

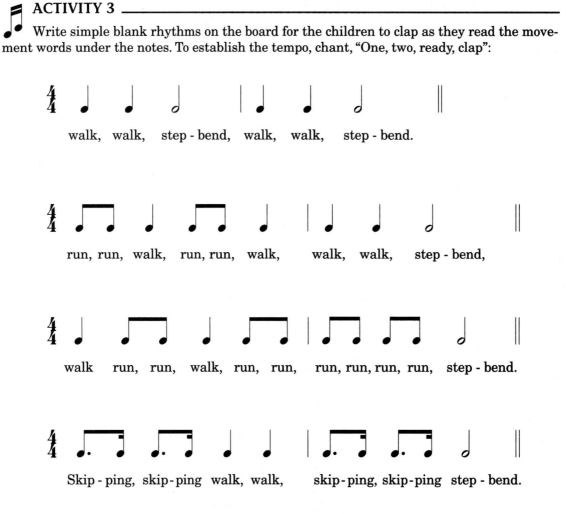

walk,   walk,   step - bend,   walk,   walk,   step - bend.

run, run, walk, run, run, walk,   walk,   walk,   step - bend,

walk   run, run, walk, run, run,   run, run, run, run, step - bend.

Skip - ping, skip - ping walk, walk,   skip - ping, skip - ping step - bend.

This note-reading skill is readily acquired since it is based on the echoing of rhythmic patterns (pages 45–58 and pages 120–131) and adds only the visual symbol.

ACTIVITY 4

When the reading-aloud and clapping responses are prompt and accurate, transfer the game to instruments. Omit the oral reading and have different groups of children read and play blank rhythms one, two, or more times to a tempo you establish at the beginning by chanting, "One, two, ready, play." Use the examples in activity 3 over again, and invent new ones to reinforce this skill.

ACTIVITY 5

These new reading skills now may be used in a creative way by composing and writing instrumental scores for songs added to the children's repertoire. Here is an example:

SEE MY PONY

Key: F
Starting tone: F

Folk Tune

1. Teach this song.
2. Guide the children as they find out that the song has five phrases: three long ones (1, 2, and 5) and two short ones (3 and 4). The three long ones are identical in rhythm and melody; so are the two short ones. These discoveries all may be made *by ear* as the song is sung and analyzed.
3. Look at the song in written form on the music staff, using an overhead projection, a large wall chart, or individual duplicated copies. Ask children to identify *visually* what has already been explored by listening.
4. Discuss with the children the instrumentation they would like for each phrase of the song. Point out that they may have instruments play the beat, pattern, or accent. As they make their suggestions, notate them on the chalkboard, having them clap and play back what they have proposed. Distribute the instruments and try out several of the suggested arrangements, using a consensus of opinion for a final score.
5. After class, write the score on a large chart using felt pen and newsprint and the symbols for instruments suggested earlier (pages 196–197). Your class's final orchestration and score might appear as follows with a checkmark √ indicating phrase endings:

SEE MY PONY

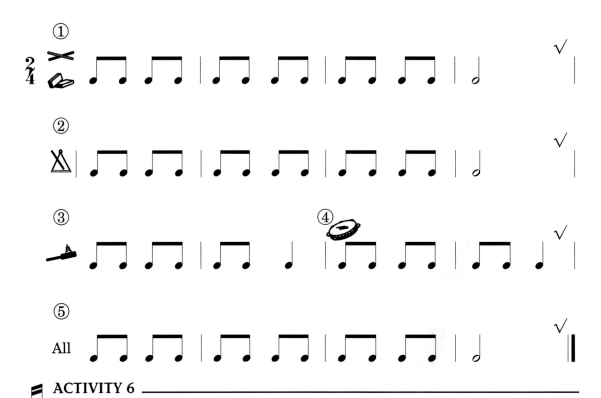

♪ **ACTIVITY 6** ────────────────────────────────

Since the previous score is a pattern score only, develop two more scores for this song, one with drums playing the beat and another with cymbals playing on the accent, as follows:

SCORE FOR DRUMS

SEE MY PONY

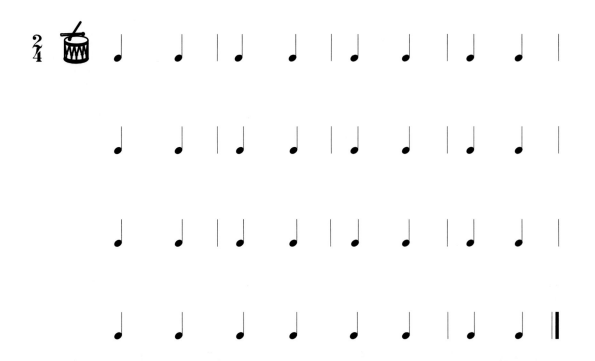

SCORE FOR CYMBALS

SEE MY PONY

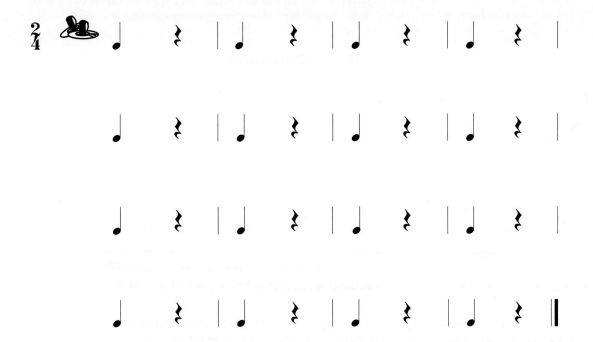

Point out that the cymbal players have a quarter note (♩) and a quarter rest (marked 𝄽)

throughout their entire score. You now have three scores and six groups of players for this song. If individual group practice is necessary for accuracy, have the rest of the children sing the song. For full performances, tape the entire class singing and add live playing. Also, tape the class playing and add live singing. Some children will be able to sing and play simultaneously. Tape this also.

◆ ─────────────────── ◆

Songs in this book that lend themselves to score writing include:

"Clap, Clap, Clap Your Hands" p. 75
"What Shall We Do?" p. 78
"Here We Come A-Walking" p. 102
"Bluebird, Bluebird" p. 103

♫ **ACTIVITY 7** _____

♪ As proficiency in reading rhythmic notation grows, children enjoy a version of the once-popular TV game "Name That Tune!" Write the rhythmic patterns of several familiar songs on large sheets of newsprint; *keep the titles a secret.* Have different instruments ready and play the rhythmic phrases in sequence. At the end of the segment, invite children to identify what song has been played, using only the pattern clues. Suggestions include:

HOT CROSS BUNS

HUSH LITTLE BABY

MARY HAD A LITTLE LAMB

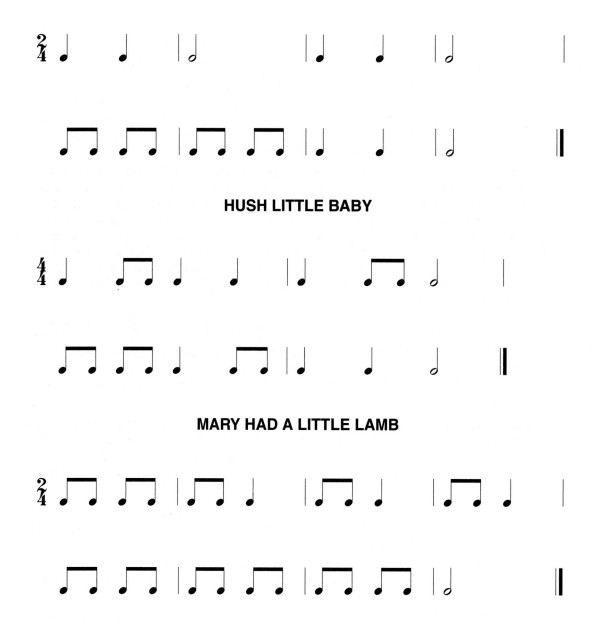

These blank rhythms used at infrequent intervals serve to keep the children alert to the relationship of sight to sound. Unlike orchestration scores, these quick charts should have a short life in the classroom, yielding place to new "Name That Tune" clues as more songs are learned by the children. In this way, learned patterns are used and remembered. Classroom teachers with the desire and ability to extend the children's skills may wish to study and prepare short, simple recorded pieces, as suggested for phrasing. Share them with the children and prepare scores and "Name That Tune" charts for ones they like.

◆ ——————————————————————— ◆

Children who acquire facility in all the rhythmic activities involving percussion instruments possess beginning skills in listening for and playing musical phrases, following a conductor's direction, and playing from and creating visual symbols for musical orchestration through scores and charts. All these activities, while interesting and enjoyable in themselves, build each child's skills, ability, and musicianship.

Tuned Instruments

Tuned or pitched instruments form part of the early childhood music program and are used for melody and harmony making by both teacher and children.

Step bells.   A C-major octave of tuned metal bars on a wooden frame. The instrument looks like a xylophone but has a hinged rod under the bar with the highest pitch, which enables it to stand up like a flight of stairs. The bells are played with a rubber or wooden mallet and are useful in pitch activities.

Resonator bells.   Tuned bars made of tempered steel, constant in pitch. Each bell is attached to a wooden (or heavy plastic) bar that adds resonance and allows bells to be held and played individually with a rubber mallet. The bells are available in various combinations. A useful set contains the chromatic scale in black and white bars from middle C to G. The bells are graduated in size and come in a fitted case with a set of rubber mallets. Resonator bells are versatile instruments that can be used for teaching and learning about pitch, melody experimentation, improvisation, accompaniments (especially in the pentatonic scale), melodic ostinati (repeated short melodic fragments), and harmonic playing.

Piano.   A well-tuned piano is useful in the primary classroom even if the teacher's skills are minimal. All teachers of young children should learn to read and play simple melodies on the piano and use it for atonal and pentatonic improvisations. Children like to play the piano, working out melodies and tonal effects by ear and experimentation. With help (such as a colored symbol on each note of a pentatonic scale), they can work out and notate in color their own melodic creations.

Several of the instruments in the Orff Instrumentarium, while more specialized and expensive, are excellent for use by the regular classroom teacher. All have beautiful tone quality and are available in different tonal ranges and sizes. They are always played with two mallets. Many publications are available to help teachers use them in simple, creative, and beautiful ways (see Appendix D).

Xylophone.   Hardwood bars mounted over resonating boxes. Each bar is removable, allowing the teacher to set up tone patterns and pentatonic or diatonic scales. They are often played with padded mallets.

Glockenspiel.   Removable metal bars on a wooden frame. When the bars are struck, they have a bright, clear tone like the bells of a marching band. The structure and use of the glockenspiel is similar to that of the xylophone.

Metallophone.   Versatile barred instrument made of thick metal with deep resonance and rich tone.

Introducing Melody Instruments

Introduce melody instruments by making them available one at a time for children to explore freely and creatively. Since they are more complex than percussion instruments, show each one to the group first, illustrating how it should be handled, played, taken apart, and re-assembled for proper care.

The Pentatonic Scale.   When introducing resonator bells or Orff instruments, you are wise to put out only the third, fifth, and sixth tones of the scale (E, G, and A in the key of C) for a while, later adding the first and second tones (C and D) to form the pentatonic scale. Keep to this scale for creative experiments and use the full diatonic scale for accompaniments. Since the letter name of the note is engraved on each bar of these instruments, children can begin early to write down sequences of tones that please them. For young children, the pentatonic scale is the ideal medium for the creation of melodies. The activities that follow are sequentially arranged, leading from complete rhythmic and tonal freedom to melodic improvisation within a rhythmic framework.

 ACTIVITY 1 _____

HEY THERE MISTER MONDAY

Key: C pentatonic
Starting tone: G

Barbara Andress

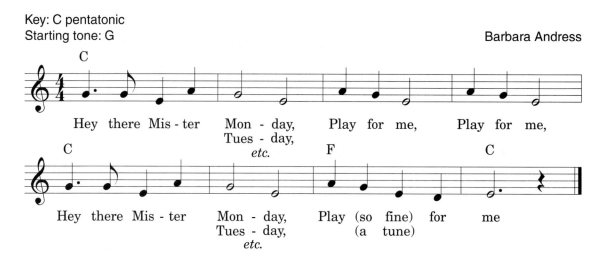

1. Teach this song.
2. When the song is familiar, prepare the C pentatonic scale on a melody instrument*
   as follows:

Resonator bells: Arrange the bells on the floor or a table:

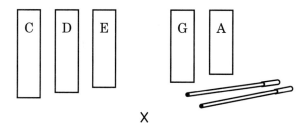

X

*In all the activities that follow, any of the instruments shown here may be used where the term *bells* appears. The player sits at *X* with the low tones to the left, high to the right.

Orff xylophone, glockenspiel, metallophone: Remove the diatonic bars, leaving this arrangement:

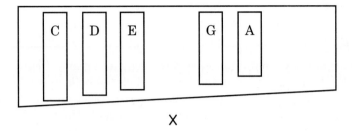

Step bells or piano keyboard: Use washable felt pen or colored adhesive tape to show which keys to use:

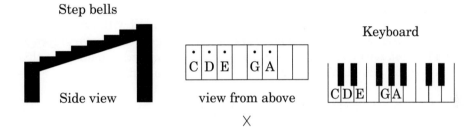

3. When the children know the song well, seat them in a circle and ask them to name the tune they hear. Play the first phrase of the melody, using a light, bouncing touch:

The children will recognize it quickly. Ask them to sing with you, repeating the phrase and continuing through the Monday stanza.
4. Tell them you will now play a tune for Mr. Monday. Improvise a short sequence, using the bells in any order and rhythm. Remember to use repeated tones, to skip over bells, and to move stepwise from bell to bell.
5. Pause here to point out how easy it is to make up tunes on the bells, and give one or two more examples. This will help the children both visually and aurally.
6. Ask who would like to play a tune for Mr. Tuesday and have the volunteer *take your place* at the bells during the unaccompanied singing of the Tuesday stanza. The child then plays her improvisation.

Use only the children who wish to try this activity on the first run through. Later each child may choose a successor by walking to him and giving him the mallets during the singing of the next verse. Greet every effort, however short or stiffly played, with enthusiasm and praise, commenting on the pleasant sounds the bells can make. Repeat the activity over two or three days until all who wish have had a chance to play. Later you may wish to play the melody yourself to accompany the singing. Another variation is to sing a Mr. Weekend verse, instead of Saturday and Sunday verses, and to ask two children to improvise side by side simultaneously. For this it is helpful to put out another set of bells:

The bells should also be made available during free time. Often children will extend this activity on their own, even working out how to play the melody. If you observe this happening, move in with encouragement and help as needed.

ACTIVITY 2 _____

Set out the bells in the C pentatonic. Teach the song and game "I Have a Little Cupboard" (page 253). Explain that the song can be played on the bells and a little tune made up and played while a person goes to the cupboard to find the object inside. Demonstrate this, improvising the melody yourself. Choose two children, one to go to the cupboard and another to improvise a tune. This may be repeated with pairs of volunteers or with each child passing on the mallets to a neighbor or friend. Work out similar activities with other pentatonic songs.

ACTIVITY 3 _____

Leave the bells out for free experimental use and be at hand with paper and pencil or crayons to help children write down (in any way) improvisations they have played and would like to have in written form. Even five-year-olds become interested and adept at this activity, and older children can add blank rhythm notations to their melodic sequences. For example:

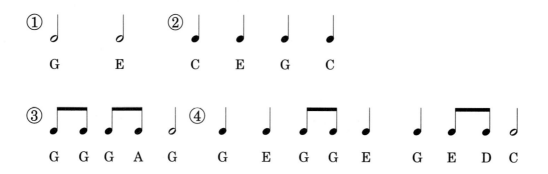

Do not worry if this writing activity does not develop. Free melodic improvisation is the important thing.

♪ ACTIVITY 4 _____

Give as many children as possible a C pentatonic scale. Encourage each child to use two mallets as in the Orff approach (see Glossary). Chant the names of two members of the group and improvise a melody in that rhythmic pattern, using any sequence of notes. Start with a simple combination:

Bill   and   Don   Sal - ly   and   Jane

After each example, ask for improvisations on the names from a few individual children. Ask all the players to improvise together, repeating the names two or four times. This gives a new musical experience: combining several strands of music that are varied in melody and united rhythmically. This is usually an exciting and rewarding experience for children, leading to exploration with more complex patterns. Here are some suggestions.

♦ Use two sets of name patterns alternately:

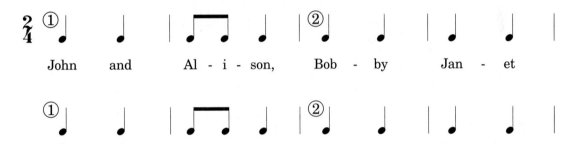

John   and   Al - i - son,   Bob - by   Jan - et

♦ Repeat each pattern:

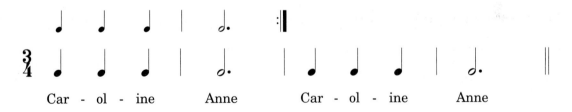

Car - ol - ine   Anne   Car - ol - ine   Anne

♦ Speak and play two patterns in a sequence:

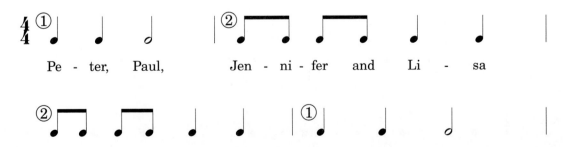

Pe - ter,   Paul,   Jen - ni - fer   and   Li - sa

Use other sets of words to provide a rhythmic structure, such as days, months, fruits, vegetables, colors, shapes, vehicles, cities, and countries. Use the children's suggestions. Repeat the words, clapping them out if they are not spoken rhythmically at first, and then take turns around the group or improvise in twos or using as many as have instruments. Here are four suggestions to start you off:

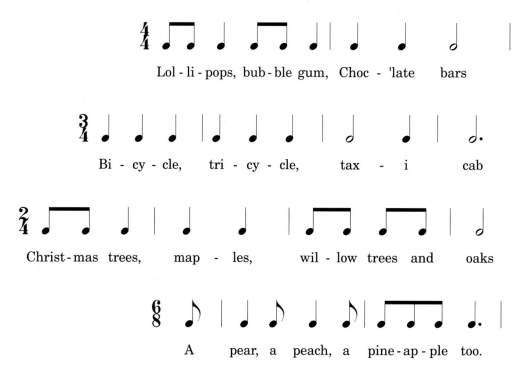

Sometimes set up the bells in a different pentatonic scale such as F (FGA CD) or G (GAB DE).

ACTIVITY 5

When the children are confident and skillful at improvising to verbal rhythms, they are ready to dispense with the crutch of words. Give them clapping rhythms and have the improvisation move around the instrumental group without loss of the underlying beat. Build from simple to more complex rhythmic patterns:

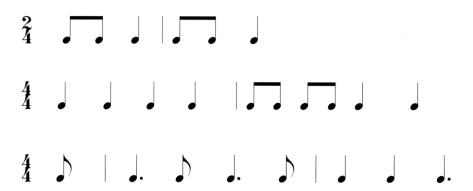

Be sure to change the key used from day to day to give variety to the tonality and range available and to teach that pentatonic scales may be built on any tone. Sometimes use the black resonator bells or piano keys in F♯ pentatonic: F♯ G♯ A♯ C♯ D♯. The black triplets and twins on the keyboard are particularly easy to use.

ACTIVITY 6

Sing a simple and familiar pentatonic song and then improvise melodically in the same rhythmic pattern as the words but with any note sequence. After singing, you may wish to clap the rhythmic pattern before improvising on it. As soon as the concept is grasped, leave out the clapping and go straight from singing into creating melodies, either individually or in the group. Suitable songs in this book are "Starlight, Starbright," "Rain, Rain," and "Ring Around the Rosie" (pp. 123–124).

Melodic and Harmonic Accompaniments

Two groups of pitched or tuned instruments are appropriate for use with young children: those described in the preceding section, which are used primarily for playing melodies and melodic accompaniments, and instruments that are used mostly for harmonizing or chord playing to accompany singing. The second group includes the autoharp, guitar, ukulele, and banjo. The piano, resonator bells, and Orff instruments may also be used for simple chording. (Of course, if the classroom teacher has expertise on any musical instrument, it should be used as an integral part of the music program in innovative and creative ways.) Children enjoy learning and playing accompaniments that have a melodic or harmonic basis.

Melodic Ostinati.   An *ostinato* is a small musical fragment, often taken from the song itself, that is repeated "obstinately" throughout the entire song to enrich the effect.

ACTIVITY 1

Set out the resonator bells in C pentatonic. Review the song "I Have a Dog."

I HAVE A DOG

Key: C pentatonic
Starting tone: E

American Folk Song

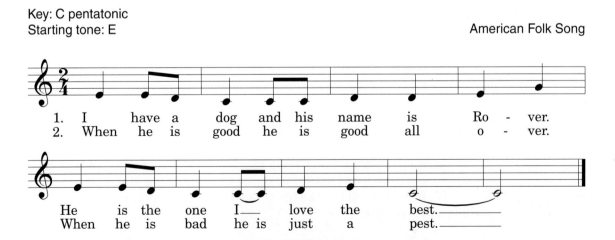

Ask the children to listen for an addition to the music. Repeat the song, playing this two-tone ostinato on the E and G bells to a steady 2/4 beat:

Ostinato 1

Discuss the accompaniment with the children, helping them to discover that it is Rover's name, just as it is heard in the song. Give children turns at playing the ostinato, choosing first those whose rhythmic sense you know to be secure, and then including any who wish to try. Be sure to keep a steady, slow tempo. At the end of this session, show the children what they have been playing, writing it on the chalkboard. Make a flash card of the notes as they watch you, using the word *ostinato.*

Next time, review the song and ostinato 1 and have the children listen for a new one:

Ostinato 2

Teach it in the same way as before. Notate the accompaniment on the chalkboard and make the flash card after the listening and playing experience. While writing, mention that 𝄇 means "play it again" or "repeat."

Here is a third accompaniment to be taught as before, when the first two can be played with ease:

Ostinato 3

After playing, when you write the pattern for children to see, mention that the mark or sign 𝄽 means "don't play now" or "rest." Use these ostinati interchangeably to accompany the song, but maintain good singing quality.

With primary children, experiment with combining ostinati—having two children playing simultaneously 1 and 2, 2 and 3, 1 and 3. When this activity goes well and instruments are available, have the children play all three ostinati, bringing them in in sequence and starting the song when all three are playing steadily. The flash card of each child's ostinato may be set before him.

Vary the song by changing the dog's name. Have the children choose two-syllable names with the same rhythmic pattern, such as Lassie, Muffin, or Duchess. Write and tape different names onto the flash card. Remember to use the cards as a record of what has been done, not as a device for teaching a new pattern.

•————————————————————•

You need not use flash cards for every ostinato, since the aural activity is more valuable. However, the occasional use of visual aids *after* the experience is good incidental teaching, leading toward future learning.

♪ ACTIVITY 2 _____

Here are two more songs with suggested melodic ostinati. Teach the song first and when it is well known, proceed as with activity 1.

This first song needs a G pentatonic scale. Put out GAB DE.

WHO'S GOT A FISHPOLE?

Key: G pentatonic
Starting tone: G

Southern Singing Game

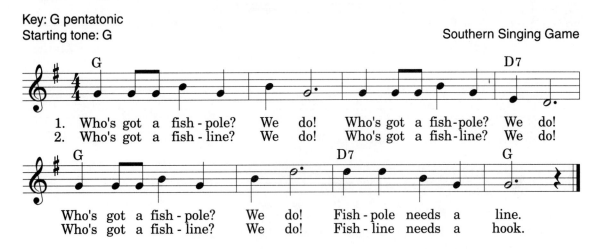

1. Who's got a fish-pole? We do! Who's got a fish-pole? We do!
2. Who's got a fish-line? We do! Who's got a fish-line? We do!

Who's got a fish-pole? We do! Fish-pole needs a line.
Who's got a fish-line? We do! Fish-line needs a hook.

3. Who's got a fish-hook? We do! *(3 times)*
   Fish-hook needs some bait.

4. Who's got a cricket? We do! *(3 times)*
   Cricket catch a fish!

Ostinato 1

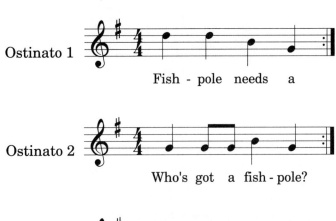

Fish - pole needs a

Ostinato 2

Who's got a fish - pole?

Ostinato 3

We do!

The following song needs an F pentatonic scale. Put out FGA CD.

CHATTER WITH THE ANGELS

Point out that in ostinato 3 the word *angels* is repeated, while it is sung only once each time it occurs in the song. Also point out that one of the ostinato patterns for both songs is the beat of the song. This helps keep the tempo steady.

Pentatonic songs in this book that lend themselves to this treatment include:

Other well-known pentatonic songs that may be used include:

"All Night, All Day"
"Angel Band"
"Hot Cross Buns"
"Jennie Jenkins"
"Land of the Silver Birch"
"Riding on the Bus, Miss Mary Jane"

Melodic Accompaniments

Some songs in both diatonic and pentatonic scales are suited to melodic accompaniments that are not ostinati. The following song uses a melodic insert between phrases.

HERE IS A VERY GOOD WAY

Key: F
Starting tone: F
Folk Song

Here is a ver - y good way (clap, clap)

We can be hap - py to - day (clap, clap)

If you can fol - low a - long (clap, clap)

Lift up your voic - es in song. (clap, clap.)

Two melodic inserts may be played instead of the claps (♩ ♩) at the end of each phrase. At the end of phrases 1, 2, and 3, play the following:

At the end of phrase 4, play:

Set out only the necessary bells and teach the patterns by rote, without visual aids.

Other songs are suitable for this treatment. Put out the bells needed for the patterns indicated and have them played by rote instead of sung.

"Are You Sleeping?": Play the echo to phrases 1, 2, and 4.

"Looby Loo": Play this with the same melodic patterns as "Here Is a Very Good Way,"

changing the rhythm to ⁶/₈ 𝄾 ♪ ♩ 𝄾 .

"Old MacDonald Had a Farm": Sing this starting on F♯. Play E-I-E-I-O on the three tones A♯, G♯, and F♯ (the black triplets on keyboard or bells).

Harmonic Accompaniments

Harmony occurs when more than one tone is sounded simultaneously. Children *hear* harmony when you add to their singing a simple accompaniment, played on the bells (or other melody instrument). Children *make* harmony when they are able to accompany their own singing. Six examples follow.

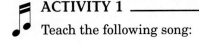 **ACTIVITY 1** ————————————————————————————————

Teach the following song:

GO TELL AUNT RHODY

Key: D
Starting tone: F
American Folk Song

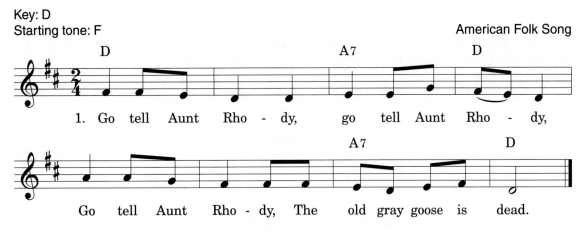

1. Go tell Aunt Rho - dy, go tell Aunt Rho - dy,
Go tell Aunt Rho - dy, The old gray goose is dead.

    2. The one she's been saving *(3 times)*
       To make a feather bed.

    3. The goslings are crying *(3 times)*
       Because their mother's dead.

    4. She died in the duck pond *(3 times)*
       Standing on her head.

Use D and A bells to add this harmonic accompaniment:

Note: D is taken from the I chord and A from the V_7 chord of the scale. (See Appendix B for chord identifications.)

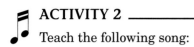

ACTIVITY 2 _____

Teach the following song:

MARY HAD A BABY

Key: F pentatonic
Starting tone: F

Spiritual

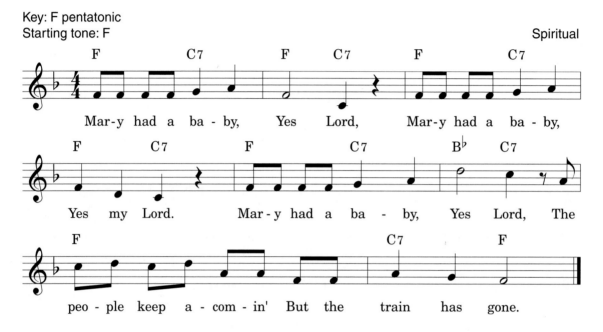

2. Angels were a-singing.

3. Shepherds came a-running.

4. That's how come it's Christmas.

Set out the F and E bells and teach the following accompaniment:

Note: F is taken from the I chord and E from the V$_7$ chord of the scale. This may be written

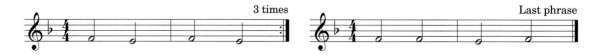

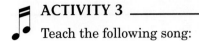 **ACTIVITY 3** —————————————————————————————
Teach the following song:

ARROZ CON LECHE
(Rice with Milk)

Key: F
Starting tone: C   Argentinian

1. A - rroz con le - che me quie - ro ca - sar Con
u - na se - ño - ri - ta que se - pa bai - lar. Con es - ta, sí, con
es - ta, no, Con es - ta se - ño - ri - ta me ca - so yo.

2. Que sepa coser, que sepa planchar,
Que sepa abrir la puerta para ir a jugar.
Con esta, sí, con esta, no,
Con esta señorita me caso yo.

In this song a young man is looking for a young woman to be his wife.
Set out the F and C bells and teach the following accompaniment:

Note: F is taken from the I chord and C from the V_7 chord of the scale.

ACTIVITY 4 _____

Teach the following song:

WIND, WIND, WIND THE THREAD

Key: G
Starting tone: D

Danish Singing Game

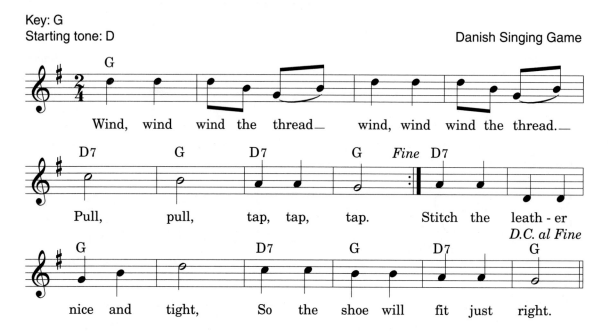

Set out D, F♯, G, and A bells and teach the following accompaniment:

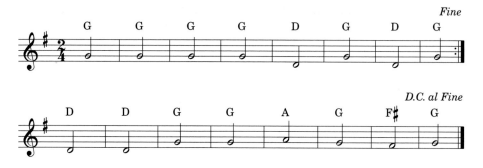

Note: G is taken from the I chord; D, A, and F♯ from the V_7 chord.

Primary age children whose music program contains much movement and playing enjoy playing harmonic accompaniments composed of block chords. Here, two or three children, each with one bell, strike their bells at exactly the same time, giving a rich texture to the music. Sounding the chords on every strong beat, the accompaniment will be as follows:

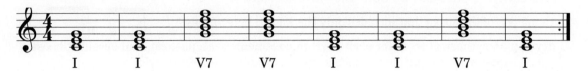

Repeat this chord sequence for the refrain.

ACTIVITY 5

Here is another familiar song. This time it is in the key of G major. Review and accompany "Bow, Bow, O Belinda" (page 97).

ACTIVITY 6

Review "Riding in the Buggy" (page 135). Give bells to two groups of children as in the diagram.

RELATED ACTIVITIES FOR STUDENTS

1. Choose several songs from this book and develop for each an orchestration to teach phrase-wise playing. Write your orchestrations on newsprint and teach them to your class. (Examples: "What Shall We Do?" "Bluebird, Bluebird")

2. Using one of the songs that includes only the known note values (♩ , ♫ , ♩. , ♩ , 𝅗𝅥), develop an orchestral score for each rhythmic element: beat, pattern, and accent. Choose appropriate instrumentation for each score. (Example: "See My Pony")

3. Choose a pentatonic song from this book and develop at least one ostinato pattern. Be sure to study the examples given in this chapter as models. Test your ostinato on the resonator bells. Write out the song and the ostinato so that it can be used by either classmates or children.

4. Choose two songs from this book, one using the I and V_7 chords and the other using the I, IV, and V_7 chords (see Appendix B). Create an accompaniment for the songs using the resonator bells either as a sequence of single tones or as chords. (Example: "Go Tell Aunt Rhody")

5. Choose a favorite children's story from your childhood or from your study of children's literature. Use both pitched and unpitched rhythm instruments to create appropriate sound effects to enhance your telling of the story. Make a cue sheet for yourself, indicating with sketches of the instruments the points in the narration where each is to be used.

Listening to the
Music of Others

To meet our goals of enjoyment, appreciation, and understanding we encourage active participation based on the child's growing listening ability. *The ability to listen, however, involves not only hearing but focusing the mind on the sounds perceived.* This ability to pay attention is not innate but is a learned skill, and the young child needs training and help to acquire it.

The activities in Chapters 4 through 8 assume that listening skills grow from active, successful involvement in chanting, singing, moving, and playing. In addition to providing a firm experiential foundation in music making, however, we also involve children in the active appreciation of music made by others, both live and recorded.

Today's children have little live music at home in comparison with youngsters of two or more generations ago. Then, families often sang together and played a variety of instruments. Parents today have fewer children, less leisure time, and more accessible and inexpensive sources of relaxation and enjoyment. Nursery rhymes and folk songs are not passed along to children within the family as much today. Of course some parents continue to make music at home, share it with their children, and take their children to suitable musical events. Many families do this for a specific purpose—the preservation of a cultural or religious tradition—and thereby help their children to gain listening skills as well as a thorough understanding of music.

Regardless of children's experiences with live music, most of them are surrounded by recorded music. They hear it in the grocery store, the bus terminal, the airplane, the automobile, the home, and public buildings. David Evans points out that "adults and children are used to hearing music as a background, with people talking, making noises and listening only in bits. So they get into the habit of listening in the imperfect way, cutting out a whole chunk of music. They may even get into the habit of talking as soon as they *hear* music."[1]

When children age three or four arrive in day-care centers and nursery schools skilled at tuning music out, teachers may unintentionally compound the problem. Often they will play a tape or a record as a background for snack time, rest time, art activities, or free play; to provide a familiar setting; to meet the requirement for a music component in their program; or even to control the children's own noise level. Recorded music used in this way detracts from the child's ability to understand and value music.

During the primary years the use of recorded background music in the classroom diminishes. In out-of-school life, however, cassette and CD players and portable radios continue to provide a background for informal peer-group meetings, organized sports, and recreational activities.

Whatever the child's former musical experience, our goal is to intensify and increase his enjoyment of the music of others. While not everyone will grow up to perform, all children have the potential and the right to experience and value music.

Creating a Listening Climate

It is important to maintain a positive climate for music listening throughout the early childhood years. We do this by letting children see our own enjoyment of music and our respect for it, not as a background for "more important" things but as a valuable entity in itself, worthy of our most courteous attention. Children should experience music of all kinds: classical, contemporary, folk, ethnic, jazz, pop, instrumental, and vocal. They should hear the best of each kind in short and vivid servings. We must listen with them to both their own and others' music, talk with them about the music, and relate it to the familiar in their lives to stretch them toward new experiences. They need our help to respond to music in overt ways that are consonant with their active natures through discussion, appropriate movement, playing instruments, and imitating what they have heard. These expressions may engage their minds but must not be so rigorous as to distract them from the listening activity itself.

In our visually oriented society, as Ian Lawrence points out, "listening to music . . . is not easy for the beginner, and many people, including experienced adults, find that their mind is easily distracted by what they are seeing during the music." [2] We experience the truth of this in ourselves and in others, especially very young children. This difficulty is naturally overcome when "the listener sees the musicians actually make the sounds he is hearing, and the close relationship between the two helps him to concentrate on the music."[3] Our sequence of listening activities, therefore, begins with live music making in the classroom.

Sharing Live Music

Singing

ACTIVITY 1 _____

Gather your class around you in an informal group. Announce simply, "I have something for you to listen to." Sing a short song you know well that you enjoyed as a young child. Tell the children that you learned this song when you were their age and discuss it briefly. They may enjoy hearing it again, perhaps joining in on any catchy phrases. One or two of the group may have songs to sing that they have learned at home. Let each one come and stand by you to sing her solo. Encourage attentive listening and appreciative comments on such features as clear words, the story line, repetition, rhythm, or mood. Explain that when people share or trade songs with each other they often call that time a "song swap." Thank the children for sharing, and promise more opportunities for song swaps.

ACTIVITY 2 _____

Sing two or three well-contrasted songs and discuss how they differ: tempo, rhythm, mood, contrast, and subject matter. The stress is on hearing these songs rather than teaching them. If, however, a song is requested a second time, comply. Some children may join in on repeated parts and clap or tap the beat or a rhythmic fragment. Acknowledge this participation without requiring it.

ACTIVITY 3 _____

Introduce a song swap using a theme song. Ella Jenkins's song, "You'll Sing a Song and I'll Sing a Song" from the CD/cassette tape of the same name, is an excellent choice, or use *Stories and Songs*, page 165. Explain that children themselves will be the swappers. Have three or four volunteers sing for the group; follow with discussion as in activity 2. To optimize listening skills, these songs should not come from the classroom repertoire. With your guidance, the children may keep a written record of performers and song titles including your own contributions.

ACTIVITY 4 _____

Once a month help the children to plan a five- to fifteen-minute program of song swaps. They should choose from the list prepared in activity 3. Each contributor is asked to sing her particular song again, a written program is prepared, and all the class is invited to be the audience.

At first, be the announcer yourself and make brief appreciative comments on each contribution. It is a good idea to end this miniconcert with your theme song.

Children soon look forward to these occasions and take an interest in planning a balanced program. Even at five years of age, some will be keen and able announcers. Be sure to continue as a music maker yourself, using this opportunity to expand the listening skills of your class.

Here are some suggested songs for the teacher to perform for a song swap:

"Frog Went A-Courting"

"I've Been Working on the Railroad"

"Kum Bah-Ya"

"Michael, Row the Boat Ashore"

"There Was an Old Lady Who Swallowed a Fly"

"This Land is Your Land"

"Way Down South in the Yankety-Yank"

"When I First Came to This Land"

Sea chanteys, cowboy songs, and spirituals are also appropriate.

Instruments

Guest Artists.   As children begin listening to and performing for each other, you will hear of class members who are beginners on musical instruments. There may be siblings, family members, and friends who play the piano, flute, guitar, chord organ, recorder, drums, trumpet, and other instruments. Invite their participation in your miniconcerts and ask each guest to demonstrate his instrument. Visit a local church to hear the organ or walk past the high school when the band is playing outside. Make sure these sessions are short and include hands-on activities if possible. Try to take some photographs for a series of posters or a music scrapbook. Surround the pictures with words children use to describe what they hear.

Ongoing Live Music Activities.   Children grow naturally in music listening ability when they themselves make music for others to hear. The two processes nurture each other and lead to new musical experiences, including listening to recorded music.

Before suggesting activities based on recordings, we wish to emphasize the importance of continuing the live listening and music-making activities already described throughout the primary school years. A natural extension of these will involve other classes in song swaps and miniconcerts, listening and musical participation in settings outside the classroom, and visits by performing musicians.

Sharing Recorded Music

Listening to Ourselves

Early experiences in listening to recorded music should involve children hearing tapes of their own music making. This can begin as early as age three or four. Hearing oneself speak and sing stimulates the participant to want to do more and better, to hear others, and to try new combinations of music.

Most teachers have access to a tape recorder with a built-in microphone. Equip yourself with some good-quality blank tapes early in the school year.

♫ ACTIVITY 1 ─────────────────────────────

Give the children informal opportunities to record and hear their voices speaking, chanting, and singing, alone and in groups. Probably, some will already be familiar with this activity and capable of operating the recorder themselves. This experimental time is important in building confidence and establishing natural, un-self-conscious behavior.

ACTIVITY 2

Use the tape recorder often during live music experiences. Let children listen to the playbacks and lend them to others both at school and at home. This is important since it forms a meaningful and personal link between live and recorded music.

The ability to keep the music we make, so that we may hear it again and share it with others, encourages interest in the recorded music of those whom we do not know, for now we understand how the recording came to be. Further, it opens a new avenue for the recall of sensory experience that is fundamental to the young child's learning mode. Plan, therefore, to begin a tape library in your class and keep it up to date. Erase inferior material only after it has served its purpose as a learning tool.

Listening to Others

The use of recorded material is often the weakest part of an early childhood music program. Some teachers use it as background for other activities; to fill quiet moments; or even to invite active singing, moving, or playing instruments. But very few use recorded music for sharing vivid, good-quality compositions appropriate to children's interests and abilities or for developing musical understanding and enjoyment.

The sequence of live and recorded experiences just described addresses this problem. Children who have participated in these activities know how to listen to others' music and how to share their own. They have learned that music is recorded to be enjoyed again and again, that it becomes part of the lives of listeners beyond their own daily experiences, and that music can be made in many ways.

With this background they are ready to listen to recordings of music they have not yet heard, performed by people they do not know. The listening activities that follow incorporate two strands: musical elements and different kinds of music and music making. These strands can be woven into ongoing activities in singing, moving, and playing. A composition that illustrates more than one musical topic can be played again with a different focus for a different occasion. Your own enthusiasm can keep enjoyment high for a second, third, or fourth playing, so that a selection is greeted with "Oh good, you're going to play the one we heard last week again," rather than "Oh, no, we heard that already!"

Focus attention with judicious use of visuals, and keep the selections short, using volume control to fade out at an appropriate point. A short excerpt may hold children's attention, while longer selections may cause them to tune out. Most of the music suggested is in the standard repertoire and may be found in numerous recordings on cassettes and CDs. In addition, we list pieces from Belwin's *Bowmar Orchestral Library* series and their recording *The Small Listener.** Music stores and college and public libraries have personnel and cross-referenced catalogs to help you locate these and alternative selections for the following activities.

Listening for Musical Elements

The following sequence of listening experiences should be used over a period of several days so that children have the opportunity to extend their knowledge each day without becoming tired.

Mood

ACTIVITY 1

Sing two well-contrasted familiar songs such as "Ev'rybody Ought To Sing" (page 147) and "Hush, Little Baby" (page 210). Discuss briefly how each song creates a different feeling—the first happy, the second peaceful. Show these feelings by contrasting hand movements as

---

*The *Bowmar Orchestral Library* is available on CD or cassette from the CPP Belwin Co. of Miami, Florida. In addition, *Adventures in Music,* an integrated elementary listening program from Bowmar, is an excellent resource—with teacher's guides.

you sing the music. Play "Polka" by Strauss and "Little Girl Rocking Her Dolly" by Rebikoff (*The Small Listener,* Bowmar). Invite the use of hand motions as appropriate. Help children discover that these two pieces have the same feelings as the songs just sung even though they do not use words. Titles may be created or given.

ACTIVITY 2

From your miniconcert tapes (activity 2, page 231) help the children choose two selections showing joyful and restful moods.

ACTIVITY 3

Play the two selections from activity 2 and compare them with the selections used in activity 1.

ACTIVITY 4

Improvise contrasting moods on pentatonic resonator bells in G, F, or C (review melodic improvisation on pages 212-217) and in movement to either improvisation or recording.

ACTIVITY 5

Conclude the sequence by listening again to the two selections from activity 2.

Phrase

ACTIVITY 1

Review moving to phrases (page 182, activities 1, 2, and 3) and playing phrases (page 207). Have the children sit on the floor, well spaced. Listen to the first part (the four long phrases) of "Morning" from Grieg's *Peer Gynt Suite (Bowmar).*

ACTIVITY 2

Your miniconcert tapes may yield other dancelike music or marches. Play these examples. Talk about them, humming and clapping snatches and comparing them to "Morning," which may now be heard to the end of the recording.

ACTIVITY 3

Choose a recording such as "The Swan" from *Carnival of the Animals* by Saint-Saens (*Bowmar*) or "Barcarolle" from *Tales of Hoffmann* by Offenbach. These compositions have long, clear phrases. Darken the room and have the children lie down in their own spaces. Explain that the music and you together will tell a story about sunbeams in the sky. Flashlights will act out the story on the ceiling and the children will follow each sunbeam with their arms and hands as it moves about above their heads.

Tell a simple story about a sunbeam that comes up in the sky one morning and gets lost. Describe, in words and with your light, how it plays at first, then starts to hunt for a companion, uphill and down, around and about. Toward evening a second little sunbeam appears on the scene. Ultimately, the two meet and go off together as the sun sets and the world goes to sleep.

Practice telling the story with both music and the flashlights. Use a variety of shapes and tempi as the sunbeam moves. *Be certain to make a marked change of direction with the light at the end of each phrase of the music.* When the second sunbeam appears, let the two work their way toward each other from opposite sides of the ceiling so that they meet overhead.

 ACTIVITY 4 _____

Conclude this sequence by listening to the sunbeam music as part of a miniconcert.

Form

 ACTIVITY 1 _____

Sing "Twinkle, Twinkle, Little Star." Establish that it begins and ends with the same melodic phrase. Use cutouts and a pocket chart or flannel board to reinforce the idea of ABA form. Substitute A and B shapes for the cutouts and transfer the idea to other known songs such as "See, See, See!" (page 82) and "See My Pony" (page 207). End this activity by singing or playing a short, quiet piece in ternary (ABA) form such as "The Ash Grove" or "All Through the Night," both traditional Welsh melodies.

 ACTIVITY 2 _____

Review the idea of a musical sandwich (ABA) by playing the appropriate pieces from your miniconcert tapes. Use cutouts or ABAs for reinforcement.

 ACTIVITY 3 _____

Prepare a tape of ABA music with a light, clear rhythm such as "Dance of the Sugar Plum Fairy" from the *Nutcracker Suite* by Tchaikovsky (*Bowmar*). The children stand in a circle, each one holding a knot in a chain of colored scarves tied together, while you hold one end:

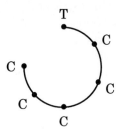

As the music plays part A, you lead the group lightly and rhythmically away from the circle in a curving path around the room. The children follow, holding the scarves at shoulder level as they step to the beat and listen to the melody. As the end of A nears, you bring them back into a circle and take the hand of the last child.

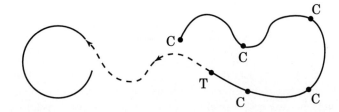

During part B, the group continues to move lightly and rhythmically, almost in place. Each child uses just the small area around him to respond to the music. On the return of A, let go of the last child's hand and once more take the group around the room, ending appropriately in a circle.

ACTIVITY 4

On a second hearing of this piece, sit in a circle holding the scarves which are now joined in a ring. Pass the knots from one to the next silently and rhythmically, reversing direction when a new section is heard. This quiet activity tunes children in to the music.

ACTIVITY 5

Add the ABA piece chosen to the listening repertoire of the class.

Dynamics

ACTIVITY 1

Review several familiar chants. Experiment with them at different dynamic levels:

1. Chant softly.
2. Chant loudly.
3. Start chanting softly, gradually get louder, and then reverse.
4. Begin the chant with one voice, adding voices at key points until all are chanting, then reverse.

Illustrate the dynamic markings for each of the following:

1. Soft (p, pp, ppp)
2. Loud (f, ff, fff)
3. Crescendo (<)
4. Decrescendo (>)

ACTIVITY 2

Choose several songs from the children's repertoire such as "Hush You Bye" (page 146) and "Join Hands All Around the World" (page 148). With the children's help, identify the appropriate dynamic markings for each song. Sing the songs using the dynamic markings chosen. Vary singing the songs with different dynamics and discuss the results. Experiment with crescendos and decrescendos to see if they enhance the music. Use the tape recorder to help decide which versions children prefer.

ACTIVITY 3

Select two recorded compositions that are contrasting in dynamics. You may wish to use jazz, a contemporary pop piece, or a well-known march, and contrast it with a gentle folk song or popular ballad. Listen to as much of each recording as holds pupil interest. Discuss the dynamics. You may want to have some children use movement or an art medium to express the dynamic levels of each piece.

ACTIVITY 4

Discuss the changing sights and sounds of a parade approaching from a distance, passing directly in front, and going away. Listen to "Parade" by Tansman, from Bowmar's *The Small Listener,* to illustrate how the dynamics of the music represent just such an event. Dynamic markings on cards may be put into a pocket chart during a second listening in this sequence:

| *pp* | *p* | *f* | *ff* | *f* | *p* | *pp* |

ACTIVITY 5

Listen to other pieces containing strong contrasts in dynamics, such as "Hall of the Mountain King" by Grieg. Children may rearrange the cards to reflect what they hear.

ACTIVITY 6

Add the contrasting pieces used in the preceding activities to your miniconcert library. The essential instructional sequence in these activities is as follows:

1. Review an activity already well known and relate it to the new experience being presented.
2. Introduce new material for the listening program using a supportive activity such as moving, playing, singing, or using visuals.
3. Reduce and ultimately remove teaching aids.
4. Add the music selected to the listening repertoire.

◆ ———————————————— ◆

Study other musical elements in the sequential manner described above (e.g., tempo, pitch [high, low, the same], rhythm [beat, accent, pattern], articulation [staccato, legato], and harmony) (see Related Activities for Students).

Listening to Different Kinds of Music

When your children (are going to) have the opportunity to hear a live instrumental performance—in their own room, at a school assembly, or in their local community—it is particularly helpful to use a recording or videotape beforehand. This will introduce them to the instruments they will be seeing and hearing, and will prepare their eyes and ears.

Flute

Selection: "Dance of the Toy Flutes," *Nutcracker Suite,* Tchaikovsky (*Bowmar*)

ACTIVITY 1

Tell the story of Marie and the magic nutcracker.

ACTIVITY 2

Display a large picture of the flute (see Appendix D for sources) and describe the three dancing toy flutes of the story. Play the selection. On first hearing fade out after section A.

ACTIVITY 3

Review orally the ABA, or musical sandwich, form and listen to the whole movement, noting the return of the flutes. Prepare six theme cards of the first measure of theme 1. Use them in a pocket chart to announce each appearance of this theme.

♫ **ACTIVITY 4** _____

Another hearing may stress the staccato articulation of the flutes in A and the smooth legato of the trumpets in B.

♫ **ACTIVITY 5** _____

Listen to more flute solos performed by James Galway or Jean-Pierre Rampal.

♫ **ACTIVITY 6** _____

Listen to other dances from *The Nutcracker Suite,* "Land of the Sugar Plum Fairy."

String Family

Selection: "Romanze," *Eine Kleine Nachtmusik,* Mozart (*Bowmar*)

♫ **ACTIVITY 1** _____

Tell about Mozart's childhood as a musical little boy in Salzburg, making him a real person to your class. Describe how people in those days loved relaxing music played outdoors in the summertime since they had no portable radios. Mozart composed such music, and the selection is an example. Play the "Romanze" in its entirety.

♫ **ACTIVITY 2** _____

Discuss and illustrate the string family with pictures, and instruments if possible. Recall related experiences. Point out that only the instruments in the string family are heard in the "Romanze." Identify which instruments sing the higher and which the lower melodies, and describe the size and tone of each instrument. Play the opening A section and identify which stringed instrument plays the main theme. Repeat the playing of this opening theme and encourage children to hum or sing along.

♫ **ACTIVITY 3** _____

Start off with a puzzle. Clap the rhythmic pattern of the opening theme:

See if the group can recognize the pattern and can clap and hum it. A clue such as the three repeated opening tones may be helpful. Use blank rhythm cards to indicate the many occurrences of this motif during a complete hearing of the piece.

♫ **ACTIVITY 4** _____

Listen to contrasting string music such as square dance or fiddling tunes. You might play Guion's "Arkansas Traveler" or Copland's "Hoe-Down" (both on *Bowmar*).

Piano

Selection: Choose from the repertoire of great jazz artists such as Scott Joplin and Ray Charles.

ACTIVITY 1

Play a Scott Joplin fragment and note how the children respond to the strong rhythmic thrust and syncopation. Let them use their own words to describe how the music makes them feel. Do the same with a Ray Charles arrangement of an upbeat tune.

Tell a little about both of these men. Joplin, whose ragtime music was popularized in the movie *The Sting,* played and composed all his life. Charles plays modern jazz and is blind. Both men are black. Talk about what their music has in common.

ACTIVITY 2

Plan one or two miniconcerts of contemporary jazz and pop music, listening for piano parts or other keyboard instruments. Arrange a demonstration of electronic keyboards and stringed instruments such as guitars.

ACTIVITY 3

Make opportunities for children to improvise and experiment with keyboard instruments. In addition to the piano, portable chord organs, resonator bells, xylophones, metallophones, and glockenspiels might be available. Review with children the pentatonic scale (page 212). Show how to play it on the easy-to-locate black keys. On these twins and triplets one child may play an ostinato from a familiar song or one of her own creation, while another may improvise a melody to go along with it. Recording and playing back these compositions may lead children to revising their compositions and learning notation.

ACTIVITY 4

Explore with the children the world of classical piano music using live performers as well as recordings by such famous artists as Rubinstein, Horowitz, Watts, and Van Cliburn.

Voice

ACTIVITY 1

Replay several songs from your miniconcert tapes, identifying the singers. Be sure to include some adults who have sung for the group, as well as duets and trios. Talk about how we recognize the voices of those we know and what the differences are between children's, men's, and women's voices. Elicit descriptive words and reinforce those that identify vocal similarities and differences.

ACTIVITY 2

Make some short tapes of familiar singers such as Mr. Rogers, Kermit, Raffi, and other favorites. Try to avoid words or tunes that give away the identity of the singer. Have the children guess who the artists are. They may also record themselves trying to imitate one of these singers or someone else in the class.

ACTIVITY 3

Using well-contrasted recordings of solo singers (such as Marian Anderson and Julie Andrews), illustrate the differences between contralto and soprano voices. Extend these activities to contrast male voices and small ensembles versus massed choirs to demonstrate the great versatility of the human voice as a musical instrument.

As you continue your listening program, draw freely and creatively on fine recordings, interweaving them with the other strands of your music program. We have not tried to be prescriptive but have tried to show you some possible routes to follow. We have, however, dwelt in greater detail on live music listening and tape-recording first, to enhance children's personal listening enjoyment of commercial and other recordings. We have done this because we believe this is a practical and dynamic way to initiate young listeners into a lasting love and understanding of the vast world of music that awaits them.

NOTES

1. Evans, David. (1978.) *Sharing sounds.* London: Longman's, p. 130.
2. Lawrence, Ian. (1975.) *Music and the teacher.* London: Pitman and Sons, p. 14.
3. Ibid.

RELATED ACTIVITIES FOR STUDENTS

1. Survey the holdings in your college or university library for instrumental recordings designed for children's listening. From the offerings available, choose and carefully document five individual compositions. List for each composition the musical purposes that it could serve in a classroom listening experience.

2. Choose one of the following topics: tempo, rhythmic pattern, harmony, or pitch. Select and carefully document a short recorded composition suitable for teaching the topic. Based on the model used in this chapter, construct a sequence of activities to extend and reinforce the children's previous understanding of this topic.

3. Choose and document two well-contrasted popular compositions that you like and know well. If your choices are songs, be sure the words are suitable for young children. Develop a set of listening activities for children based on the model given in this chapter to demonstrate contrasts in style. Take into account other concepts such as mood, instruments, and rhythm.

4. Listen to the following marches (all on *Bowmar*):

   "Stars and Stripes Forever," Sousa.

   "March of the Little Lead Soldiers," Pierne.

   "March of the Siamese Children," Rodgers.

   "March" from *The Love for Three Oranges,* Prokofiev.

   Choose and document one of the marches. Plan a sequence of listening activities involving (a) basic movement (pages 179-181) and (b) using instruments to mark the accent or the strong beat (pages 207-209). The overall goal should be to reinforce the ability to listen to the rhythmic component of music.

Part Three

The Curriculum and Music

Music is a vital subject in its own right in today's school curriculum. Along with its sister arts it forms the aesthetic component of education for the whole child. It brings with it a particular body of knowledge, a vast range of participatory experiences and skills, and the opportunity to express and create. It is essential that music continue to be taught as a school subject to all children, not overshadowed by the role it plays in today's integrated curriculum. Parts One and Two of this book are dedicated to that purpose.

The role music plays in the overall curriculum, although a supporting one, is significant. Part Three of this book focuses on this aspect of music education. Current thinking on curriculum includes integrated subject matter, the whole language approach, thematic teaching, and a literature-based literacy program. All of these afford music a larger role in today's classrooms. Classroom teachers find songs, singing games, rhymes, and chants to be usable tools in their literacy programs, as well as in the content areas.

Chapter 10 introduces the activity cluster as a strategy for combining music with other curriculum areas. The chapter is divided into two sections. Section 1 provides four activity clusters dealing with language learning for emergent and early readers in the whole language approach to literacy. Section 2 contains three activity clusters integrating particular content areas of the curriculum. Both strategies have as their goal enhanced meaning for the learner. We hope that classroom and music teachers will cooperate in creating many new activity clusters of their own, based on the prototypes we present.

CHILDREN WITH SPECIAL NEEDS

It is our experience that children with special needs benefit from integrated learning and a holistic approach to curriculum. These approaches offer such children greater flexibility and a wider range of goals, increasing their opportunities to succeed. Implement these strategies sensitively, basing your plans on the examples provided and bearing individual needs in mind. Meaningful learning should be the goal for all children.

Chapter 10

Music and Integrated Learning

In our view, integrated learning is learning that crosses the lines separating traditional subject areas. We implement this by means of activity clusters, as a flexible and creative way of organizing content. *Activity clusters* consist of several developmentally appropriate activities with a common strand to give them unity, clustered around a starting point or "motivator." These activities may come from a variety of areas or disciplines. Language-based clusters draw on the language arts, literature, and, of course, music. Integrated curriculum clusters draw on one or more traditional subject areas and, of course, music.

Integrated learning draws deeply from story, in both oral and written form, bringing books into close relationship with music and other subject areas. We therefore introduce this chapter with a song that may be used in many different contexts and at different levels.

READ A BOOK TO ME

Key: G
Starting tone: B

Tom Pease

This upbeat chorus is part of Tom Pease's song about a week without TV. The whole story unfolds on his tape: *I'm Gonna Reach**. Since we do not have room for all eight verses, we are grateful for his permission to share the chorus, which children love, and we append one verse of our own, for emergent readers!

> I want to learn to read the way the grown-ups do.
> I want to read the pictures and the story too.
> So bring me stories every day
> And very soon I'll know the way
> To read-a-read-a-read-a-read-a-book to you!

*Tomorrow River Music, Box 165, Madison, WI 53701

Section 1: The Music and Language Connection

The relationship between language and music is a natural and close one, and there are many parallels between them. Especially in the early years, the two go hand in hand. Words, rhythm, melody, and movement combine to enhance learning and increase the young child's active participation in it. Primary age children enjoy practicing and extending their new skills and knowledge through finger plays, rhymes and chants, singing games, and songs. Teachers capitalize on this by making strong connections between all kinds of music and whole language activities in their classrooms. Figure 1 shows clearly that the objectives of both the music specialist and the classroom teacher may be realized from the same starting point: a musical activity.

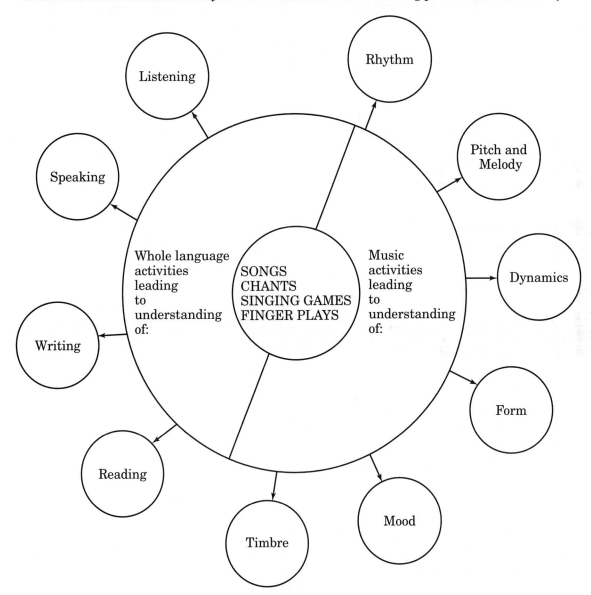

Figure 1 ♦

Three clusters of field-tested activities are included in this section. Each cluster addresses a topic, has music at its core, and extends the musical experience to language and literature-related activities. All of them involve listening, expressing ideas and feelings, using previous knowledge and experience, decoding and interpreting symbols, and working cooperatively. In addition, specific musical and language learnings occur in every activity cluster. These are listed at the end of each one. Be sure to use the activity clusters as prototypes, rather than follow them minutely. As you do, you'll see the music-language connection grow stronger every day.

ACTIVITY CLUSTER 1: COLORS _____

AT THE EASEL

Key: C
Starting tone: G

Thomas Moore*

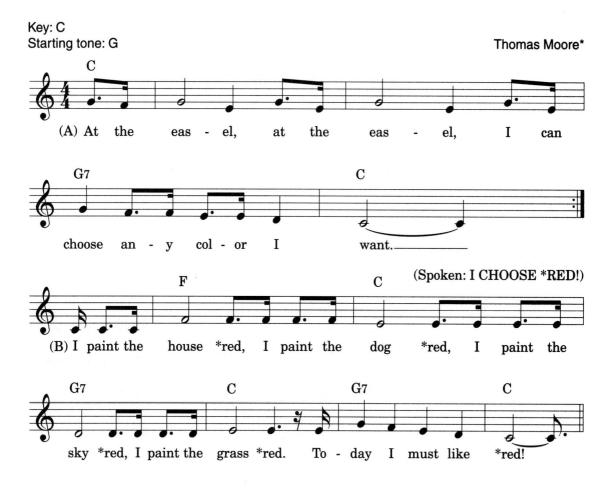

(A) At the eas - el, at the eas - el, I can

choose an - y col - or I want._____

(Spoken: I CHOOSE *RED!)

(B) I paint the house *red, I paint the dog *red, I paint the

sky *red, I paint the grass *red. To - day I must like *red!

_____
*Thomas Moore Records, 4600 Park Rd. #1000, Charlotte, NC 28209

1. Teach the song "At the Easel." Add a clapping rhythm on beats 2 and 4:

$$\frac{4}{4} \mid \quad - \quad \overset{\times}{|} \quad - \quad \overset{\times}{|} \quad \mid$$
$$\quad 1 \quad 2 \quad 3 \quad 4$$

2. Share a book about the color red:
   Finding Red by Betsy Imershein (Harcourt Brace Jovanovich)
   Red Is Best by Kathy Stinson (Annick Press)
   Who Said Red? by Keiko Narahashi (Macmillan)

3. Teach the song "Red Is Best."

RED IS BEST

Key: C
Starting tone: E

Traditional Melody
Words: J. Haines

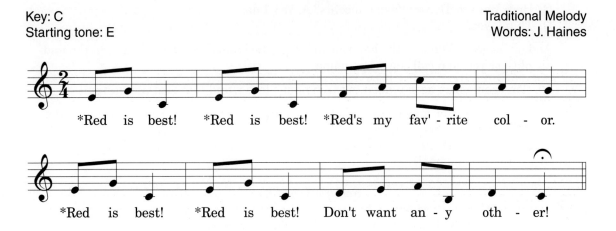

4. Review both songs, adding colors of children's choice.
5. Use word cards to change the colors at asterisks.
6. Discuss how colors affect feelings; ask children to make associations.
7. Sing the songs in different moods to match the colors: gray (mysterious voices), yellow (smiley, sunny), purple (rich, royal), green (like Kermit!).
8. Form small groups of those with the same favorite color. Have each group make its own "Color Is Best" book or poster, share it, and sing either song to the class.
9. Children who are unsure of their colors may learn by playing the singing game "Balloons for Sale!"

BALLOONS FOR SALE!

Key: F
Starting tone: C

J. Haines

The children sit in a circle with the balloon man in the center. He holds a bunch of colored balloons and walks around as the children sing. At the end of the song he sells a balloon to the child where he stopped, as follows:

Q. Would you like to buy a balloon today? A. Yes, please.
Q. What color would you like? A. Red, please.
Q. Here you are. Do you have ten cents? A. Yes, I do.
Q. Thank you!

And on he goes. When all the balloons are sold, the balloon man may stand in the middle of the circle and call the colors home.

10. This game may be extended to teach name, letter, and numeral recognition.

This activity cluster may be extended to include work on other colors by changing the songs and finding other books. Start with *Of Colors and Things* by Tana Hoban (Greenwillow), *Mouse Paint* by Ellen Walsh (Harcourt Brace Jovanovich), and *Seven Blind Mice* by Ed Young (Philomel).

Specific Learnings

Music	*Language*
Off-the-beat rhythm	Color knowledge
Singing of fifth and descending scale-wise	Name, letter, and numeral recognition
Chord tones: tonic and dominant	Changing text and meanings
Adapting rhythm to text	Writing and illustrating own text
Matching style to mood	New words, new feelings

ACTIVITY CLUSTER 2: DAYS OF THE WEEK —————————————

TODAY IS MONDAY

Key: F
Starting tone: C

J. Haines

1. Teach or review the song "Today Is Monday" (see also the Spanish version "Hoy, Hoy Es Lunes," page 143).
2. Write *work* and *play* on the chalkboard.
3. Add and sing other words that the children offer, substituting them for *work* and *play*.
4. Add three or four more pairs of the children's words to the list. The list may be similar to the following:

work	play
song	story
recess	snack
reading	writing
fun	p.e.

Sing each verse. Put children's initials by their contributions.

5. Have the children make observations about the words in the list. Kindergarteners may make comments such as the following:

They're all different.

Three start with *s.* Two start with *r.* One has a double letter.

Two have *-ing.*

One has two initials.

Two end with *y.*

There are words with two, three, four, five, six, and seven letters.

There are three *a*'s, four *e*'s, three *i*'s, three *o*'s, and one *u.*

Why does *writing* start with *w* and sound like *reading* and *recess?*

6. Write (each phrase in) the verse on a strip of oaktag, as shown below. The underlined words are movable and should be on separate strips.

> Today is *Monday,*
> Today is *Monday.*
> What shall we do today?
> We'll have a *work* time,
> We'll have a *play* time.
> That's what we'll do today.

7. Write the names of other days of the week and words from the children's list on
   cards. Have the children create new verses by adding their word cards to the verses.
8. Teach the following song:

OH, MRS. GRADY

Traditional melody
Adapted by Aden G. Lewis
and J. Haines

Key: F
Starting tone: C

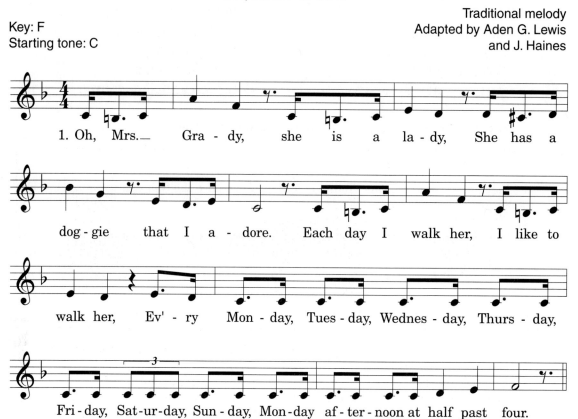

1. Oh, Mrs.— Gra - dy, she is a la - dy, She has a dog - gie that I a - dore. Each day I walk her, I like to walk her, Ev' - ry Mon - day, Tues - day, Wednes - day, Thurs - day, Fri - day, Sat - ur - day, Sun - day, Mon - day af - ter - noon at half past four.

2. Oh, Mrs. Grady, she is a lady,
   She has a pony that I adore.
   Each day I ride her,
   I like to ride her,
   Ev'ry Tuesday, Wednesday,
     Thursday, Friday,
   Saturday, Sunday,
     Monday, Tuesday
   Afternoon at half past four.

3. Oh, Mrs. Grady, she is a lady,
   She has a kitty that I adore.
   Each day I pet her,
   I like to pet her,
   Ev'ry Wednesday, Thursday,
     Friday, Saturday,
   Sunday, Monday,
     Tuesday, Wednesday
   Afternoon at half past four.

4. Oh, Mrs. Grady, she is a lady,
   She has a piggie that I adore.
   Each day I feed her,
   I like to feed her,
   Ev'ry <u>Thursday</u>, Friday,
     Saturday, Sunday,
   Monday, Tuesday,
     Wednesday, Thursday
   Afternoon at half past four.

5. Oh, Mrs. Grady, she is a lady,
   She has a bunny that I adore.
   Each day I stroke her,
   I like to stroke her,
   Ev'ry <u>Friday</u>, Saturday,
     Sunday, Monday,
   Tuesday, Wednesday,
     Thursday, Friday
   Afternoon at half past four.

6. Oh, Mrs. Grady, she is a lady,
   She has a monkey that I adore.
   Each day I brush her,
   I like to brush her,
   Ev'ry <u>Saturday</u>, Sunday,
     Monday, Tuesday,
   Wednesday, Thursday,
     Friday, Saturday
   Afternoon at half past four.

7. Oh, Mrs. Grady, she is a lady,
   She has a baby that I adore.
   Each day I hug her,
   I like to hug her,
   Ev'ry <u>Sunday</u>, Monday,
     Tuesday, Wednesday,
   Thursday, Friday,
     Saturday, Sunday
   Afternoon at half past four.

9. Post clue cards such as the following for each verse:

doggie   walk

pony   ride

kitty   pet

10. Create seven cards for the days of the week. Have seven children hold the cards up in sequence starting with the new day in each verse.
11. Share the book *One Monday Morning* by Uri Shulevitz (Macmillan).
12. Give a percussion instrument to each of nine children who play the nine characters in the book. Read the story again. Each child sounds his instrument every time his character is mentioned.
13. Share the books *Cookie's Week* by Cindy Ward (Scholastic) and *Today is Monday* by Susan Baum (HarperCollins).
14. Review the song "Sardines" (page 56). Use five vowel sounds and two-beat motions instead of claps.
15. Make word cards and strips available for independent use.

Specific Learnings

Music	*Language*
Two new songs for repertoire	Two new stories
Repeated tones	Synonyms and antonyms
Chromatic intervals	Word analysis

♪ ACTIVITY CLUSTER 3: NAMING, RHYMING, AND OPPOSITES —————

WHERE IS THE CEILING?

Key: E♭
Starting tone: B♭

J. Haines

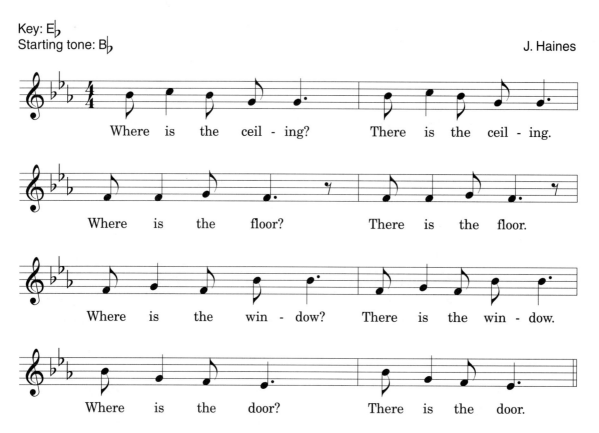

Where is the ceil - ing? There is the ceil - ing.

Where is the floor? There is the floor.

Where is the win - dow? There is the win - dow.

Where is the door? There is the door.

2. Where is the table?
   There is the table.
   Where is the chair?
   There is the chair.
   Where is your face?
   Here is my face.
   Where is your hair?
   Here is my hair.

3. Where is your mouth?
   Here is my mouth.
   Where is your nose?
   Here is my nose.
   Where is your head?
   Here is my head.
   Where are your toes?
   Here are my toes.

4. Where is your ankle?
   Here is my ankle.
   Where is your thigh?
   Here is my thigh.
   Where is down low?
   Here is down low.
   Where is up high?
   Here is up high.

5. Where are your hands?
   These are my hands.
   Where are your feet?
   These are my feet.
   Where is your chest?
   This is my chest.
   Please take your seat.
   This is my seat.

1. Teach the song "Where Is the Ceiling?" It may be sung as a question-answer song between the teacher and the class, or between a lead child or group and the class. The verses may be sung in any order and new ones made up. Make sure the words and motions in each answer are accurate. "Show me" may be used instead of "Where is." This song helps to assess comprehension and diction in children who speak English as a second language.

2. Teach the following singing game. First prepare a carton to use as a cupboard. Put one or more objects in it. Include familiar objects: small toys; cards with names, letters, or numerals; shapes; animal or food pictures; and so on. Give a pretend key to a child who goes to the cupboard as the song is sung. On the third phrase she opens it up, chooses an object, and after "What do you see?" announces the name of the object. She passes the key on and the game is repeated. Children may also be asked to find specific objects in the cupboard, showing and naming them after the question.

I HAVE A LITTLE CUPBOARD

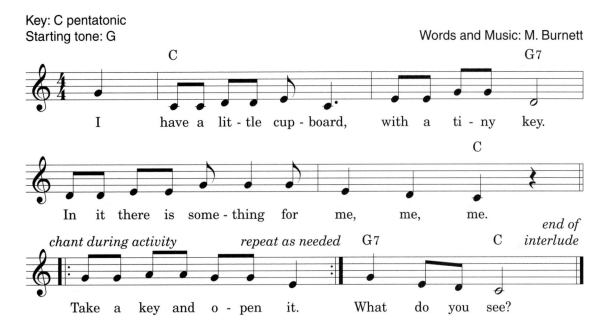

Key: C pentatonic
Starting tone: G

Words and Music: M. Burnett

3. Share Tana Hoban's *Of Colors and Things* (Greenwillow) or Jane Miller's *Farm Alphabet* (Prentice Hall).

4. On a neighborhood walk, start individual children singing "I can see a (bicycle, big red truck, yellow dog, and so on)" to the tune of "Do You Know the Muffin Man?"

5. Share the following poem. Chant it rhythmically with a patsch. The first verse will be memorized in no time.

ALLIGATOR PIE

Dennis Lee

Alligator pie, alligator pie,
If I don't get some I think I'm gonna die.
Give away the green grass, give away the sky,
But don't give away my alligator pie.

Alligator stew, alligator stew,
If I don't get some I don't know what I'll do.
Give away my furry hat, give away my shoe,
But don't give away my alligator stew.

Alligator soup, alligator soup,
If I don't get some I think I'm gonna droop.
Give away my hockey-stick, give away my hoop,
But don't give away my alligator soup.

6. Mime the second line of each verse as you teach this poem. Verse 1: Let head roll forward, close eyes. Verse 2: Look up, shrug shoulders, raise arms. Verse 3: Flop forward limply, from the waist. (This may help you avoid the children vulgarizing verse 3.)
7. Fours and fives enjoy changing "alligator" to the names of other creatures. Post a list of the animals they name along with each child's initials.
8. Fives and sixes, after starting with alligator, can select more unusual animal names in alphabetical order, such as brontosaurus, caterpillar, dinosaur, elephant, and so on.
9. Sixes and sevens can select animals from different classes, such as swimmers, flyers, egg-layers, meat-eaters, and fur-bearers, or based on the number of syllables in the animals' names.
10. Sevens and eights can fill the board with a list of alligator dishes, such as cake, bread, and jam, and then vote to select one they will rhyme with. Have them compose whole verses, assisting as needed. The two "give away" items should be a related pair. Offer the following to start them off:

Alligator bread, alligator bread,
If I don't get some I think I'll go to bed.
Give away my needle, give away my thread,
But don't give away my alligator bread.

11. Post the new verses and chant from them.
12. Share Raffi's book *Down by the Bay* (Crown).

13. Teach the song "I Can Say Up," first as an echo song, then as a question-answer song. Use the verses in any order but always sing verse 10 last.

I CAN SAY UP, I CAN SAY DOWN

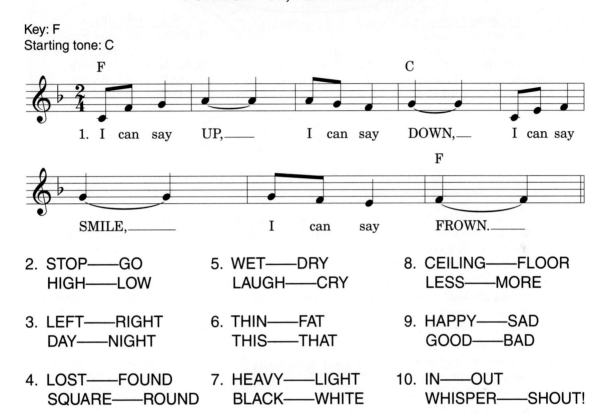

Key: F
Starting tone: C

2. STOP——GO   5. WET——DRY   8. CEILING——FLOOR
   HIGH——LOW   LAUGH——CRY   LESS——MORE

3. LEFT——RIGHT   6. THIN——FAT   9. HAPPY——SAD
   DAY——NIGHT   THIS——THAT   GOOD——BAD

4. LOST——FOUND   7. HEAVY——LIGHT   10. IN——OUT
   SQUARE——ROUND   BLACK——WHITE   WHISPER——SHOUT!

14. Help the children to make up more verses as a class. Give them clues: for example, you might supply the ending words for phrases 1 and 3, such as "COME" and "FAST" or "HOT" and "YOUNG." Ask them what words they could use for phrases 2 and 4.
15. Share the book *Becca Backward, Becca Frontward* by Bruce McMillan (Lothrop, Lee, and Shepard) or *The Sheepish Book of Opposites* by George Mendoza (Grosset and Dunlap).
16. Have children work in twos to illustrate a page of opposites for a big class book, and then make miniatures for take-home reading.

Section 2: Music and the Integrated Curriculum

The current stress on thematic teaching and integrating the curriculum contributes to the making of meaning by the learner. Activity clusters offer a practical way of crossing curricular boundaries and using several subject areas to reinforce a central topic. We use a musical activity as the "motivator," planning each cluster in diagram form.

Gather together several activities that share a common factor; choose a sure-fire musical activity as your starting point; put it in the center of your cluster and encircle it with the others. Note, as you do this, the different subject areas represented by these activities. It is desirable to integrate material from three or more areas of the curriculum, as in the examples that follow.

ACTIVITY CLUSTER 1: PEANUT BUTTER

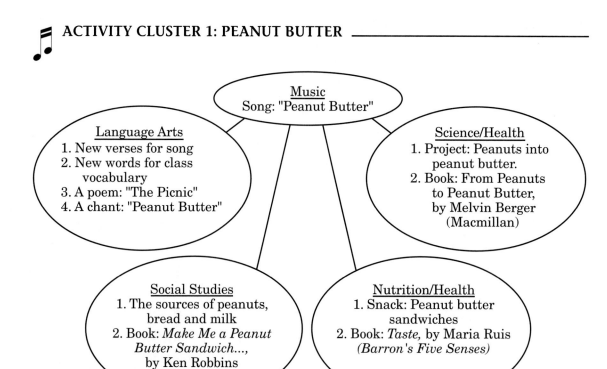

1. Teach the song "Peanut Butter."

PEANUT BUTTER

Key: c
Starting tone: C

Eileen Packard

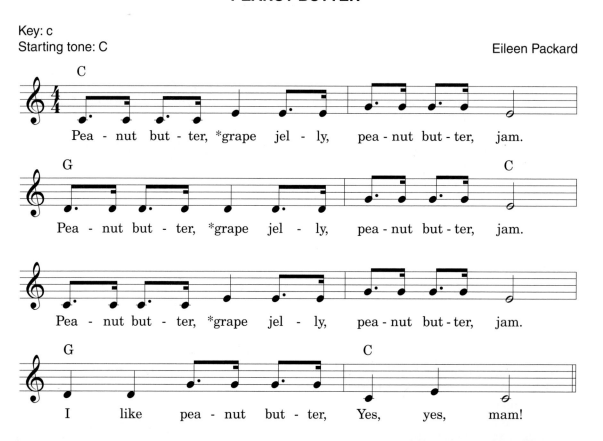

The following interdisciplinary activities, used in any order and over several days, will develop new knowledge and skills.

2. Ask children for ideas to replace "grape jelly." Sing the new verses they create and add the words to the class vocabulary charts.
3. Teach the chant "Peanut Butter" to accompany number 4 below. This chant combines both speech and song.

PEANUT BUTTER

Key: E
Starting tone: F♯

Refrain   Camp Song

Pea - nut,____   pea - nut   but - ter,__   jel - ly!

1. First you   dig   the   pea - nuts,   and you   dig 'em,   you dig 'em.

You   dig   'em,   dig   'em,   dig   'em,   then   you

crush 'em,   you   crush 'em.   You   crush 'em, crush 'em, crush 'em, then you

spread 'em,   you   spread 'em.   You   spread 'em,   spread 'em,   spread 'em. *Refrain*

2. Then you pick the berries,
   and you pick 'em, you pick 'em . . .
   then you crush 'em, you crush 'em . . .
   then you spread 'em, you spread 'em . . . *Refrain*

3. Then you bite the sandwich,
   and you bite it, you bite it . . .
   and you munch it, you munch it . . .
   Then you swallow, you swallow . . . *Refrain*

4. Make peanut butter for a snack. Note quantities used and changes observed.
5. Serve and eat the peanut butter on bread and share the poem "The Picnic":

THE PICNIC

Dorothy Aldis

We brought a rug for sitting on.
Our lunch was in a box.
The sand was warm. We didn't wear
Hats, or shoes or socks.

The waves came rolling up the beach.
We waded. It was fun!
Our sandwiches were different kinds.
I dropped my jelly one!

6. Discuss the sense of taste, using the book *Taste* by Maria Ruis (*Barron's Five Senses Series*).
7. Share two information books at any appropriate time: *From Peanuts to Peanut Butter* by Melvin Berger (Macmillan) and *Make Me a Peanut Butter Sandwich and a Glass of Milk* by Ken Robbins (Scholastic).

♫ ACTIVITY CLUSTER 2: THE MUSICIANS OF BREMEN: A FOLK TALE _____

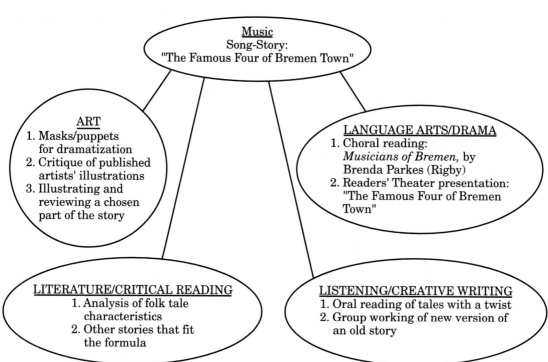

1. Teach this song as the theme for a Readers' Theater presentation:

Oh   Brem - en Town is   down the road. And that's the place to   go.
We'll   go   and sing in Brem - en Town. We'll be   all right, you know.

2. Discuss briefly the story referred to here. It should be familiar, but may have some variations.
3. Lead a choral reading of Parkes' Big Book, *Musicians of Bremen* (Rigby) and explain that *The Famous Four of Bremen Town* follows the same outline.
4. Give out the text and have all survey it for the song, singing it each time it is found. Note the change of words in the last repeat.

THE FAMOUS FOUR OF BREMEN TOWN*

The parts are indicated as follows:

1: Donkey
2: Dog
3: Cat
4: Rooster
N: Narrator

All children speak the lines underlined and sing the animals' chorus and citizens' finale.

N: Once upon a time there was a donkey. He'd lived on his farm <u>for years and years and years.</u>

> <u>The Donkey grew too old to work,</u>
> <u>But still he liked to bray.</u>
> <u>They didn't want him any more,</u>
> <u>And so he ran away.</u>

1: HEE-HAW! HEE-HAW!
N: On the very next farm there was a dog. He'd lived on his farm <u>for years and years and years.</u>

> <u>The Dog, he grew too old to work,</u>
> <u>But still his bark was grand.</u>
> <u>They didn't want him any more,</u>
> <u>So he joined Donkey's band.</u>

2: WOOF-WOOF! WOOF-WOOF!
N: The donkey and the dog sang to each other:

Animals' chorus

Oh   Brem - en Town is   down the road. And that's the place to   go.
We'll   go   and sing in Brem - en Town. We'll be   all right, you know.

1: HEE-HAW! HEE-HAW!
2: WOOF-WOOF! WOOF-WOOF!

N: On the very next farm there was a cat. He'd lived on his farm <u>for years and years and years.</u>

<u>The Cat, he grew too old to work,</u>
<u>But still his meow was hearty.</u>
<u>They didn't want him any more,</u>
<u>So he joined Donkey's party.</u>

3: MEE-OW! MEE-OW!
N: The donkey and the dog and the cat sang to each other:.

Animals' chorus

Oh   Brem - en Town is   down the road. And that's the place to   go.
We'll   go   and sing   in   Brem - en Town. We'll be   all right, you know.

1: HEE-HAW! HEE-HAW!
2: WOOF-WOOF! WOOF-WOOF!
3: MEE-OW! MEE-OW!
N: On the very next farm there was a rooster. He'd lived on his farm <u>for years and years and years.</u>

<u>The Rooster grew too old to work,</u>
<u>But still his crowing rang.</u>
<u>They didn't want him any more,</u>
<u>So he joined Donkey's gang.</u>

4: COCK-A-DOODLE-DOO!
N: The donkey and the dog and the cat and the rooster sang to each other:

Animals' chorus

Oh   Brem - en Town is   down the road. And that's the place to   go.
We'll   go   and sing   in   Brem - en Town. We'll be   all right, you know.

1: HEE-HAW! HEE-HAW!
2: WOOF-WOOF! WOOF-WOOF!
3: MEE-OW! MEE-OW!
4: COCK-A-DOODLE-DOO!

N: The four musicians started off.
            They were a funny foursome.
            They brayed and barked and meowed and crowed.
            The noise was really awesome!

All four together:

    1: HEE-HAW! HEE-HAW!
    2: WOOF-WOOF! WOOF-WOOF!
    3: MEE-OW! MEE-OW!
    4: COCK-A-DOODLE-DOO!

    N: The sun went down. They felt so tired—
                           No food, no place to sleep.
                           At dead of night they saw a light
                           Within the forest deep.

    1:                     "I see a house,"
    N: the Donkey said.
    2:                     "Let's look!"
    N: the Dog replied.
                           And from the windowsill they saw
                           Three robbers were inside.

    3:                     "They're eating food! And counting coins!"
    4:                     "Let's scare them, if we can!"
    1–4:   "They'll run if we sing loud enough!"
    N: And so the song began.

Together:

    1: HEE-HAW! HEE-HAW!
    2: WOOF-WOOF! WOOF-WOOF!
    3: MEE-OW! MEE-OW!
    4: COCK-A-DOODLE-DOO!

    N: The robbers left! The four moved in!
                           They ate and went to bed.
                           And soon the thieves came creeping back.
                           <u>"We'll turn them out!"</u> they said.

                           But all at once a monster sprang!
                           It flapped its wings and crowed!
                           It kicked and bit and scratched until
                           It drove them down the road!

Together, twice through:

    1: HEE-HAW! HEE-HAW!
    2: WOOF-WOOF! WOOF-WOOF!
    3: MEE-OW! MEE-OW!
    4: COCK-A-DOODLE-DOO!

Citizens' finale

Now Brem - en has a con - cert at the end of ev' - ry day.
The neigh - bors come and lis - ten, But the rob - bers stay a - way!

Together:

> 1: HEE-HAW! HEE-HAW!
> 2: WOOF-WOOF! WOOF-WOOF!
> 3: MEE-OW! MEE-OW!
> 4: COCK-A-DOODLE-DOO!

◆ ———————————————————————— ◆

5. Divide the class into four groups and model an animal sound for each group. Practice the sounds.
6. On the first reading, narrate all the text with the children adding animal sounds and song as indicated. (**Note:** Very young children can participate in this song-story up to this point.)
7. Add the group readings as underlined and repeat the whole piece. Several rehearsals will be needed. (A child may take the Narrator's role.)
8. Children may make masks or stick puppets for the presentation.
9. Invite an audience to hear the Readers' Theater present "The Famous Four of Bremen Town."
10. Children may compare illustrations of the story by different artists, giving reasons for their preferences.
    (*The Bremen Town Musicians* by Ruth B. Gross, Scholastic Book/Cassette; *Musicians of Bremen* by Brenda Parkes, Rigby Big Book; *The Bremen Town Musicians* by Brenda Parkes, Rigby Big Book; *The Bremen Town Musicians* by Bernadette Watts, North-South Books, hardback)
11. Children enjoy choosing and illustrating their own favorite parts of the story and critiquing their own work.
12. Outline the formula followed in this and many folk tales, and find others that use the same pattern.
13. Share folk tales with a new twist, such as *The Paper Bag Princess* by Robert Munsch (Annick Press) and *The True Story of the Three Little Pigs* by Jon Scieszka (Viking).
14. Lead a group to experiment with creating a new twist to an old tale.

♫ ACTIVITY CLUSTER 3: USING NUMBERS ——————————————

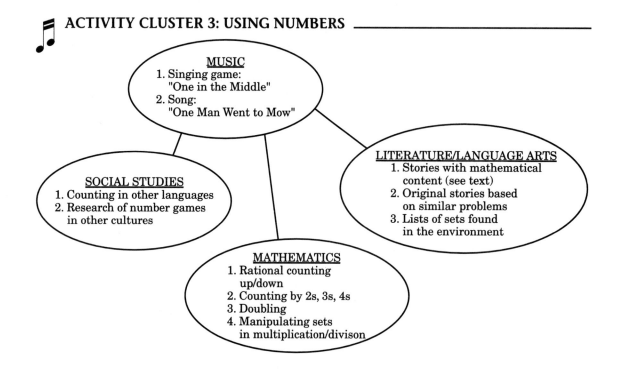

1. Teach the following two songs over several days:

ONE IN THE MIDDLE

Key: F pentatonic
Starting tone: F

American Singing Game

2. Swing you another and another one in.

3. Two in the middle . . .

The children hold hands in a circle and walk clockwise. One child in the middle, the leader, walks at random, pretending to look for a way out. On verse 2, the children stand still and clap the beat while the leader chooses a second child and draws her into the circle, and they swing each other around. On each repeat of the game, the last child chosen brings a new child in until as many are inside as the circle can contain. Then all drop hands and move around freely singing: "All in the middle and we dance about."

ONE MAN WENT TO MOW

Key: E♭ major
Starting tone: G

Folk Song

1. One man went to mow, Went to mow a mead-ow.

One man and his dog Went to mow a mead-ow.

2. Two men went to mow, Went to mow a mead-ow.

Two men, one man and his dog Went to mow a mead-ow.

3. Three men went to mow . . .
Three men, two men, one man and his dog etc.

Intersperse the following activities as appropriate:

2. Share the following and/or other stories focusing on division and multiplication:
   The Doorbell Rang by Pat Hutchins (Morrow)
   The Half-Birthday Party by Charlotte Pomerantz (Clarion)
   Discuss similar problems and write original stories.
3. Share the following and/or other stories focusing on set theory:
   What Comes in 2's, 3's, and 4's? by Suzanne Aker (Simon and Schuster)
   Create a class/list book of sets found in the environment.
4. Develop/reinforce the mathematical skills of rational counting, counting by 2s, etc.,
   doubling, and simple division and multiplication.

5. Count in other languages. Where possible, initiate this activity through class members with non-English-language skills. Some samples follow:

	Spanish	Swahili	Navajo	French
1	uno	moja	t'ááta'í	un
2	dos	mbili	naaki	deux
3	tres	tatu	táá'	trois
4	cuatro	nne	díí'	quatre
5	cinco	tano	'ashdla'	cinq
6	seis	sita	hastáá	six
7	siete	saba	tsosts'id	sept
8	ocho	nane	tseebíí	huit
9	nueve	tisa	náhást'éí	neuf
10	diez	kumi	neeznáá	dix

6. Teach these number games/songs: Obwisana (page 27) and Uno, Dos y Tres (page 84).
7. Research and play number games from other cultures.

RELATED ACTIVITIES FOR STUDENTS

1. Choose one of the activity clusters in this chapter and arrange to teach a group of children several of the activities.

2. Choose a whole language or an integrated curriculum topic and create an activity cluster around it, referring to the models presented.

3. Add one song/chant/singing game to three of the clusters in the chapter, with teaching notes.

4. Add one appropriate book to three of the clusters presented, documenting it carefully and stating its value in the cluster.

In Conclusion

The teaching of music has a twofold purpose. It opens the door for children to enter the world of music with understanding, so that they may experience, interpret, and enjoy the music. It also enables them to create music for themselves and for others.

Each child has the ability to convey some idea, some concept, or some feeling that expresses his or her unique combination of talents and abilities and unique experiences. This expression, the outpouring of the self, needs a form to give it existence outside of its creator. Our task, therefore, is not only to establish the supporting, accepting atmosphere that gives children the desire to experience and create but also to teach them the vocabulary of music which gives them a means for expression. When this is achieved, children have access to music not only to enrich their lives but to meet their needs, stimulate their minds and senses, and suit their individual creative purposes.

We hope that Part One of this book deepens your understanding of children, of music, and of your role as a teacher. We hope you also share our discovery that children who experience the varied musical activities of Parts Two and Three grow in their love of music. They sing, move, play, and listen sensitively and well. They have quick ears, responsive bodies, and a repertoire of skills and competencies on which they draw with confidence and in innovative ways. These are the rewards of leading young children to music!

Appendix A

Examples of Incidental and Planned Teaching

The following examples of incidental and planned music lessons are geared for different age groups. They apply to different group settings and use different materials and kinds of musical activity. Each one has at least one musical skill as its major goal, along with others that the reader may identify. They are offered only as suggestions or guidelines; what works for one teacher and setting may not work for another. We urge you to take your planning seriously, do it thoroughly, commit your music to memory, and have your materials ready.
Be sure to review:

1. Criteria for Choosing a Song, p. 132
2. Teaching a New Song, p. 132
3. Three Ways to Start a Song, p. 133

While these preparations will not guarantee success with every lesson, they will minimize problems you may encounter. Above all, they will give you confidence that can make each teaching experience rewarding and joyful.

Incidental Teaching

Here are several examples of incidental teaching.

♪ EXAMPLE 1 ────────────────────────────────────

A group of city day-care children is finishing a midmorning snack that is to be followed by a walk. The teacher chants:

These chants may be repeated, sung in a different order, used to incorporate children's names, or turned into questions requiring answers. As the children gather, the teacher begins the song "I Live in a City," singing the refrain several times as the group leaves the building and crosses the school yard. On returning, he sings the refrain again before story time, and many of the children now join in, singing and clapping. This experience encourages in-tune singing and introduces a new song with a strong rhythmic beat, in an incidental way.

♪ EXAMPLE 2 ────────────────────────────────────

A group of kindergarten children sit with a teacher developing a language experience chart about signs of spring. An observant child sees a robin on the grass outside the window and excitedly draws attention to it. The teacher immediately begins the song "As I Looked Out My Window," changing the words of the third phrase to "I saw Robin Redbreast." He repeats the song once or twice. By then, the children begin to join in the echo parts. Later the event is included in the group's story. This incident is used to teach a new song, enhancing listening and tone-matching skills.

♪ EXAMPLE 3 ────────────────────────────────────

A second grade class stands in two lines at the classroom door ready to go to the lunch room, with two or three minutes to spare. The teacher says, "Let's sing 'Where is the Ceiling?' while we're waiting. This line sings the questions, this line sings the answers." The song is sung through and repeated with reversed roles before the lunch bell rings. Here a familiar song is sung in a new way, incidentally involving children in the beginning skills of part singing.

♫ EXAMPLE 4 _____

A third grade class rides the school bus back from a field trip. The children are tired, noisy, and quarrelsome. The teacher initiates a clapping pattern with those sitting nearby:

This is quickly picked up by the rest of the group. Soon the teacher announces clearly, "Now let's clap this rhythm":

When this is established, the patterns are clapped in turn by those on alternate sides of the bus. The teacher, now up front, conducts the activity and brings the volume down to a quieter level. Then the teacher begins to sing the familiar song "Chatter with the Angels." Since the children know this song well and have played melodic ostinati to it in the classroom, they have little difficulty in singing along, while alternate groups clap the rhythmic ostinati as before. Here the teacher changes a difficult negative situation into a good one by skillful use of incidental teaching.

Planned Teaching

The following lesson plans will be helpful as a guide in formulating your own plans. Notice that you begin by stating your objective and build your plan around that statement. At times you will have more than one objective; in addition to your musical goal, some objectives may relate to other areas of your program. This is appropriate; music may be integrated with other curricular areas and program goals (see Chapter 10).

Lesson Plan 1

The following is a ten-minute lesson plan for three- and four-year-olds in a nursery school setting.

Musical Objective. The children will participate in a group musical activity and movement with the beat in a new action song.

Materials
"Tommy Thumb's Up" (p. 77)
"Freight Train, Freight Train" (p. 45)
"We'll All Clap Hands Together" (p. 75)
"Good News!" (p. 79)

Procedures
1. *Familiar material and warm-up activities:*
Finger Play: "Tommy Thumb's Up"
Chant: "Freight Train, Freight Train"
2. *Reinforcement of previous skill:*
Movement to the beat
Repeat "Freight Train," substituting clapping for rhythmic hand rubbing.
Conclude with a loud clap on the three different ending words.

3. *New learning:* "We'll All Clap Hands Together"
Continue hand clapping and introduce the new song, maintaining a clear, steady beat. Discuss other body sounds, repeating the song with each action identified by the children. Add one or two silent rhythmic movements such as "We'll nod our heads" or "We'll blink our eyes."

4. *Culminating activity:*
Change the words for the song just used to "We'll go for snack together," repeating until all children are seated. Conclude with one verse of "Good News!" with "Snack is coming" as new words for this familiar song.

Evaluation. Can most children clap on the beat in the new song? Can many children clap and sing at the same time? Can some children perform other movements with a steady rhythm? Can some children suggest and model successfully new rhythmic movements?

Lesson Plan 2

The following is a twenty-minute lesson plan for six-year-olds in a classroom setting.

Musical Objective. The children will increase their ability to sing in tune.

Materials
> "I Have a Song" (p. 129)
> "As I Looked Out My Window" (p. 126)
> "Oh My, No More Pie" (p. 56)
> "A Little Black Dog" (p. 99)
> "Starlight, Starbright" (p. 123)
> Resonator bells/xylophone

Procedures

1. *Familiar material and warm-up activities:* "I Have a Song"

   Sing the song once, without repeats. Repeat the song using the repetition of each phrase as an echo between teacher and children. Repeat song with a child in the teacher's role and an individual child echoing.

2. *Reinforcement of previous skill:* Accurate tone matching

   Review "As I Looked Out My Window" and add echo-singing procedure as above.

3. *New learning:* "Oh My, No More Pie"

   Direct the children to echo each phrase they hear you sing. Sing the whole song, supporting the pitch with a half-note ostinato on the D resonator bell:

Divide the class into two groups. Repeat the song, singing to each group in turn in echo fashion. When (and if) the singing is secure, assign the accompaniment to a child with a strong rhythmic sense. Reverse the order of the groups and repeat the song if practice is needed or interest is high.

4. *Culminating activity:*

   Concentrated singing activity like this needs to be followed by a vigorous singing game: "A Little Black Dog." End the lesson with the familiar song "Starlight, Starbright." Reinforce the lesson's objective during the singing of this song.

Evaluation. Can most children echo the minor third interval (*sol-mi*) in tune? Can the majority of children echo new song material with reasonable accuracy? Can the class sing a song in tune with an instrumental accompaniment?

Note: "Oh My, No More Pie" is learned quickly because of the sequential rhyme scheme and three-tone melody. In the follow-up lesson, a child will be able to take the leadership role in the song.

Lesson Plan 3

The following is a thirty-minute lesson plan for eight-year-olds in a classroom setting.

Musical Objective. The children will create, play, and sustain a melodic ostinato as an accompaniment to group singing.

Materials
"Hush You Bye" (p. 146)
"Chatter with the Angels" (p. 220)
"Three Bears' Jive" (p. 59)
"Who's Got a Fishpole?" (p. 219)
Resonator bells/xylophone

Procedures
1. *Familiar material and warm-up activities:*

   Sing "Hush You Bye," adding a clapping ostinato appropriate to the abilities of your children.

2. *Reinforcement of previous skill:*

   Review the song "Chatter with the Angels," including the familiar melodic ostinato on the resonator bells or xylophone:

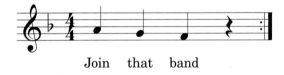

Join   that   band

   Extend this activity by having a small group sing the melodic ostinato "ALL DAY LONG" and play it on the bells to accompany the remainder of the class. Switch groups and repeat if interest is high.

3. *Relaxation and change of pace:*

   Act out the familiar song-story "The Three Bears' Jive."

4. New learning: Based on the known song "Who's Got a Fishpole?"

Sing the song through, checking intonation, diction and tempo. Elicit from the children two or three parts of the song for melodic ostinati, notating them on the board. Play each suggestion as the children sing the first verse. After discussion, choose the most suitable ones, erasing others. Allocate instruments available and practice one of the ostinati chosen as an accompaniment to the singing. If proficiency warrants, a second pattern may now be learned and added. Now the song may be sung by two groups in question-and-answer fashion with one ostinato accompanying the questions, the other accompanying the answers, and both groups playing on the last phrase. The children must listen to the three strands of music being played and sung. Remind instrumentalists to sing the song as they play the ostinati to develop their musical skill. This will need practice but it is very rewarding and should be extended.

Note: The culminating activity of this lesson is the performance of the song with its instrumental accompaniments.

Evaluation. Can most children sing and clap accurately a rhythmic ostinato? Can most children sing and play accurately a melodic ostinato? Do all children understand what an ostinato is? Can some find usable patterns from known material? How many different melodic accompaniments can the group sustain while singing?

Lesson Plan 4

The following is a thirty-minute lesson plan for seven- and eight-year-olds in a classroom setting.

Musical Objective. The children will demonstrate through movement, graphically and verbally, their understanding of ABA form in music.

Materials

"This Train" (p. 139)
"Freight Train, Freight Train" (p. 45)
Recording of "Dance of the Sugar Plum Fairy" by Tchaikovsky

Procedures

1. *Familiar material:*

   Song: "This Train"

   Chant: "Freight Train, Freight Train" (omit "yes, no, maybe so")

2. *Reinforcement of previous skill:*

   Sing and chant the above in the following order, patching the beat throughout:

   a. "This Train" (A)

   b. "Freight Train" (B)

   c. "This Train" (A)

3. *New learning:*

   Work out a four-beat clapping pattern to the middle section ("Freight Train"). Repeat the entire sequence as in step 2,

substituting the new motions to "Freight Train." Lead a discussion on the musical sandwich the children have created, having them draw or diagram it on the chalkboard or describe it in words: "We sang and patsched. We chanted and clapped. We sang and patsched." Introduce the term ABA to describe this musical form.

4. *Application:*

   Apply this new understanding to a listening activity by playing a recording of "Dance of the Sugar Plum Fairy" by Tchaikovsky (*Bowmar Orchestral Library*) or any similar ABA instrumental piece. Ask the children to listen to it, remembering what they have just experienced.

   Note: Explain your plan to work out this selection in movement (as a Reinforcement Activity) in the next lesson.

5. *Culminating activity:*

   A lively song of the children's choice.

Evaluation. Did the children participate in the activities of step 3 using the chalkboard, oral language, or movement? Did the children use appropriate graphic symbols, movements, or words to show their understanding of ABA form? Was the repetition of part A shown by a repetition of movements or symbols used the first time?

Appendix B

Accompanying Children's Singing

Children's singing may be supported and enhanced by instrumental accompaniments. If you play the piano or electronic keyboard, use your skill to accompany songs once they are known and sung tunefully. Avoid teaching a song by the repeated playing of its melody; use the voice as your teaching tool.

Chording instruments also add harmonic and rhythmic color to class singing. The two most frequently used are the autoharp and the guitar. Most songs in this book include appropriate chord patterns above the staff.

The Autoharp

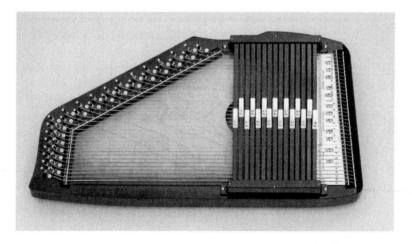

The autoharp is a stringed instrument with a flat sounding box that is played horizontally using the fingertips and a plectrum. Both fifteen- and twenty-one-bar models are suitable for classroom use.

For strumming you may use a pick or the back of the fingertips of the right hand. A felt pick or the fingers produce the best tone for accompanying young voices. The autoharp must be kept in good tune. As a beginner you will be wise to have this done for you by a music teacher, a music specialist, or a good music store technician. Later you will be able to do it yourself.

The Omnichord, made by Suzuki, is an electronic instrument suitable for classroom use. With no strings to strum, buttons are used for chording and for six rhythmic accompaniments. In addition, a harp effect can be created by stroking across a touchplate, and there are controls for volume and tempo. It requires no tuning, and batteries or an adapter provide the power.

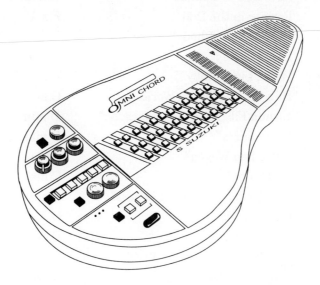

The following table lists the most frequently used keys with their basic chords:

Chord Table

Key name	I chord	IV chord	V_7 chord
G major	G maj.	C maj.	D_7
C major	C maj.	F maj.	G_7
F major	F maj.	$B^\flat$ maj.	C_7
D major	D maj.	G maj.	A_7
A minor	A min.	D min.	E_7
D minor	D min.	G min.	A_7
G minor	G min.	—	D_7

The I chord is built on the first tone or tonic of the major scale. The IV chord is built on the fourth tone or subdominant tone of the major scale. The V_7 chord is built on the fifth tone or dominant tone of the major scale, with an added seventh tone. The chord table will enable you to play many one-, two-, and three-chord songs by ear:

One-Chord Songs	*Key*
"Are You Sleeping?"	F maj.
"Row, Row, Row Your Boat"	C maj.
"Skip One Window"	C maj.
"There's a Hole in My Bucket"	F maj.

Two-Chord Songs	
"Bow, Bow O Belinda"	G maj.
"Farmer in the Dell"	F maj.
"Go Tell Aunt Rhody"	F maj.
"Hokey Pokey"	G maj.
"Hush, Little Baby"	F maj.
"He's Got the Whole World"	C maj.
"Joshua Fit the Battle of Jericho"	D min.
"Kookaburra"	D maj.
"Little Red Wagon"	F maj.
"Looby Loo"	C maj.
"My Hat It Has Three Corners"	C maj.
"Paw-Paw Patch"	G maj.
"Oh Chiapanacas"	F maj.
"One, Two, Three, Four, Five"	F maj.
"Polly Wolly Doodle"	D maj.
"Skip to My Lou"	C maj.
"Six Little Ducks"	F maj.

Three-Chord Songs	
"Happy Birthday"	F maj.
"Happy Wanderer"	C maj.
"Home on the Range"	F maj.
"I'm Gonna Sing"	G maj.
"O Susanna"	F maj.
"Old MacDonald Had a Farm"	F maj.
"This Land is Your Land"	F maj.
"This Old Man"	F maj.
"Who Built the Ark?"	G maj.
"Jingle Bells"	F maj.
"Silent Night"	C maj.
"Camptown Races"	C maj.
"Old Brass Wagon"	F maj.
"Red River Valley"	F maj.
"Twinkle, Twinkle, Little Star"	D maj.

Many songs with more than three chords can be played on the autoharp. After you have mastered the three-chord songs and feel confident enough to use the autoharp with children, look through this book for songs with four or more chords. Many songs in other books for children are also chorded. Expand your repertoire and your facility in playing so that you can use your autoharp to enhance your music program. Happy playing!

The Guitar

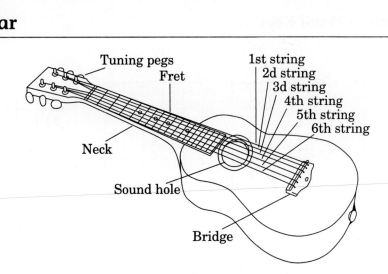

GUITAR TUNING   GUITAR FINGERING

Piano keyboard   Guitar strings   Left Hand finger numbers:

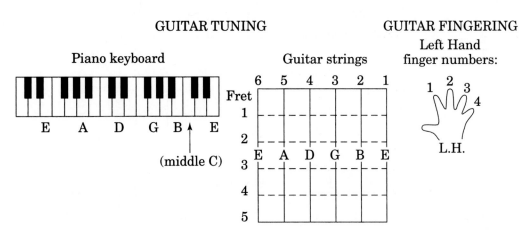

Guitar Chords in Major Keys

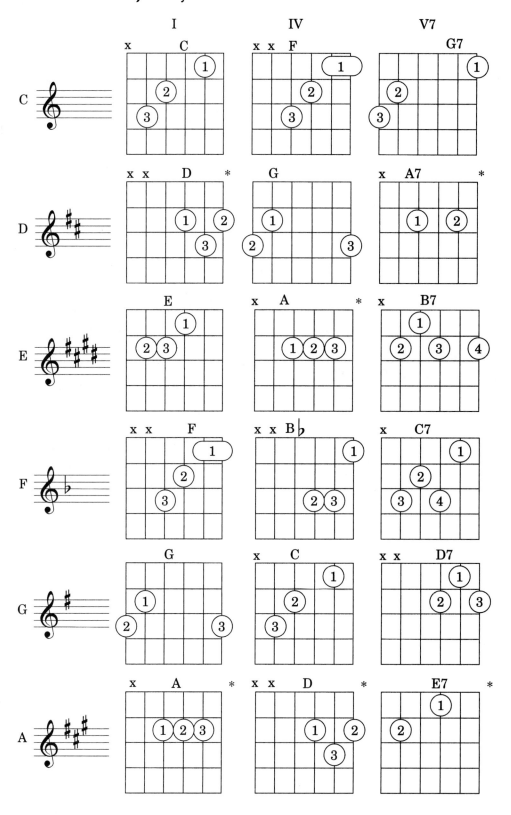

Strings marked with an *X* are not sounded. Strings with no finger number and no *X* are played as open strings. An asterisk (*) indicates chords easily fingered by beginners.

Guitar Chords in Minor Keys

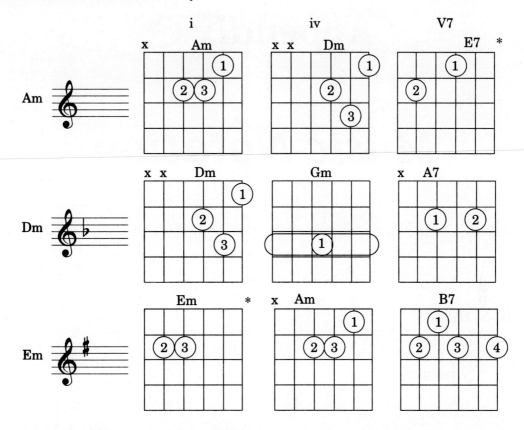

Strings marked with an X are not sounded. Strings with no finger number and no X are played as open strings. An asterisk (*) indicates chords easily fingered by beginners.

Appendix C

Music Notation

Basic Symbols

The Staff

Clef Signs

G or Treble Clef

F or Bass Clef

Names of Lines and Spaces

G or Treble Clef

F or Bass Clef

The Grand Staff (Key of C Major)

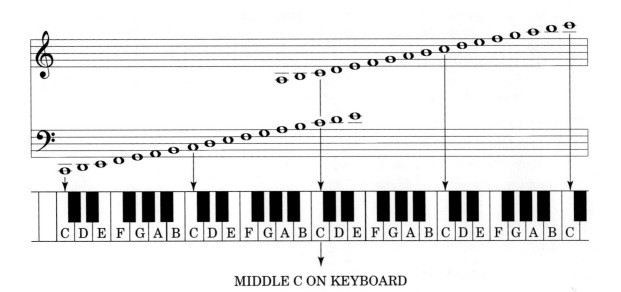

MIDDLE C ON KEYBOARD

Key Signatures or Tonal Centers

To identify major and minor tonal centers from key signatures, use the following guidelines:

- In a key signature of sharps, the sharp farthest right is the seventh tone, or *ti*. The next line or space above is the eighth tone, or *do*, the tonal center for the major key. The next line or space below is the sixth tone, or *la*, the tonal center for the minor key.
- In a key signature of flats, the flat farthest right is the fourth tone, or *fa*. Count downward on the lines and spaces to the first tone, or *do*, for the major tonal center; then count upward five steps to *la*, the sixth tone, for the minor tonal center.

Accidental signs written before the note have the following effects:

♭ (flat): lowers the pitch one half step

♯ (sharp): raises the pitch one half step

♮ (natural): cancels a flat or sharp

Notes and Rests

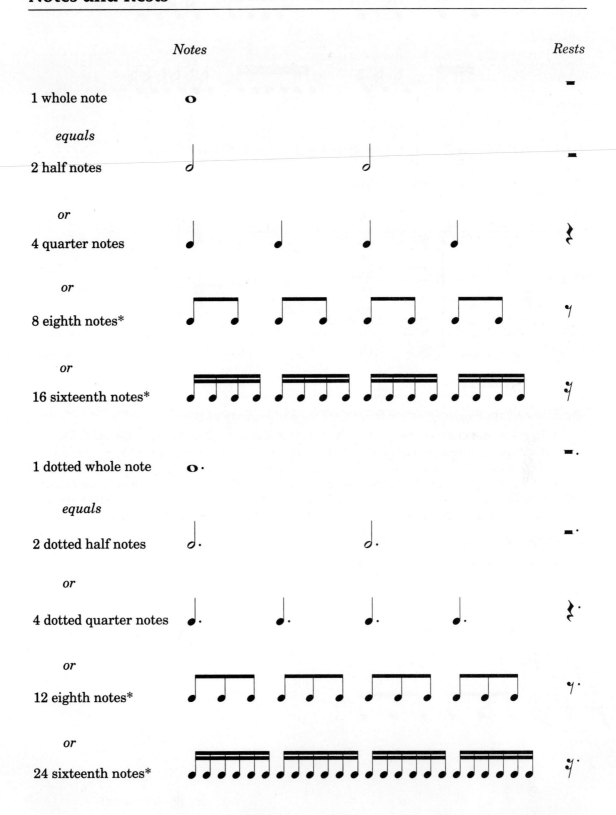

	Notes	Rests
1 whole note	o	—
equals		
2 half notes		—
or		
4 quarter notes		♩
or		
8 eighth notes*		
or		
16 sixteenth notes*		
1 dotted whole note	o·	■·
equals		
2 dotted half notes		■·
or		
4 dotted quarter notes		♩·
or		
12 eighth notes*		
or		
24 sixteenth notes*		

Notes (indicated with an asterisk) may also be written separately from each other. When this is done, the flags are changed as shown:

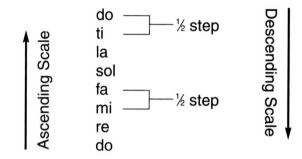

Tonic Sol-Fa Syllables for the Diatonic Major Scale

This scale may be read in either direction:

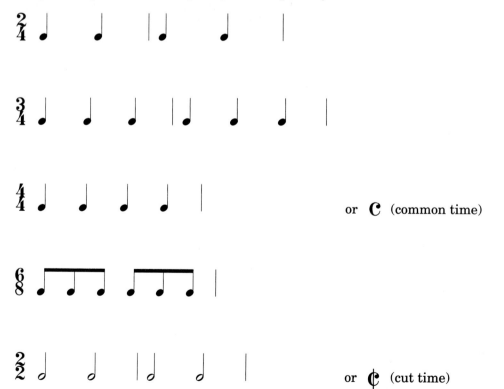

Time Signatures

The following time signatures are frequently used in primary music:

$\frac{2}{4}$ ♩   ♩ |♩   ♩ |

$\frac{3}{4}$ ♩   ♩   ♩ |♩   ♩   ♩ |

$\frac{4}{4}$ ♩   ♩   ♩   ♩ | or **C** (common time)

$\frac{6}{8}$ ♫♪ ♫♪ |♫♪ ♫♪ |

$\frac{2}{2}$ 𝅗𝅥   𝅗𝅥 |𝅗𝅥   𝅗𝅥 | or **¢** (cut time)

The top numeral indicates the number of beats in a measure. The bottom numeral tells which kind of note is the basic beat.

Appendix D

Sources and Resources

Bibliography

Child Development

College students are directed to library holdings and course recommendations for current readings on child growth and development.

Bee, Helen. (1997). *Life span development* (2nd ed.) New York: Addison-Wesley

Bredekamp, Sue, ed. (1997). *Developmentally appropriate practice in early childhood programs serving children from birth through age 8.* Washington, DC: National Association for the Education of Young Children.

Edwards, Linda C. (1990). *Affective development and the creative arts.* Upper Saddle River, NJ: Merrill/Prentice-Hall.

Elkind, David. (1994). *A sympathetic view of the child from birth to sixteen* (3rd ed.). Boston: Allyn and Bacon.

Hendrick, Joanne (1995). *The whole child* (6th ed.). Upper Saddle River, NJ: Merrill/Prentice-Hall.

Music Texts

The decision as to where to list particular books is a rather subjective one. Readers should note that some books in the "Music Texts" section contain useful resource material as well as good text. Similarly, some of the listings under "Music Resource Books" contain sound textual material.

Anderson, William M. et al. (1998). *Integrating music into the elementary classroom.* Belmont, CA: Wadsworth.

Andress, Barbara. (1998) *Music for children.* Orlando, FL: Harcourt Brace and Company.

Andress, Barbara, and Linda Walker, eds. (1992). *Readings in early childhood music education.* Reston, VA: Music Educators National Conference.

Aronoff, Frances W. (1980). *Music and young children* (2nd ed.). New York: Holt, Rinehart and Winston.

Atterbury, Betty W. (1990). *Mainstreaming exceptional learners in music.* Upper Saddle River, NJ: Merrill/Prentice-Hall.

Barrett, Janet et al. (1997). *Sound ways of knowing: Music in the interdisciplinary classroom.* New York: Schirmer.

Bayless, Kathleen M., and Marjorie Ramsey. (1991). *Music: A way of life for the young child* (4th ed.). Upper Saddle River, NJ: Merrill/Prentice-Hall.

Bennett, Peggy D., and Douglas R. Bartholomew (1997). *Songworks,* Belmont, CA: Wadsworth.

Campbell, Patricia Shehan, and Carol Scott-Kassner. (1995). *Music in childhood.* New York: Schirmer.

Carder, Polly, ed. (1990). *The eclectic curriculum in American music education.* Washington, DC: Music Educators National Conference.

Evans, David. (1978). *Sharing sounds: Musical experiences with young children.* New York: Longman.

Frazee, Jane, with Kent Kreuter. (1987). *Discovering Orff.* New York: Schott.

Jaques-Dalcroze, Emile. (1921). *Eurhythmics, music, and education.* New York: G. P. Putnam's Sons.

Katz, Susan A., and Judith Thomas. (1992). *Teaching creativity by working the word.* Upper Saddle River, NJ: Merrill/Prentice-Hall.

McDonald, Dorothy T., and Gene M. Simons. (1989). *Musical growth and development: Birth through six.* New York: Schirmer.

Mead, Virginia H. (1994). *Dalcroze eurhythmics in today's music classroom.* Valley Forge, PA: Schott.

Michon, Rozmajzl, and René Boyer-White. (1997). *Music fundamentals, methods and materials for the elementary classroom teacher* (2nd ed.). White Plains, NY: Longman's.

Moog, Helmut. (1976). *The musical experience of the pre-school child.* London: Schott.

Moomaw, Sally. (1984). *Discovering music in early childhood.* Boston: Allyn and Bacon.

Moomaw, Sally. (1997). *More than singing: Discovering music in preschool and kindergarten.* St. Paul, MN: Redleaf Press.

Palmer, Mary, and Wendy L. Sims. (1993). *Music in prekindergarten: Planning and teaching.* Reston, VA: Music Educators National Conference.

Steen, Arvida. (1992). *Exploring Orff.* New York: Schott.

Upitis, Rena. (1990). *This too is music.* Portsmouth, NH: Heinemann.

Upitis, Rena. (1992). *Can I play you my song?* Portsmouth, NH: Heinemann.

Music Resource Books

Abramson, Robert M. (1973). *Rhythmic games for perception and cognition.* New York: Music and Movement Press.

Andress, Barbara L. (1973). *Music in early childhood.* Washington: Music Educators National Conference.

Birkenshaw, Lois. (1986). *Music for fun, music for learning* (3rd ed.). Toronto: Holt, Rinehart and Winston.

Birkenshaw-Fleming, Lois. (1989). *Come on everybody, let's sing!* Toronto: Gordon V. Thompson Music Pub.

Bradford, Louise Larkins. (1978). *Sing it yourself: 220 pentatonic folk songs.* Sherman Oaks, CA: Alfred.

Burnett, Millie. (1975). *Dance down the rain, sing up the corn.* Allison Park, PA: Musik Innovations.

Burnett, Millie. (1990). *All about me* (I like to sing, Vol. 1), Van Nuys, CA: Alfred.

Campbell, Patricia S., Ellen McCullough-Brabson, and Judith C. Tucker. (1994). *Roots and branches.* Danbury, CT: World Music Press. (Multicultural book with cassette/CD)

Choksy, Lois, and David Brummit. (1987). *120 singing games and dances for elementary schools.* Upper Saddle River, NJ: Merrill/Prentice-Hall.

Cohn, Amy L. (1993). *From sea to shining sea: A treasury of American folklore and folk songs.* New York: Scholastic.

Ebinger, Virginia Nylander. (1993). *Ninez—Spanish songs, games and stories of childhood.* Santa Fe, NM: Sunstone Press.

Feierabend, John, and Gary Kramer. (1987). *Music for very little people* (with optional cassette). Farmingdale, NY: Boosey and Hawkes.

———. (1989). *Music for little people* (with optional cassette). Farmingdale, NY: Boosey and Hawkes.

Findlay, Elsa. (1971). *Rhythm and movement: Applications of Dalcroze eurhythmics.* Evanston, IL: Summy Birchard.

Hall, Mary Ann. (1989). *Take a bite of music, it's yummy!* Westport, CT: Music for Children.

Jenkins, Ella. (1993). *This is rhythm.* Chicago: Sing Out Pub.

Joyce, Mary. (1993). *First steps to teaching creative dance to children* (3rd ed.). Palo Alto, CA: Mayfield.

Palmer, Hap. (1993). *Musictivity: Sing me a story* (book and CD). Milwaukee, WI: Hal Leonard.

Regner, Hermann, ed. (1977). *Music for children.* Princeton, NJ: European-American Music Corp. Orff-Schulwerk (American ed.), Vol. 2: Primary.

Saliba, Konnie K. (1991). *Accent on Orff: An introductory approach.* Upper Saddle River, NJ: Merrill/Prentice-Hall.

Seeger, Ruth. (1980). *American folk songs for children.* New York: Doubleday.

Sullivan, Molly. (1982). *Feeling strong, feeling free: Movement exploration for young children.* Washington, DC: National Association for the Education of Young Children.

_____. (1991). *Teaching music with a multicultural approach.* Reston, VA: Music Educators National Conference. (four videos also available)

Weikart, Phyllis. (1989). *Teaching movement and dance.* (3rd ed.). Ypsilanti, MI: High/Scope Press.

Weikart, Phyllis. (1989). *Movement plus music, activities for children ages 3–7* (2nd ed.). Ypsilanti, MI: High/Scope Press.

Weikart, Phyllis S. (1997). *Movement plus rhymes, songs and singing games* (2nd ed.). Ypsilanti, MI: High/Scope Press.

Music Series Books

Jane Beethoven, Dulce Bohn, Patricia Shehan Campbell, Carmen E. Culp, Jennifer Davidson, Lawrence Eisman, Sandra Longoria Glover, Charlotte Hayes, Martha Hilley, Mary E. Hoffman, Hunter March, Bill McCloud, Marvelene Moore, Catherine Nadon-Gabrion, Mary Palmer, Carmino Ravosa, Mary Louise Reilly, Will Schmid, Carol Scott-Kassner, Jean Sinor, Sandra Stauffer, Judith Thomas. (1995). *The music connection.* Morristown, NJ: Silver Burdett Ginn.

Coordinating Authors: Judy Bond, Marilyn Copeland Davidson, Mary Goetze, Vincent P. Lawrence, Susan Snyder. Authors: René Boyd-White, Margaret Campbell-du Gard, Robert de Frece, Doug Goodkin, Betsy M. Henderson, Michael Jothen, Carol King, Nancy L. T. Miller, Ivy Rawlins. *Share the music.* (1995). New York: Macmillan/McGraw-Hill School Publishing Company.

Edwin E. Gordon. *Jump right in! The music curriculum.* (1986). Chicago: G.I.A. Publications.

Eunice Boardman Meske, Barbara Andress, Mary Pautz, Fred Willman. *Holt Music.* (1988). New York: Holt, Rinehart and Winston.

Sources of Music Materials

There are many places to find excellent CDs, tapes, instruments, and music materials for young children. Following is a representative list of companies who sell quality music education materials. They all offer good service and will answer any questions you might have.

Elderly Instruments
1100 N. Washington
Lansing, MI 48906

Magnamusic-Baton, Inc.
10370 Page Industrial Blvd.
St. Louis, MO 63132

Music is Elementary
P.O. Box 24263
Cleveland, OH 44124

Peripole Bergerault, Inc.
2041 State St.
Salem, OR 97301

Rhythm Band, Inc.
P.O. Box 126
Fort Worth, TX 76101

West Music Company (also World Music
  Publications)
P.O. Box 5521
1208 Fifth St.
Coralville, IA 52241

Professional Organizations and Publications

Association for Childhood Education
  International (ACEI)
11141 Georgia Ave., Suite 200
Wheaton, MD 20902
Journal: *Childhood Education*

Day Care and Child Development Council
  of America Inc. (DCCDCA)
1401 K St., N.W.
Washington, DC 20005

Educational Resources Information
  Center/Early Childhood Education
  (ERIC/ECE)
805 West Pennsylvania Avenue
Urbana, IL 61801

Foundation for Music-Based Learning
P.O. Box 4274
Greensboro, NC 27404-4274
Journal: *Early Childhood Connections*

Music Educators National Conference
  (MENC)
1902 Association Dr.
Reston, VA 22091
Journal: *Music Educators Journal*

National Association for the Education of
  Young Children (NAEYC)
1834 Connecticut Ave. N.W.
Washington, DC 20009
Journal: *Young Children*

United States Department of Education
Office of Child Development
Children's Bureau
Washington, DC 20201
Journal: *Children Today*

Glossary

AB   A musical design that has two contrasting segments, A and B; also called *binary form.*

ABA   A musical design with three segments, A, B, and a repetition of A—forming a musical "sandwich"; also called *ternary form.*

Accelerando   Increase of speed in music.

Accent   Stress of one tone over others, making it stand out; often the first beat of the measure.

Accidental   Sign written before a single note (or measure) that alters the pitch of the note for one measure only and does not appear in the key signature. The accidentals are ♯ (sharp), ♭ (flat), and ♮ (natural).

Accompaniment   Music that goes along with a more important part; often harmony or rhythmic patterns accompanying a melody.

Arhythmic movement   A sequence of motions based on no perceptible or constant beat or pattern.

Atonal music   Music that has no home tone, tone center, or key; that is, music that has no identifiable family of tones.

Auditory awareness   The ability to distinguish between the presence and absence of sound.

Auditory discrimination   The ability to distinguish between sounds, with respect to their source, direction, duration, and pitch.

Auditory sequencing   The ability to reproduce a sequence of sounds in the order presented and perceived.

Autoharp   A stringed instrument with chord bars that are pressed down as the strings are strummed so that only the tones belonging to the desired chord are heard; in the classroom used chiefly for harmonic accompaniment.

Axial movement   A wide range of physical motions, large or small, performed while the body remains in one location.

Bar line   A vertical line through the staff to delineate a measure of music.

Beat   The continuing and steady pulse that is heard or felt in most music, moving the music forward in time.

Blank rhythms   Rhythmic patterns without specific pitches; often represented visually by notes and rests not written on the staff.

Cadence   A point in the melodic or harmonic structure of music that marks the end of a phrase or musical idea.

Call and response   A form of singing or chanting in which a phrase given as a solo is answered by a group, either as an echo or a contrast.

Canon   A song in which two (or more) groups sing the same melody but start at different times, each singing the song once. A *round* is a canon that is repeated, each voice going back to the beginning.

Chanting   May be described as halfway between speech and song. The words are uttered very rhythmically, and the pitches, sometimes identifiable, lie within a small range.

Chord   A chord consists of three or more musical tones. If they are sounded together, they form a *block chord;* if sounded in sequence, they form an *arpeggio,* or harplike chord.

Chording instruments   Instruments that have, or can be tuned to, specific pitches to provide chordal accompaniments to melodies or chants. Examples include the autoharp, piano, guitar, ukulele, and banjo.

Chord tones   The tones of a scale that are used to build a specific chord. They often appear in sequence in the melodies of songs, providing easy intervals or jumps that help to develop in-tune singing.

Chromatic scale   A sequence of twelve tones using only half steps or semitones.

Chromatic tone cluster   A group of tones sounded simultaneously that contains tonal and half-tone intervals not found in the chord structure of an established key; such clusters often consist of tones played at random on the piano for a special effect.

Color-coding   The use of familiar colors attached to tuned or melody instruments to enable young children to record on paper melodies or tonal sequences that they first create by playing.

Crescendo   Gradual increase in volume, written ━━◁━ .

Cumulative song   As the name implies a song that starts out naming one item and accumulates an additional one with each repeat.

Dalcroze, Emile Jaques   A Swiss musician and educator (1865–1950) who created an approach to music through movement.

Decrescendo   Gradual decrease in volume, written ▷━━━ .

Descending minor third   The interval of two and a half tones between *sol* and *mi;* frequently the first interval intoned by young children.

Diatonic scale   A sequence consisting of five whole tones and two half steps, using all the pitch names (see *Major scale* and *Minor scale*).

Dominant seventh chord (V₇)   A four-tone chord built on the fifth step of the scale and including the interval of a seventh as its fourth tone.

Duration   The length of time a tone, chord, or rest is sustained.

Dynamics   Degrees of loudness and softness, changes in volume, and the stress of one tone over others—all giving variety and meaning to music.

Echo singing   Singing that requires the exact repetition, in rhythm, pitch, and words, of a phrase or melodic fragment.

Ensemble   A group of musicians who sing or play together.

Eurhythmics   The expressive use of the body as an instrument, increasing musical responsiveness and understanding.

Fermata   The musical sign (⌢) that indicates the holding of a tone, chord, or rest for longer than its normal duration.

Finger play   Gestures that accompany and dramatize strongly rhythmic words (spoken, chanted, or sung).

Flat   A musical symbol (♭) that lowers a written pitch by one half step. When the symbol appears in a key signature, it lowers the pitch throughout the piece.

Form   A component of all the arts, musical form is the structure or plan on which a piece of music is based, giving it both design and unity.

Four chord (IV)   The three-tone chord built on the fourth tone or subdominant of the scale: *fa-la-do.*

Glissando   A rapid upward or downward scale played by sliding over every tone of the instrument. On the piano the thumbnail is often used to obtain the desired effect.

Glockenspiel   A metal instrument resembling the xylophone with bars (often removable) of varying length that are played with mallets. The bars produce accurate and bell-like pitches. The instrument is often associated with the Orff Schulwerk approach to music.

Half tone   The smallest interval notated and used in Western music; also called a *half step* or *semitone.*

Harmony   The sound resulting from two or more tones being sung or played simultaneously, as in part singing or playing a chording instrument.

Improvisation   Spontaneously created music, either sung or played on an instrument, that may or may not have an underlying melodic, rhythmic, or harmonic structure. The pentatonic scale lends itself well to melodic improvisation for children.

Inner ear   Refers to the ability to hear sounds (musical and other) within the mind when they are not actually being perceived through a sense of hearing.

Instrumentation   The selection of instruments most suitable for playing a particular piece of music.

Interval   The difference in pitch between two tones, or the number of whole and half tones separating them.

Key   The scale in which a piece of music is heard or written. The first or lowest tone of the scale gives the key its name and is also the focal point or home tone of the music. Keys may be in the major or minor mode.

Key chord   The three-tone chord built on the first tone (I) of the scale; also called the *tonic* or *home chord.*

Key signature   In written form, the sharps or flats at the beginning of a piece of music to show the tonic or home tone and the scale of the music (see Appendix C).

Kodaly, Zoltan   A Hungarian composer and educator (1882–1967) who developed music education for children from three years of age on. Singing and rhythmic activities form the basis of his method, which stresses ethnic pentatonic songs, special syllable names for note values, and hand signs to reinforce the sol-fa syllables. The method bears his name.

Legato   Singing or playing sounds in a smooth, connected manner. See also *Staccato.*

Locomotor movements   Motions that move the body from one place to another in space and through time. Basic locomotor movements include even motions, such as walking of many kinds and speeds, running, rolling, twisting, hopping, jumping, and sliding, and uneven movements, such as skipping and galloping.

Lyrics   Words designed to be sung to a melody or chant. They may be poetry or prose, but they will be clearly rhythmic and have a close relationship with the melody line.

Major scale   A sequence of tones with one half step between the third and fourth tones and another between the seventh and eighth tones (the octave); the other five intervals are whole steps. The sol-fa names for the tones are *do, re, mi, fa, sol, la, ti, do.*

Measure   A group of equal beats defined by bar lines. The first beat of each group is usually accented, and the beats recur consistently throughout a composition, as designated by the time signature.

Melody   A sequence of single pitches moving through time with rhythmic organization.

Metallophone   A xylophone-type instrument with removable tuned metal bars that are played with mallets; part of the Orff Instrumentarium.

Meter   A basic grouping of beats, usually within a measure.

Minor scale   A scale having a half step between the second and third tones known as a minor third.

Mood   The feelings music can arouse, usually described with adjectives such as *happy, sad, carefree, martial, lazy, frightening,* and so on.

Natural sign   A musical symbol (♮) that cancels a flat or sharp.

Notation   A system of symbols used to record music in written form, including the duration and pitch of each tone.

Note values   Visual symbols that can be translated into sounds of different duration (see Appendix C).

Octave   The eighth tone of the diatonic scale bearing the same name as the first and in perfect consonance with it, sounding like it at a different pitch.

Omnichord   An electronic instrument for chording and rhythm accompaniments.

Orchestration   A plan that designates which instruments in an ensemble (orchestra or band) will play and in what combinations.

Orff, Carl   A German composer and educator (1895–1982) whose schoolwork in music (the Orff Schülwerk) parallels the development of both music and the human being. Speech, movement, and folk music combine with percussive and tuned instruments of Orff's design (the Orff Instrumentarium) to achieve a total musical experience.

Ostinato   A short rhythmic or melodic pattern that is closely related to the music it accompanies and is repeated "obstinately." (Plural: *ostinati.*)

Patschen   Rhythmic thigh-slapping often accompanying chants or songs associated with Orff's Schulwerk. (Verb: *patsch.*)

Pentatonic scale   A five-tone scale (*do-re-mi-sol-la*) without the semitones found in the diatonic scale, most easily located on the black piano keys (G♭, A♭, B♭, D♭, E♭). The scale can originate on any tone and is useful for playing ostinati and melodic improvisation.

Percussion instruments   Instruments that are played by shaking or striking and may be either pitched or unpitched.

Phrase   The unit of musical meaning; a statement in sound with a beginning and ending, comparable to a sentence in the spoken word.

Phrase-wise approach   A method of teaching rote songs in which a phrase is dictated by the teacher and imitated by the learners. When all segments are learned, the song is put together.

Pitch   The lowness or highness of a musical tone, determined by the number of vibrations per second.

Pulse   The underlying, steady rhythm present in all music, whether heard or sensed; another name for *beat.*

Range   The distance between the highest and lowest tones in any musical passage.

Repeat sign   Written ⫾‖ , this sign means go back and sing or play again either from the beginning or from the sign ‖⫾.

Repertoire   The number of items known in any particular category, such as finger plays, rote songs, part songs.

Resonator bells   A series of tuned metal bars (diatonic or chromatic) mounted on individual blocks of wood or plastic and played with rubber mallets.

Rest   A symbol used to indicate the duration of a pause or silence in music; each note value has a corresponding rest sign (see Appendix C).

Rhythm   The aspect of music that relates to the duration of sounds in time; the ordering of long and short tones to give both unity and diversity to music.

Rhythmic pattern The varied sequence of long and short tones within a musical passage, often contrasting with the regular and steady beat.

Ritardando Slowing down of speed in music.

Rondo A musical form consisting of a repeated section with two or more contrasting sections; its form is ABACADA.

Rote songs Songs that are committed to memory by repetition, usually with little intellectual effort beyond imitation. They are especially useful for young children and others who cannot read or in informal recreational settings.

Scale A sequence of tones or pitches arranged in ascending or descending order. The arrangement of whole and half steps of the tones denotes the specific type of scale, such as major, minor, or pentatonic.

Score The written notation of music showing all the parts to be played or sung.

Sharp A musical symbol (♯) that raises a written pitch by one half step. When it appears in a key signature, it raises the pitch throughout the piece.

Sol-fa Using *do, re, mi, fa, sol, la,* and *ti* to sing a song instead of lyrics or note names. The method is used primarily to develop singing at sight and tonal intervals. The tones are also called *tonic sol-fa syllables,* and the method, *solfège.*

Sound localization The ability to respond to the directionality of a perceived sound.

Staccato The performing of short, detached sounds, indicated by a dot under or over the note (♩ ♩ ♩ ♩). See also *Legato.*

Staff A series of five horizontal lines on and between which musical notes are written to indicate their pitch (see Appendix C).

Starting tone The pitch on which a piece of music begins.

Step-wise progressions Changes within a melody in which each new tone is only one pitch above or below its predecessor.

Tempo The rate or speed of music.

Timbre The quality or color of a sound produced by an instrument or by the voice.

Time signature Two numerals written at the beginning of music that indicate the number and note value of the beats in each measure (see Appendix C).

Tonality The relationship of the pitches of a scale to the tonic chord or tonal center.

Tone calls Short musical passages (usually pentatonic) sung in dialogue form to develop accurate singing.

Tone matching The ability to sing a tone (or sequence of tones) on the exact pitch(es) given.

Tonic chord (I) A three-tone chord built on the tonic of the scale. The major chord is *do-mi-sol;* the minor chord is *la-do-mi.*

Tuned instruments Instruments that give an identifiable pitch when played.

Unison The playing or singing of the same notes or pitches in a melody by all participants.

Verse-chorus form A series of stanzas sung to the same melody alternating with a refrain in which the words remain the same.

Vocables Sung syllables or words with no literal translation.

Whole-song approach A method of teaching rote songs in which the whole song is sung by the teacher with learners joining in as the song becomes familiar.

Whole tone A full-step interval between two tones comprised of two half steps up or down.

Xylophone A diatonic or chromatic percussion instrument with removable tuned wooden bars that are played with mallets; used in the Orff Instrumentarium.

Subject Index

Accompaniment(s). *See also* Appendix B
  harmonic, 223–227
  instrumental, 217–221
  melodic, 221–222
  ostinato
    defined, 217
    melodic, 217–221
Active listening. *See* Auditory skills
Activity clusters for integrated learning
  defined, 245
  sample clusters, 246–265
Adding songs to stories, 165
  "Billy Goats Gruff," 169
  "Gingerbread Boy," 167
  "Three Bears," 169
  "Three Little Kittens," 166
  "Three Little Pigs," 168
Andress, Barbara, 10
Arts education legislation, xvi
Attitude toward music
  children's, 14
  teacher's, 18
Auditory skills
  awareness, 9–10, 172–175
  discrimination, 9–10, 175–176
  memory, 9–10
  sequencing, 9–10, 176–178
  through movement, 9–10
Autoharp. *See* Appendix B
  accompaniments for songs, 275
  how to play, 274–275
  songs for, 276

Birkenshaw, Lois, 9, 34

Call-and-response singing. *See* Singing
Carson, Rachel, 15
Chanting and chants, 45–55. *See also* Speech,
    rhythmic; Tone matching
Children, characteristics of. *See* Growth
    characteristics
  developmental stages, 5–8
  special needs, 33–38
Children, special needs of, 33–38

  emotional problems, 34
  hearing, 33
  learning problems, 34
  mobility, 34
  understanding, 34
  vision, 33–37
Chords
  use of primary in accompaniments, 223–227
Circle, how to make, 94
Circle games. *See* Singing games
Classroom instruments, 11, 12–13
  categories, 196 *See also* Instruments;
    Percussion instruments, 196–198
  storage, 196
Classroom setting, 19
  free space in, 94
Creativity
  active listening, 12
  moving, 12
  original songs, 12. *See* Songs
  playing, 12
  repertoire, 82–89
  singing, 12
Curriculum
  eclectic, 20
  integrated, 244–266

Dalcroze, Emile Jaques, 187, 290
Diversity, cultural. *See* Multicultural music
    education
Diversity, individual. *See* Children, special
    needs of
Dynamics
  definition and use of, 14, 186–189
  listening activities for, 236–237
  materials for teaching, 236–237
  in movement, 186–189

Echo-singing. *See* Singing
Elements of music, 13–15
Elkind, David, 8
Environmental sounds, 5, 172–173
Equipment. *See* Music materials
Evans, David, on listening, 230

Index of Songs, Chants and Poems

Song titles with asterisks are pentatonic.

Index
of Multicultural Songs